SOCCER
Records · Facts and Champions
Jack Rollin

Title page: Argentina's goalkeeper **Nery Pumpido** holds aloft the FIFA World Cup trophy after his country's successful victory in the 1986 final.

Editor: Beatrice Frei
Design: David Roberts
Picture Editor: Alex Goldberg

© **Jack Rollin and Guinness Publishing Ltd, 1985, 1988**

First published in 1985
Second edition 1988

Published in Great Britain by Guinness Publishing Ltd,
33 London Road, Enfield, Middlesex

Phototypeset in 11/12pt Century Schoolbook and 8pt Helvetica by Ace Filmsetting Ltd, Frome, Somerset

Picture Acknowledgements
All-Sport: Title page, 11, 16, 18, 19, 21, 34, 42, 44, 48, 62, 68, 89 (top), 126
All-Sport/Simon Bruty: 38, 46, 77, 97
All-Sport/David Cannon: 10, 29, 52, 56, 58, 60, 70
All-Sport/Chris Cole: 78
All-Sport/Mike King: 127
All-Sport/Vandystadt: 26
Colorsport: 17 (left), 20, 23, 30, 32, 33 (bottom left), 40, 50, 66, 129 (bottom left)
Evening Echo: 4
Keystone Collection: 72, 80, 105, 116
Popperfoto: 14 (top), 17 (right), 22, 31, 33 (top left) 33 (right), 37, 54, 79, 82, 83 (top), 85, 90, 125, 129 (top left), 129 (top right), 129 (bottom right), 130, 137
Sporting Pictures: 14 (bottom), 28, 74, 89 (bottom), 95, 130 (right)
Bob Thomas/Sports Photography: 25

Printed and bound in Great Britain by Hazell Watson & Viney Ltd, Member of the BPCC plc, Aylesbury, Buckinghamshire.

'Guinness' is a registered trade mark of Guinness Superlatives Ltd

British Library Cataloguing in Publication Data

Rollin, Jack, *1932–*
   Soccer: the records, facts and champions—2nd ed.
   1. Association football
   I. Title
   796.334

ISBN 0-85112-360-0

CONTENTS

SPECIAL FEATURES

Gary Lineker **34**, Helmut Schoen **36**, Dundee United **38**, Barcelona **40**, Bobby Charlton **42**, Liam Brady **44**, Ray Clemence **46**, Everton **48**, Johan Cruyff **50**, Coventry City **52**, William Ralph 'Dixie' Dean **54**, Danny McGrain **56**, Uruguay **58**, Phil Neal **60**, Pat Jennings **62**, Peter Beardsley **64**, Gerd Muller **65**, Glasgow Rangers **66**, Mirandinha **68**, Wladyslaw Zmuda **70**, Just Fontaine **72**, Peter Patrick Lorimer **74**

Colour Features, to include the climax to the 1988 European Championship with results (facing p. 64)

JACK ROLLIN was born in London in 1932 and educated at King's, Harrow. There he played soccer, while later at Westcliff-on-Sea High School it was rugby. Within ten days of joining the Royal Air Force he was playing in a Welsh Cup tie for RAF Bridgnorth and in the services he learned shorthand and typing. He considers that his certificate of service contains the only complimentary words ever written about him: '. . . has proved to be efficient and accurate in his duties. He has gained some experience of office organization, filing systems and general clerical duties which should be of value in the future. He has shown a keen interest in team sports and games and maintained a good standard of physical fitness. He is invariably smart in appearance and alert. Recommended for employment in a junior administrative capacity.'

He also claims to have the unusual record of serving under two monarchs, King George VI and Queen Elizabeth II and spending a week on special guard duty for a third, Queen Juliana of the Netherlands.

In 1958 an ankle injury ended his own playing career during which, at the age of 14, he had been offered a trial with the United States club Chicago Maroons. He wisely declined a one-off reappearance in 1971 against the European Cup finalists Panathinaikos of Greece.

For 10 years Jack Rollin was Editor of the weekly magazine *Soccer Star* and its companion monthly *World Soccer* before becoming a freelance journalist again which he had been originally, covering the 1954 World Cup in Switzerland.

After 1970 he researched football for BBC Television, acted as an assistant to commentators on 'Match of the Day', spoke on radio and appeared on television programmes. He has contributed to *Radio Times* and in 1975 he won the Designers and Art Directors Association Silver Award for *Radio Times World Cup Special* for the most outstanding specialist feature of the year.

In 1972 he became one of the compilers of *Rothmans Football Yearbook* and is currently in his second spell as Editor of the book. He has provided advice on the football sections of the *Guinness Book of Records*, *Encyclopaedia Britannica* and *Britannica Book of the Year* and reports football regularly for the *Sunday Telegraph*. He co-edited the paper's year book for five years.

Jack Rollin contributed to three part-works: *The Game* (8 vols. 1970); *Book of Football* (6 vols. 1972) and *Football Handbook* (1979–80). His articles have appeared in programmes for matches at Wembley since 1963. He has produced handbooks which include *World Soccer Digest* 1961, 1962 and 1963 and *World Cup Digest* 1966. In 1978 he carried out the international research for the BBC Television series 'The Game of the Century' and produced the first edition of *The Guinness Book of Soccer Facts and Feats*.

Other books he has written: *England's World Cup Triumph* (1966), *A Source Book of Football* (1971), *The History of Aldershot Football Club* (1975), *World Cup Guide* (1982), *Who's Who in Soccer* (1984, 1986), *Soccer at War 1939–45* (1985) and *Soccer: The Records* (1985). In 1988 another Guinness original title is published: *Soccer Shorts*. In 1974 he contributed the South American section for John Moynihan's *Football Fever*.

The author is married to June and has a daughter Glenda. He is a member of the Association of Football Statisticians.

Introduction

This second edition of *Soccer – The Records* has been completely revised and updated. It also contains a number of new features.

The essential ingredients of the first edition, which included the best of the all-time records at various levels, are retained and there are entirely new in-depth illustrated stories of world famous players and teams past and present. Among those selected in this section are Gary Lineker, who scored six goals in the 1986 World Cup and was the leading marksman in the Mexico tournament; Peter Beardsley, the most expensive signing in Britain; Mirandinha, the first Brazilian to play in the Football League; Bobby Charlton, the record marksman for England in internationals and Barcelona, the best supported club on the continent of Europe.

All major tournaments including the World Cup, European Championships and the three leading European club competitions are given extensive coverage and the analysis of Football League champions is fully comprehensive. There are more wide-ranging details of South American Championship winners, those in the African Nations Cup and the World Club Championship. All the derby results of the chief rivals in England and Scotland are listed, as are also the highest wins and heaviest defeats inflicted by teams on both sides of the border. Wherever possible, team names are those existing at the time of a particular entry. For example Hartlepools United up to 1968, then Hartlepool.

Attendance figures for Football League seasons as well as those in the European Cup and the Cup Winners' Cup are also featured and goalscoring achievements at domestic and other levels can be found.

Among the innovations are the highest aggregate of League appearances for each Football League club, clubs who have suffered no home defeat or away win in a particular season and the post-war players who have graced the game at the age of 40.

The author would like to acknowledge the assistance and contribution of Christine Phillips and the late C. R. Williamson.

Milestones

1848 The first rules drawn up at Cambridge University.

1855* Sheffield, the oldest soccer club still in existence, founded.

1862 Notts County, the oldest Football League club, founded.

1863 Football Association formed in London on 26 October.

1865 Tape to be stretched across the goals 8 ft (2.4 m) from the ground.

1866 Offside rule altered to allow a player to be onside when three of opposing team are nearer their own goal-line. Fair catch rule omitted.

1867 Queen's Park, the oldest Scottish club, founded.

1869 Kick-out rule altered and goal-kicks introduced.

1871 Start of the FA Cup. Goalkeepers first mentioned in laws.

1872 First official international, between Scotland and England at Glasgow.
The Wanderers win the FA Cup Final.
Corner kick introduced.

1873 Scottish FA formed and the start of the Scottish Cup.

1874 Umpires first mentioned in laws.
Shinguards introduced.

---

* The date of Sheffield's foundation was given as 1855 in the Sheffield City Almanack (1902). And in the issue of the *Sheffield Telegraph* dated 29 September 1954 an article quoted H. B. Willey, a previous Secretary of the club, as follows: 'I used to have the Minute Book for 1855 but it was borrowed and never returned.'

1875 The cross-bar replaces tape on the goalposts.

1876 FA of Wales formed.
The first international between Scotland and Wales.

1877 The London Association and the Sheffield Association agree to use the same rules.
A player may be charged by an opponent if he is facing his own goal.

1878 Referees use a whistle for the first time.

1879 First international between England and Wales.
Cliftonville, the oldest Irish club, founded.

1880 Irish FA formed and the start of the Irish Cup.

1882 Ireland's first internationals with Wales and England.
International Football Association Board set up.
Two-handed throw-in introduced.

1883 First international between Scotland and Ireland.
The first British International Championship.

1885 Professionalism legalized in England.
Arbroath beat Bon Accord 36–0 in Scottish Cup; still a record score for an official first-class match.

1886 International caps first awarded.

1888 Football League formed.

1889 Preston North End achieve the League and FA Cup 'double'.

1890 Irish League formed.
First hat-trick in the FA Cup Final, by Blackburn's William Townley. Goal nets invented.
Scottish League formed.

1891 Referees and linesmen replace umpires.
Introduction of the penalty kick.

1892 Penalty taker must not play the ball twice.
Extra time allowed for taking a penalty.
Goal nets used in FA Cup Final for the first time.
Division Two of the Football League formed.

1893 Scotland adopts professionalism.

1894 First FA Amateur Cup Final.
Division Two of Scottish League formed.
Referee given complete control of the game.
Unnecessary for players in future to appeal to him for a decision.
Goalkeeper can only be charged when playing the ball or obstructing an opponent.

1895 FA Cup stolen from a Birmingham shop window. It was never recovered.
Goalposts and cross-bars must not exceed 5 in (127 mm) in width.
Player taking throw-in must stand on touch-line.

1897 Aston Villa win both the League and the FA Cup.
The Corinthians tour South America.
The word 'intentional' introduced into the law on handling.

1898 Players' Union first formed.

1899 Promotion and relegation first used in the Football League, replacing Test Matches.

1901 Tottenham Hotspur win the FA Cup while members of the Southern League.

1902 Terracing collapses

during the Scotland–England match at Ibrox Park, killing 25.

1904 FIFA formed in Paris, on 21 May.

1905 First £1000 transfer. Alf Common moves from Sunderland to Middlesbrough.
First international in South America, between Argentina and Uruguay.
England joins FIFA.

1907 Amateur FA formed.
Players' Union (now Professional Footballers' Association (PFA)) re-formed.

1908 England play in Vienna, their first international against a foreign side.
The first Olympic soccer tournament in London, won by the United Kingdom.

1910 Scotland, Wales and Ireland join FIFA.

1912 Goalkeeper not permitted to handle ball outside his own penalty area.

1913 Defending players not to approach within ten yards of the ball at a free-kick.

1914 Defending players not to approach within ten yards of ball at corner kick.

1916 The South American Championship first held.

1920 Division Three (Southern Section) of the Football League formed.
Players cannot be offside at a throw-in.

1921 Division Three (Northern Section) formed.

1922 Promotion and relegation introduced in the Scottish League.

1923 First FA Cup Final at Wembley: Bolton beat West Ham before a record crowd.

1924 A goal may be scored direct from a corner kick.

1925 Offside law changed to require two instead of three

defenders between attacker and goal.
Player taking throw-in must have both feet on touch-line.

1926 Huddersfield Town achieve the first hat-trick of League Championships.

1927 Cardiff City take the FA Cup out of England for the first time.
Mitropa Cup begins.
J. C. Clegg, President of the FA, knighted.

1928 British associations leave FIFA over broken-time payments to amateurs.
First £10 000 transfer: David Jack goes from Bolton to Arsenal.
Dixie Dean scores 60 goals for Everton in Division One, a Football League record.

1929 England lose 4–3 to Spain in Madrid, their first defeat on the continent.
Goalkeeper compelled to stand still on his goal-line at penalty-kick.

1930 Uruguay win the first World Cup, in Montevideo, Uruguay.
F. J. Wall, secretary of the FA, knighted.

1931 Goalkeeper permitted to carry ball four steps instead of two.
Instead of free-kick after a foul throw-in it reverts to opposing side.
Scotland lose 5–0 to Austria in Vienna, their first defeat on the continent.

1933 Numbers worn for the first time in the FA Cup Final.

1934 Italy win the second World Cup, in Rome, Italy.

1935 Arsenal equal Huddersfield's hat-trick of League Championships.
Arsenal centre-forward Ted Drake scores seven goals against Aston Villa at Villa Park, a Division One record.

1936 Defending players not permitted to tap the ball into goalkeeper's hands from a goal-kick.

Luton centre-forward Joe Payne scores ten goals against Bristol Rovers, a Football League record.
Dixie Dean overhauls Steve Bloomer's 352 goals in the Football League.

1937 A record crowd of 149 547 watch the Scotland v England match at Hampden Park.
Defending players not permitted to tap the ball into goalkeeper's hands from free-kick inside penalty area.
Weight of ball increased from 13–15 oz (368–425 g) to 14–16 oz (397–454 g).
Arc of circle 10 yd (9 m) radius from penalty spot to be drawn outside penalty area.

1938 Italy retain the World Cup, in Paris, France.
Laws of the game rewritten.
Scotland's Jimmy McGrory retires, having scored 550 goals in first-class football, a British record.

1946 British associations rejoin FIFA.
The Burnden Park tragedy: 33 killed and over 400 injured during an FA Cup tie between Bolton and Stoke.

1949 Aircraft carrying Italian champions Torino crashes at Superga near Turin, killing all on board.
England are beaten 2–0 by Republic of Ireland at Goodison Park, so losing their unbeaten home record against sides outside the home countries.
Rangers win the first 'treble' – Scottish League, Scottish Cup and League Cup.
S. F. Rous, secretary of the FA, knighted.

1950 Uruguay win the fourth World Cup, in Rio de Janeiro, Brazil. England, entering for the first time, lose 1–0 to USA.
Scotland's unbeaten home record against foreign opposition ends in a 1–0 defeat by Austria at Hampden Park.

1951 Obstruction included as an offence punishable by indirect free-kick.

Studs must project ¾ in (19 mm) instead of ½ in (13 mm).

1952 Billy Wright overhauls Bob Crompton's record of 42 caps.
Newcastle United retain the FA Cup, the first club to do so in the 20th century.
England lose their unbeaten home record against continental opposition, going down 6–3 to Hungary at Wembley.

1954 West Germany win the fifth World Cup in Berne, Switzerland.
England suffer their heaviest international defeat, beaten 7–1 by Hungary at Budapest.
The Union of European Football Associations (UEFA) formed.
Ball not to be changed during the game unless authorized by the referee.

1955 European Cup of the Champions and Inter-Cities Fairs Cup started.

1956 Real Madrid win the European Cup.
First floodlit match in the Football League: Portsmouth v Newcastle United on 22 February.

1957 George Young retires with a record 53 Scottish caps.
John Charles of Leeds United becomes the first British player to be transferred to a foreign club for a substantial fee (Juventus, Italy).

1958 Manchester United lose eight players in the Munich air disaster on 6 February.
Brazil win the sixth World Cup, in Stockholm, Sweden.
Sunderland, continuously in Division One, relegated.
Football League reorganization: Division Three and Division Four started.

1959 Billy Wright plays his 100th game for England, against Scotland, and retires at the end of the season with a world record 105 appearances.

1960 USSR win the first European Nations Cup, in Paris, France.
Real Madrid win the European Cup for fifth consecutive time.

1961 Sir Stanley Rous becomes President of FIFA.
Tottenham Hotspur win the League and Cup, the first 'double' of the 20th century.
The Professional Footballers Association (PFA) succeed in achieving the abolition of the maximum wage.
Fiorentina win the first European Cup-Winners' Cup.

1962 Brazil retain the seventh World Cup in Santiago, Chile.
Denis Law is transferred from Torino to Manchester United, the first transfer over £100 000 paid by a British club.

1963 The centenary of the FA. England beat the Rest of the World 2–1, at Wembley.
The Football League's 'retain and transfer' system declared illegal.
Tottenham Hotspur win the European Cup-Winners' Cup, the first British success in Europe.

1964 Spain win the European Nations' Cup, in Madrid, Spain.
More than 300 killed and 500 injured in rioting during an Olympic qualifying game between Peru and Argentina at Lima, Peru.
Jimmy Dickinson (Portsmouth) becomes the first player to make 700 Football League appearances.

1965 Stanley Matthews becomes the first footballer to be knighted.
Arthur Rowley retires having scored a record 434 Football League goals.
The Football League agree to substitutes for one injured player.

1966 England win the eighth World Cup, at Wembley.
The Football League allow substitutes for any reason.

1967 Alf Ramsey, England's team manager, knighted.
Celtic become the first Scottish club to win the European Cup.

1968 Italy win the European Football Championship, in Rome, Italy.
A world record transfer: Pietro Anastasi moves from Varese to Juventus for £440 000.

Manchester United win the European Cup: Matt Busby knighted.
Leeds United become the first British club to win the Fairs Cup.

1969 Leeds win the Football League Championship with a record 67 points.

1970 Brazil win the ninth World Cup, in Mexico City and win the Jules Rimet Trophy outright.
Bobby Charlton wins his 106th England cap in the quarter-finals to overhaul Billy Wright's record.
The first £200 000 transfer in Britain: Martin Peters moves from West Ham to Tottenham Hotspur.

1971 Britain's worst-ever crowd disaster: 66 killed at a match between Rangers and Celtic at Ibrox Park.
Arsenal achieve the League and Cup 'double'.
Barcelona win the Fairs Cup outright (to be replaced by the UEFA Cup) after beating the holders Leeds United 2–1.

1972 Tottenham Hotspur defeat Wolverhampton Wanderers in the first all-British European final, the UEFA Cup.
West Germany win the European Football Championship, in Brussels, Belgium.

1973 Ajax win the European Cup for the third consecutive time.
Bobby Moore makes his 108th appearance for England, a new record.
Johan Cruyff becomes the first £1 million transfer, moving from Ajax to Barcelona for £922 300.

1974 Joao Havelange of Brazil replaces Sir Stanley Rous as President of FIFA.
West Germany win the tenth World Cup in Munich, West Germany.
Denis Law makes his 55th appearance for Scotland, a new record.

1975 Leeds United banned from competing in Europe for any of two seasons in the next four, after their fans rioted at the European Cup Final in Paris.
Terry Paine overhauls Jimmy

Dickinson's record of 764 League games.

1976 Bayern Munich win the European Cup for the third consecutive time.
Czechoslovakia win the European Football Championship in Belgrade, Yugoslavia, beating West Germany.
Pat Jennings makes his 60th appearance for Northern Ireland, a new record.
The Football League abandon 'goal average', introducing 'goal difference'.
Liverpool win their ninth League title, overhauling Arsenal's record.

1977 Liverpool win their 10th League title as well as the European Cup.
Kevin Keegan transferred from Liverpool to SV Hamburg for £500 000, the highest fee involving a British club.
Kenny Dalglish transferred from Celtic to Liverpool for £440 000, a record fee between British clubs.
First World Youth Cup, held in Tunisia and won by USSR.

1978 Liverpool retain the European Cup.
Nottingham Forest, the only Football League club not a limited company, win their first Championship title. Forest also win the League Cup.
Ipswich Town become the 40th different team to win the FA Cup.
Kenny Dalglish makes his 56th appearance for Scotland to overhaul Denis Law's record.
Argentina win the eleventh World Cup in Buenos Aires, Argentina.

1979 David Mills transferred from Middlesbrough to West Bromwich Albion for £516 000, a record fee between British clubs.
Trevor Francis, transferred from Birmingham City to Nottingham Forest for £1 million, breaks the record for a single transfer involving British clubs.
Laurie Cunningham, the West Bromwich Albion and England winger, signs for Real Madrid in a £900 000 move.
Liverpool win their eleventh League title.

Nottingham Forest become the third English club to win the European Cup.
Andy Gray, transferred from Aston Villa to Wolverhampton Wanderers, breaks the record for a single transfer involving British clubs at £1 469 000.
Argentina win the Second World Youth Cup in Japan.

1980 Liverpool retain the championship for their 12th League honour.
Nottingham Forest retain the European Cup.
Steve Archibald joins Tottenham Hotspur from Aberdeen in a £800 000 deal which makes him the most expensive transfer from a Scottish club.
West Germany regain their European championship title, beating Belgium in Rome, Italy.
John Trollope overhauls Jimmy Dickinson's record of 764 League appearances for one club, reaching a total of 770.

1981 Uruguay win the Gold Cup in Montevideo, Uruguay.
Liverpool win the League Cup after a replay.
Aston Villa become League champions for the first time since 1910.
Tottenham Hotspur win the 100th FA Cup after a replay, the first to be staged at Wembley.
Ipswich Town win the UEFA Cup and their midfield player, John Wark, equals a European record with his 14th goal in the competition.
Frans Thijssen, the Dutch midfield player from Ipswich Town, is voted Footballer of the Year by the Football Writers Association.
The honours in Scotland go chiefly to the auld firm of Celtic, League champions, and Rangers, Scottish Cup winners, though Dundee United retain the League Cup.
The Football League points system changes to three for a win starting 1981–82 season.
West Germany win the Third World Youth Cup in Australia.
Bryan Robson transferred from West Bromwich Albion to Manchester United for British record of £1.5 million.

1982 Liverpool become the first winners of the Milk Cup

(formerly League Cup) and also achieve their 13th League honour.
Tottenham retain the FA Cup again after a replay.
Celtic retain the Scottish League title, Rangers win the League Cup and Aberdeen win the Scottish Cup.
Aston Villa win the European Cup.
Italy win the 12th World Cup in Madrid, Spain.

1983 Liverpool retain the Milk Cup and win their 14th League title. Manager Bob Paisley retires after winning 20 trophies with them.
Manchester United win the FA Cup after a replay.
Aberdeen achieve European Cup-Winners' Cup and Scottish Cup honours.
Dundee United win their first Scottish League title.
Celtic win the League Cup.
Canon become the first sponsors of the Football League.

1984 Liverpool win the European Cup on penalties after extra time.
Tottenham Hotspur win the UEFA Cup on penalties after extra time in the second leg.
France win the European Championship, beating Spain in Paris, France.
Liverpool achieve their 15th League title and third successive Milk Cup trophy.
Everton win the FA Cup.
Aberdeen win the Scottish League title and their third successive Scottish Cup.
Rangers win the League Cup.

1985 Tragedy at Valley Parade, Bradford where 56 spectators are killed and more than 200 injured in a fire.
Ten people killed and 29 injured after crowd panic at Mexican Cup Final.
At the Heysel Stadium, Brussels, Belgium, rioting Liverpool supporters at the European Cup Final cause 39 deaths (31 of them Italian) and 437 injuries.
English clubs banned from European competition.
Juventus win the European Cup.
Everton win the League championship and the European Cup-Winners' Cup.

Manchester United win the FA Cup after extra time.

Kevin Moran, their defender, becomes the first player sent off in an FA Cup Final.

First £1 million receipts from the match.

Norwich City win the Milk Cup.

Celtic win the 100th Scottish Cup.

Aberdeen win the Scottish League, Rangers win the League Cup, now sponsored as the Skol Cup.

Charlton Athletic move to Selhurst Park to share ground with Crystal Palace.

1986 Argentina win the 13th World Cup in Mexico.

Liverpool win the League and Cup double in Kenny Dalglish's first season as player manager.

Football League clubs agree to reduce First Division to 20 by 1988 with no overall loss of membership.

Juventus agree to pay Liverpool a new British record fee of £3.2 million for Ian Rush with effect from 1987.

Oxford United win the Milk Cup.

Littlewoods sponsor the League Cup for three years.

The FA of Wales move their headquarters from Wrexham to Cardiff.

Two substitutes allowed in FA Cup and Littlewoods Cup matches.

Aberdeen win the Scottish Cup and the Skol Cup.

Luton Town ban away supporters.

Bristol Rovers share Bath City's ground.

1987 Everton win the League title.

Coventry City win the FA Cup; their first major trophy in 104 years.

Arsenal win the Littlewoods Cup.

Play-offs introduced in end-of-season promotion and relegation.

Rangers win the Scottish League and Skol Cup.

St Mirren win the Scottish Cup.

Two substitutes allowed in Football League.

Record fee between two English clubs: £1.9 million for Peter Beardsley from Newcastle United to Liverpool; Scottish record: £1.5 million for Richard Gough from Tottenham Hotspur to Glasgow Rangers.

Today drop their Football League sponsorship but are replaced by Barclays.

1988 Centenary of the Football League.

Liverpool win their 17th League championship.

Luton Town win the Littlewoods Cup; their first major trophy in 98 years.

Wimbledon win the FA Cup 11 years after entering the League.

Celtic win the Scottish League and Scottish Cup.

Rangers win the Skol Cup.

B & Q replace Fine Fare the sponsors of the Scottish League for three years past.

Dave Beasant propels himself across goal to keep out a penalty kick enabling Wimbledon to beat Liverpool in the 1988 FA Cup Final.

Major British records

Highest scores

First class match
Arbroath 36 Bon Accord 0, Scottish Cup 1st rd,
12.9.1885
International
England 13 Northern Ireland 0, 18.2.1882
FA Cup
Preston North End 26 Hyde 0, 1st rd, 15.10.1897
League Cup & Littlewoods Cup
West Ham United 10 Bury 0, 2nd rd, 2nd leg, 25.10.83
Liverpool 10 Fulham 0, 2nd rd, 1st leg, 23.9.86

Football League
Division 1
home West Bromwich Albion 12 Darwen 0, 4.4.1892;
Nottingham Forest 12 Leicester Fosse 0, 21.4.09; **away**
Newcastle United 1 Sunderland 9, 5.12.08; Cardiff City 1
Wolverhampton Wanderers 9, 3.9.55
Division 2
home Newcastle United 13 Newport County 0, 5.10.46;
away Burslem Port Vale 0 Sheffield United 10,
10.12.1892
Division 3
home Tranmere Rovers 9 Accrington Stanley 0,
18.4.59; Brentford 9 Wrexham 0, 15.10.63; **away**
Halifax Town 0 Fulham 8, 16.9.69; Brighton & Hove
Albion 2 Bristol Rovers 8, 1.12.73
Division 3 Southern
home Luton Town 12 Bristol Rovers 0, 13.4.36; **away**
Northampton Town 0 Walsall 8, 2.2.47
Division 3 Northern
home Stockport County 13 Halifax Town 0, 6.1.34;
away Accrington Stanley 0 Barnsley 9, 3.2.34

Len Shackleton in studied pose. His impact during an illustrious career was most marked when he scored six times on his Newcastle United debut v Newport County.

Division 4
home Oldham Athletic 11 Southport 0, 26.12.62; **away**
Crewe Alexandra 1 Rotherham United 8, 8.9.73
Aggregate
Tranmere Rovers 13 Oldham Athletic 4, 26.12.35
Div 3N
Scottish League
Premier Division
home Aberdeen 8 Motherwell 0, 26.3.79; **away**
Kilmarnock 1 Rangers 8, 20.9.80
Division 1
home Celtic 11 Dundee 0, 26.10.1895; **away**
Airdrieonians 1 Hibernian 11, 24.10.50
Division 2
home East Fife 13 Edinburgh City 2, 11.12.37; **away**
Alloa Athletic 0 Dundee 10, 8.3.47

Football League
Most wins in a season

	Team	Division	Season
31	Tottenham Hotspur	1	1960-61
32	Tottenham Hotspur	2	1919-20
30	Plymouth Argyle	3S	1929-30
30	Millwall	3S	1927-28
30	Cardiff City	3S	1946-47
30	Nottingham Forest	3S	1950-51
30	Bristol City	3S	1954-55
33	Doncaster Rovers	3N	1946-47
32	Aston Villa	3	1971-72
32	Lincoln City	4	1975-76
32	Swindon Town	4	1985-86

Most drawn games in a season

	Team	Division	Season
23	Norwich City	1	1978-79
23	Exeter City	4	1986-87

Most defeats in a season

	Team	Division	Season
31	Stoke City	1	1984-85
31	Tranmere Rovers	2	1938-39
33	Cambridge United	3	1984-85
29	Merthyr Town	3S	1924-25
33	Rochdale	3N	1931-32
32	Workington	4	1975-76

Fewest wins in a season

	Team	Division	Season
3	Stoke	1	1889-90
3	Woolwich Arsenal	1	1912-13
3	Stoke City	1	1984-85
1	Loughborough Town	2	1899-1900
6	Queen's Park Rangers	3S	1925-26
6	Merthyr Town	3S	1929-30
4	Rochdale	3N	1931-32
2	Rochdale	3	1973-74
3	Southport	4	1976-77

Fewest defeats in a season

	Team	Division	Season
0	Preston North End	1	1888-89
2	Leeds United	1	1968-69
0	Liverpool	2	1893-94
2	Burnley	2	1897-98
2	Bristol City	2	1905-06
3	Leeds United	2	1963-64
5	Queen's Park Rangers	3	1966-67
4	Southampton	3S	1921-22
4	Plymouth Argyle	3S	1929-30
4	Port Vale	3S	1953-54
3	Doncaster Rovers	3N	1946-47
3	Wolverhampton Wanderers	3N	1923-24
4	Lincoln City	4	1975-76
4	Sheffield United	4	1981-82

Longest winning sequence

	Team	Division	Season
12	Everton	1	1893-94 (4 games) 1894-95 (8 games)

Longest winning sequence in a season

	Team	Division	Season
11	Tottenham Hotspur	1	1960-61
14	Manchester United	2	1904-05
14	Bristol City	2	1905-06
14	Preston North End	2	1950-51

Longest unbeaten sequence

	Team	Division	Season
42	Nottingham Forest	1	Nov. 1977-Dec. 1978

Longest unbeaten sequence in a season

	Team	Division	Season
30	Burnley	1	1920-21

Most goals scored in a season

	Team	Division	Season
128	Aston Villa	1	1930-31
122	Middlesbrough	2	1926-27
127	Millwall	3S	1927-28
128	Bradford City	3N	1928-29
111	Queen's Park Rangers	3	1961-62
134	Peterborough United	4	1960-61

Most goals conceded in a season

	Team	Division	Season
125	Blackpool	1	1930-31
141	Darwen	2	1898-99
135	Merthyr Town	3S	1929-30
136	Nelson	3N	1927-28
123	Accrington Stanley	3	1959-60
109	Hartlepool United	4	1959-60

Fewest goals scored in a season

	Team	Division	Season
24	Stoke City	1	1984-85
24	Watford	2	1971-72
33	Crystal Palace	3S	1950-51
32	Crewe Alexandra	3N	1923-24
27	Stockport County	3	1969-70
29	Crewe Alexandra	4	1981-82

Fewest goals conceded in a season

	Team	Division	Season
16	Liverpool	1	1978-79
23	Manchester United	2	1924-25
21	Southampton	3S	1921-22
21	Port Vale	3N	1953-54
30	Middlesbrough	3	1986-87
25	Lincoln City	4	1980-81

Longest sequence without a win in a season

	Team	Division	Season
31	Cambridge United	2	1983-84

Longest sequence of consecutive defeats in a season

	Team	Division	Season
17	Rochdale	3N	1931-32

Scottish League

Most wins in a season

	Team	Division	Season
31	Rangers	Pr Div	1986–87
35	Rangers	1	1920–21
33	Morton	2	1966–67

Most drawn games in a season

	Team	Division	Season
18	Hibernian	Pr Div	1976–77

Most defeats in a season

	Team	Division	Season
29	Morton	Pr Div	1984–85
31	St Mirren	1	1920–21
30	Brechin City	2	1962–63

Fewest wins in a season

	Team	Division	Season
3	St Johnstone	Pr Div	1975–76
3	Kilmarnock	Pr Div	1982–83
0	Vale of Leven	1	1891–92
1	East Stirlingshire	2	1905–06
1	Forfar Athletic	2	1974–75

Fewest defeats in a season

	Team	Division	Season
4	Aberdeen	Pr Div	1983–84
4	Aberdeen	Pr Div	1984–85
4	Celtic	Pr Div	1976–77
4	Dundee United	Pr Div	1982–83
1	Rangers	1	1920–21
1	Clyde	2	1956–57
1	Morton	2	1962–63
1	St Mirren	2	1967–68

Longest winning sequence in a season

	Team	Division	Season
23	Morton	2	1963–64

Most goals scored in a season

	Team	Division	Season
90	Dundee United	Pr Div	1982–83
90	Celtic	Pr Div	1982–83
90	Celtic	Pr Div	1986–87
132	Heart of Midlothian	1	1957–58
142	Raith Rovers	2	1937–38

Fewest goals scored in a season

	Team	Division	Season
23	Clydebank	Pr Div	1977–78
23	Kilmarnock	Pr Div	1980–81
18	Stirling Albion	1	1980–81
20	Lochgelly United	2	1923–24

Fewest goals conceded in a season

	Team	Division	Season
21	Aberdeen	Pr Div	1983–84
14	Celtic	1	1913–14
20	Morton	2	1966–67

Most goals conceded in a season

	Team	Division	Season
100	Morton	Pr Div	1984–85
137	Leith Athletics	1	1931–32
146	Edinburgh City	2	1931–32

Individual British goalscoring records

Football League
10 goals, Joe Payne, Luton Town v Bristol Rovers, Division 3S, 13.4.36
Division 1
7 goals, Ted Drake, Arsenal v Aston Villa, 14.12.35; and James Ross, Preston North End v Stoke City, 6.10.1888
FA Cup
9 goals, Ted MacDougall, Bournemouth v Margate, 20.11.71
FA Cup (preliminary rounds)
10 goals, Chris Marron, South Shields v Radcliffe, 20.9.47
Scottish League
8 goals, Jimmy McGrory, Celtic v Dunfermline Athletic, 14.1.28
Scottish Cup
13 goals, John Petrie, Arbroath v Bon Accord, 5.9.1885
British International Championship
6 goals, Joe Bambrick, Ireland v Wales, 1.2.30
Career totals
Football League
434 goals, Arthur Rowley, West Bromwich Albion, Fulham, Leicester City and Shrewsbury Town, 1946–1965
Scottish League
410 goals, Jimmy McGrory, Celtic and Clydebank, 1922–1938

Quickest goals
6 seconds, Albert Mundy, Aldershot v Hartlepool United, Division 4, 25.10.58; 6 seconds, Barrie Jones, Notts County v Torquay United, Division 3, 31.3.62; 6 seconds, Keith Smith, Crystal Palace v Derby County, Division 2, 12.12.64
Fastest hat-trick
3 goals in 2½ minutes, Ephraim 'Jock' Dodds, Blackpool v Tranmere Rovers, Wartime Regional League, 28.2.43 and Jimmy Scarth, Gillingham v Leyton Orient, Division 3S, 1.11.52
4 goals in 5 minutes, John McIntyre, Blackburn Rovers v Everton, 16.9.22; Ginger Richardson, West Bromwich Albion v West Ham United, 7.11.31 (from the start of the game including three in 3 minutes)
6 goals in 21 minutes, Frank Keetley, Lincoln City v Halifax Town, Division 3N, 16.1.32
Fastest International hat-trick
3 goals in 3½ minutes, Willie Hall, England v Ireland, 16.11.38
Fastest own goal
6 seconds, Pat Kruse, Torquay United v Cambridge United, 3.1.77

International goalscoring records

For club
16 goals, Stephan Stanis (Stanikowski and sometimes known as Dembicki), Racing Club Lens v Aubry-Asturies, French Cup, 13.12.42

International Matches
10 goals, Sofus Nielsen, Denmark v France, 1908
Olympics; and Gottfried Fuchs, Germany v USSR (as
Russia), 1912 Olympics
World career records
1329 goals, Artur Friedenreich, in Brazilian football,
1910–1930
1216 goals, Edson Arantes do Nascimento (Pelé) 1956–
1974, in Brazilian football and later in USA for New York
Cosmos taking total to 1,281

Goalscoring in European competitions

European Cup individual aggregate
49, Alfredo di Stefano (Real Madrid) 1955–56 to 1963–
64; 46, Eusebio (Benfica) 1961–62 to 1973–74; and 36,
Gerd Muller (Bayern Munich) 1969–70 to 1976–77
European Cup in one season
14, José Altafini (AC Milan) 1962–63
Cup Winners' Cup
14, Lothar Emmerich (Borussia Dortmund), 1965–66
Highest scores
12–2 Feyenoord v KR Reykjavik, European Cup 1st rd,
17.9.69
11–0 Dynamo Bucharest v Crusaders, European Cup
1st rd, 3.10.73
16–1, Sporting Lisbon v Apoel Nicosia, Cup Winners'
Cup 1st rd, 13.11.63
13–0 Cologne v Union Luxembourg, Fairs Cup 1st rd,
5.10.65
Highest scores involving British clubs
13–0 Chelsea v Jeunesse Hautcharage, Cup-Winners'
Cup, 29.9.71
12–0 Derby County v Finn Harps, UEFA Cup, 15.9.76
10–0 Ipswich Town v Floriana, European Cup, 25.9.62
10–0 Leeds United v Lyn Oslo, European Cup, 17.9.69
11–0 Liverpool v Stromsgodset, Cup Winners' Cup,
17.9.74
10–0 Liverpool v Dundalk, Fairs Cup, 16.9.69
10–1 Liverpool v Oulun Palloseura, European Cup,
1.10.80
10–0 Manchester United v Anderlecht, European Cup,
26.9.56
10–1 Aberdeen v KR Reykjavik, Cup Winners' Cup,
6.9.67
10–1 Dunfermline Athletic v Apoel Nicosia, Cup
Winners' Cup, 18.9.68
10–0 Rangers v Valetta, Cup Winners' Cup, 28.9.83
12–0 Swansea City v Sliema Wanderers, Cup Winners'
Cup, 15.9.82

Alfredo di Stefano who holds the European Cup scoring
record with 49 goals. Below: **Ian Rush**, a consistent
marksman for Liverpool, Juventus and Wales.

Top British marksmen in European competitions

Leading scorers
30 goals Peter Lorimer (Leeds United) 1965–66 to
1976–77; 28 goals Denis Law (Manchester United)
1963–64 to 1968–69; 20 goals Kenny Dalglish (Celtic
and Liverpool) 1972–73 to 1983–84
**First British player to score three penalties in one
European game**
John Wark (Ipswich Town) v Aris Salonika 17.9.80
UEFA Cup. Wark scored four goals in the game
Players scoring 5 goals in one match
Ray Crawford (Ipswich Town) v Floriana, European Cup
25.9.62; Peter Osgood (Chelsea) v Jeunesse
Hautcharage, Cup Winners' Cup, 29.9.71

Golden Boot Award for Europe's leading goalscorer

Season	First	Goals	Second	Goals	Third	Goals
1967–68	Eusebio (Benfica)	43	Antal Dunai (Ujpest Dozsa)	36	Bobby Lennox (Celtic)	32
1968–69	Petar Jekov (CSKA Sofia)	36	George Sideris (Olympiakos)	35	Helmut Kogelberger (FK Austria)	31
					Antal Dunai (Ujpest Dozsa)	31
1969–70	Gerd Muller (Bayern Munich)	38	Jan Devillet (Spora Luxembourg)	31		
			Petar Jekov (CSKA Sofia)	31		
1970–71	Josip Skoblar (Marseilles)	44	Salif Keita (St Etienne)	42	George Dedes (Panionios)	28
1971–72	Gerd Muller (Bayern Munich)	40	Antonis Antoniadis (Panathinaikos)	39	Joe Harper (Aberdeen)	33
					Slobodan Santrac (OFK Belgrade)	33
					Francis Lee (Manchester City)	33
1972–73	Eusebio (Benfica)	40	Gerd Muller (Bayern Munich)	36	Petar Jekov (CSKA Sofia)	29
1973–74	Hector Yazalde (Sporting Lisbon)	46	Hans Krankl (Rapid Vienna)	36	Gerd Muller (Bayern Munich)	30
					Jupp Heynckes (Borussia Moenchengladbach)	30
					Carlos Bianchi (Reims)	30
1974–75	Dudu Georgescu (Dinamo Bucharest)	33	Hector Yazalde (Sporting Lisbon)	30		
			Ruud Geels (Ajax)	30		
			Delio Onnis (Monaco)	30		
1975–76	Sotiris Kaiafas (Omonia Nicosia)	39	Carlos Bianchi (Reims)	34	Peter Risi (Zurich)	33
1976–77	Dudu Georgescu (Dinamo Bucharest)	47	Bela Varadi (Vasas Budapest)	36	Ruud Geels (Ajax)	34
					Dieter Muller (FC Cologne)	34
1977–78	Hans Krankl (Rapid Vienna)	41	Carlos Bianchi (Paris St Germain)	37	Ruud Geels (Ajax)	34
1978–79	Kees Kist (AZ 67 Alkmaar)	34	Thomas Mavros (AEK Athens)	31		
			Laszlo Fekete (Ujpest Dozsa)	31		
1979–80	Erwin Van Den Bergh (Lierse)	39	Laszlo Fazekas (Ujpest Dozsa)	36	Walter Schachner (FK Austria)	34
1980–81	Georgi Slavkov (Trakia Plovdiv)	31	Tibor Nyilasi (Ferencvaros)	30	Karl-Heinz Rummenigge (Bayern Munich)	29
1981–82	Wim Kieft (Ajax)	32	Kees Kist (AZ 67 Alkmaar)	29	Allan Hansen (Odense BK)	28
			Delio Onnis (Tours)	29		
1982–83	Fernando Gomes (Porto)	36	Peter Houtman (Feyenoord)	30	Nikos Anastopoulous (Olympiakos)	29
					Charlie Nicholas (Celtic)	29
1983–84	Ian Rush (Liverpool)	32	Marco Van Basten (Ajax)	28	Nico Claesen (Seraing)	27
1984–85	Fernando Gomes (Porto)	39	Martin McGaughey (Linfield)	34	Vahid Halilhodzic (Nantes)	28
1985–86	Marco Van Basten (Ajax)	37	Oleg Protasov (Dnepr)	36	Toni Polster (FK Austria)	33
					Tanju Colak (Samsunspor)	33
1986–87	Rodion Camataru (Dinamo Bucharest)	44	Toni Polster (FK Austria)	39	Nasko Sirakov (Vitosha)	36

Aggregate scores by individuals

11 goals Stan Bowles (Queen's Park Rangers) UEFA Cup, 1976–77; 7 goals in two games (five in first leg) Kevin Hector (Derby County) UEFA Cup, 1976–77; 4 goals on two occasions Trevor Whymark (Ipswich Town) v Lazio UEFA Cup, 24.10.73; v Landskrona Bois, UEFA Cup 28.9.77

Goalkeeping Records

International

Dino Zoff, Italy, unbeaten in 1142 minutes from September 1972 to June 1974

British record (all competitive games)

Chris Woods, Rangers, in 1196 minutes from 26 November 1986 to 31 January 1987

Football League

Steve Death, Reading, 1103 minutes from 24 March to 18 August 1979

Most cup-winning medals

FA Cup-winning medals

5 James Forrest (Blackburn Rovers) 1884–86, 1890–91; the Hon Sir Arthur Fitzgerald Kinnaird, Kt (Wanderers) 1873, 1877–78, (Old Etonians) 1879, 1882; and Charles H R Wollaston (Wanderers) 1872–73, 1876–78

Scottish Cup-winning medals

8 Charles Campbell (Queen's Park), 1874–76, 1880–82, 1884 and 1886

Most League appearances

Football League

826 Peter Shilton (286 Leicester City, 110 Stoke City, 202 Nottingham Forest, 188 Southampton, 40 Derby County) 1966–
824 Terry Paine (713 Southampton, 111 Hereford United) 1957–77
777 Alan Oakes (565 Manchester City, 211 Chester City, 1 Port Vale) 1959–84
770 John Trollope (all for Swindon Town) 1960–80
764 Jimmy Dickinson (all for Portsmouth) 1946–65
761 Roy Sproson (all for Port Vale) 1950–72
758 Ray Clemence (48 Scunthorpe United, 470 Liverpool, 240 Tottenham Hotspur) 1966–87
757 Pat Jennings (48 Watford, 472 Tottenham Hotspur, 237 Arsenal) 1963–86

Scottish League
Division 1
626 Bob Ferrier (Motherwell) 1918–37

Left: **Peter Shilton** who overtook Terry Paine's record of League appearances during 1987–88.

Football League analysis

Most points in a season

Football League (two points system)

Division	Team	Points	Season
1	Liverpool	68	1978–79
2	Tottenham Hotspur	70	1919–20
3	Aston Villa	70	1971–72
3S	Nottingham Forest	70	1950–51
	Bristol City	70	1954–55
3N	Doncaster Rovers	72	1946–47
4	Lincoln City	74	1975–76

Football League (three points system)

Division	Team	Points	Season
1	Everton	90	1984–85
1	Liverpool	90	1987–88
2	Luton Town	88	1981–82
2	Chelsea	88	1983–84
2	Sheffield Wednesday	88	1983–84
3	Bournemouth	97	1986–87
4	Swindon Town	102	1985–86

Scottish League

Division	Team	Points	Season
Pr	Celtic	72	1987–88
1	Rangers	76	1920–21
2	Morton	69	1966–67

Fewest points (minimum 34 games)

Football League

Division	Team	Points	Season
1	Stoke City	17	1984–85
2	Doncaster Rovers	8	1904–05
	Loughborough Town	8	1899–1900

Joe Payne (left) who ranks third in the overall list of highest individual scorers in the Football League and runner-up George Camsell (right), just one goal behind Dixie Dean in a season.

3	Rochdale	21	1973-74
3	Cambridge United	21	1984-85
3S	Merthyr Town	21	1924-25
	Queen's Park Rangers	21	and 1929-30 1925-26
3N	Rochdale	11	1931-32
4	Workington	19	1976-77

Scottish League (minimum 30 games)

Division	Team	Points	Season
Pr	St Johnstone	11	1975-76
1	Stirling Albion	6	1954-55
2	Edinburgh City	7	1936-37

Highest individual goalscorers in League games

Current Football League clubs (in descending order)

Goals	Player	Team	Division	Season
60	Dixie Dean	Everton	1	1927-28
59	George Camsell	Middlesbrough	2	1926-27
55	Joe Payne	Luton Town	3S	1936-37
55	Ted Harston	Mansfield Town	3N	1936-37
52	Terry Bly	Peterborough United	4	1960-61
49	Pongo Waring	Aston Villa	1	1930-31
49	Clarrie Bourton	Coventry City	3S	1931-32
47	Harry Morris	Swindon Town	3S	1926-27
46	Peter Simpson	Crystal Palace	3S	1930-31
46	Derek Dooley	Sheffield Wednesday	2	1951-52
46	Alf Lythgoe	Stockport County	3N	1933-34
45	Jimmy Hampton	Blackpool	2	1929-30
44	Jimmy Cookson	Chesterfield	3N	1925-26
44	Arthur Rowley	Leicester City	2	1956-57
44	Albert Whitehurst	Rochdale	3N	1926-27
44	Tom Bamford	Wrexham	3N	1933-34
43	Ted Harper	Blackburn Rovers	1	1925-26
43	Jimmy McConnell	Carlisle United	3N	1928-29
43	Dave Halliday	Sunderland	1	1928-29
42	Vic Watson	West Ham United	1	1929-30
42	Ted Drake	Arsenal	1	1934-35
42	Clarrie Jordan	Doncaster Rovers	3N	1946-47
42	Pat Glover	Grimsby Town	2	1933-34
42	John Charles	Leeds United	2	1953-54
42	Allan Hall	Lincoln City	3N	1931-32
42	Cliff Holton	Watford	4	1959-60
42	Ted MacDougall	Bournemouth	4	1970-71
41	Jimmy Greaves	Chelsea	1	1960-61
41	Frank Newton	Fulham	3S	1931-32
41	Ted Phillips	Ipswich Town	3S	1956-57
41	Roger Hunt	Liverpool	2	1961-62
41	Jimmy Dunne	Sheffield United	1	1930-31
40	Billy Haines	Portsmouth	2	1926-27
40	Sammy Collins	Torquay United	3S	1955-56
40	Gilbert Alsop	Walsall	3N	1933-34 and 1934-35
40	Bobby Hunt	Colchester United	4	1961-62
39	David Brown	Darlington	3N	1924-25
39	Bill McNaughton	Hull City	3N	1932-33
39	Tom Keetley	Notts County	3S	1930-31
39	Ginger Richardson	West Bromwich Albion	1	1935-36
39	Derek Reeves	Southampton	3	1959-60
38	Tommy Johnson	Manchester City	1	1928-29
38	Arthur Rowley	Shrewsbury Town	4	1958-59
38	Wally Ardron	Rotherham United	3N	1946-47
38	Joe Smith	Bolton Wanderers	1	1920-21
38	Ronnie Blackman	Reading	3S	1951-52
38	Jack Holliday	Brentford	3S	1932-33
38	Wilf Kirkham	Port Vale	2	1926-27
38	Dennis Westcott	Wolverhampton Wanderers	1	1946-47
37	Jack Bowers	Derby County	1	1930-31
37	Ray Straw	Derby County	3N	1956-57
37	Richard Parker	Millwall	3S	1926-27
37	Ted Harper	Preston North End	2	1932-33
37	George Goddard	Queen's Park Rangers	3S	1929-30
37	Jimmy Greaves	Tottenham Hotspur	1	1962-63
36	Don Clark	Bristol City	3S	1946-47
36	Dick Yates	Chester	3N	1946-47
36	Cliff Holton	Northampton Town	3	1961-62

The youthful **Jimmy Greaves** (below, left) and **Alan Cork** (right) who hold the season's League scoring records at Tottenham Hotspur and Wimbledon respectively.

36	Wally Ardron	Nottingham Forest	3S	1950–51
36	Hughie Gallacher	Newcastle United	1	1926–27
35	George Beel	Burnley	1	1927–28
35	Craig Madden	Bury	4	1981–82
35	Terry Harkin	Crewe Alexandra	4	1964–65
35	Dixie McNeil	Hereford United	3	1975–76
35	Tom Johnston	Orient	2	1957–58
35	Bunny Bell	Tranmere Rovers	3N	1933–34
35	Sam Taylor	Huddersfield Town	2	1919–20
35	George Brown	Huddersfield Town	1	1925–26
35	Cyril Pearce	Swansea City	2	1931–32
34	David Layne	Bradford City	4	1961–62
34	Fred Whitlow	Exeter City	3S	1932–33
34	Tudor Martin	Newport County	3S	1929–30
34	Albert Valentine	Halifax Town	3N	1934–35
33	Cecil McCormack	Barnsley	2	1950–51
33	Geoff Bradford	Bristol Rovers	3S	1952–53
33	Freddie Steele	Stoke City	1	1936–37
33	Tom Davis	Oldham Athletic	3N	1936–37
32	Peter Ward	Brighton & Hove Albion	3	1976–77
32	Ralph Allen	Charlton Athletic	3S	1934–35
32	Dennis Viollet	Manchester United	1	1959–60
32	Jack Cock	Plymouth Argyle	3S	1925–26
31	Stan Richards	Cardiff City	3S	1946–47
31	Ernie Morgan	Gillingham	3S	1954–55
31	Brian Yeo	Gillingham	4	1973–74
31	Barrie Thomas	Scunthorpe United	2	1961–62
31	Bill Fenton	York City	3N	1951–52
31	Arthur Bottom	York City	3N	1955–56
31	Ralph Hunt	Norwich City	3S	1955–56
31	Jim Shankly	Southend United	3S	1928–29
31	Sammy McCrory	Southend United	3S	1957–58
30	John Aldridge	Oxford United	2	1984–85
29	Joe Bradford	Birmingham City	1	1927–28
29	Alan Cork	Wimbledon	3	1983–84
28	William Robinson	Hartlepools United	3N	1927–28
26	John Dungworth	Aldershot	4	1978–79
21	Alan Biley	Cambridge United	3	1977–78
19	Les Bradd	Wigan Athletic	4	1981–82

Current Scottish League clubs (in descending order)

Goals	Player	Team	Division	Season
66	Jimmy Smith	Ayr United	2	1927–28
53	Robert Skinner	Dunfermline Athletic	2	1925–26
52	Bill McFadyen	Motherwell	1	1931–32
50	Jimmy McGrory	Celtic	1	1935–36
49	Wee Willy Crilley	Alloa	2	1921–22
45	Harry Yarnall	Airdrieonians	1	1916–17
45	Dave Easson	Arbroath	2	1958–59
45	Davie Kilgour	Forfar Athletic	2	1929–30
45	Dunky Walker	St Mirren	1	1921–22
44	Barney Battles	Heart of Midlothian	1	1930–31
44	Sam English	Rangers	1	1931–32
43	Evelyn Morrison	Falkirk	1	1928–29
42	Jimmy Wood	East Fife	2	1926–27
42	Joe Baker	Hibernian	1	1959–60
41	Jim Renwick	Albion Rovers	2	1932–33
41	John Coyle	Dundee United	2	1955–56
41	Allan McGraw	Morton	2	1963–64
41	Alec Hair	Partick Thistle	1	1926–27
40	Willie Devlin	Cowdenbeath	1	1925–26
38	Benny Yorston	Aberdeen	1	1929–30
38	Ken Bowron	Berwick Rangers	2	1963–64
38	Kenny Wilson	Dumbarton	2	1971–72
38	Dave Halliday	Dundee	1	1923–24
38	Norman Haywood	Raith Rovers	2	1937–38
36	Billy McPhail	Clyde	2	1951–52
36	Malcolm Morrison	East Stirlingshire	2	1938–39
36	Jimmy Benson	St Johnstone	2	1931–32
36	Peerie Cunningham	Kilmarnock	1	1927–28

John Aldridge who left Oxford United for Liverpool but remained as Oxford's top scorer.

34	David Wilson	Hamilton Academicals	1	1936-37
33	Jimmy Gray	Queen of the South	2	1927-28
30	Willie Martin	Queen's Park	1	1937-38
29	Evelyn Morrison	Stenhousemuir	2	1928-29
29	Bobby Murray	Stenhousemuir	2	1936-37
28	Blair Miller	Clydebank	1	1978-79
28	Brian Third	Montrose	2	1972-73
27	Derek Frye	Stranraer	2	1977-78
26	Mickey Lawson	Stirling Albion	2	1975-76
26	Bill McIntosh	Brechin City	2	1959-60
21	John McGachie	Meadowbank Thistle	2	1986-87

Jimmy McGrory (right) who had his best scoring season for Celtic in 1935-36 and **Joe Baker** (above) who was Hibs leading marksman with their record in 1959-60.

Transfers

British players £1 million and over

£3 200 000 Ian Rush, Liverpool to Juventus, June 1987

£2 750 000 Gary Lineker, Everton to Barcelona, June 1986

£2 300 000 Mark Hughes, Manchester United to Barcelona, May 1986

£1 900 000 Peter Beardsley, Newcastle United to Liverpool, July 1987

£1 500 000 Bryan Robson, West Bromwich Albion to Manchester United, October 1981

£1 500 000 Ray Wilkins, Manchester United to AC Milan, June 1984

£1 500 000 Richard Gough, Tottenham Hotspur to Glasgow Rangers, September 1987

£1 469 000 Andy Gray, Aston Villa to Wolverhampton Wanderers, September 1979

Clive Allen shrugging off the attentions of a Watford defender and playing in Tottenham Hotspur colours. He was twice transferred for over £1 million.

£1 437 500 Steve Daley, Wolverhampton Wanderers to Manchester City, September 1979

£1 350 000 Kenny Sansom, Crystal Palace to Arsenal, August 1980

£1 250 000 Kevin Reeves, Norwich City to Manchester City, March 1980

£1 250 000 Ian Wallace, Coventry City to Nottingham Forest, July 1980

£1 250 000 Clive Allen, Arsenal to Crystal Palace, August 1980

£1 250 000 Garry Birtles, Nottingham Forest to Manchester United, October 1980

£1 200 000 Clive Allen, Queen's Park Rangers to Arsenal, June 1980

£1 200 000 Trevor Francis, Nottingham Forest to Manchester City, September 1981

£1 180 000 Trevor Francis, Birmingham City to Nottingham Forest, February 1979

£1 100 000 Gary Lineker, Leicester City to Everton, June 1985 (including additional £300 000 when transferred to Barcelona)

£1 100 000 Frank Stapleton, Arsenal to Manchester United, August 1981

£1 000 000 Mark Hateley, AC Milan to Monaco, June 1987

£1 000 000 Justin Fashanu, Norwich City to Nottingham Forest, August 1981

£1 000 000 Luther Blissett, Watford to AC Milan, July 1983

£1 000 000 Ian Ferguson, St. Mirren to Glasgow Rangers, February 1988

Milestones in British transfers
£1000 Alf Common, Sunderland to Middlesbrough, 1905

£10 000 David Jack, Bolton Wanderers to Arsenal, 1928

£100 000 Denis Law, Torino to Manchester United, 1962

£200 000 Martin Peters, West Ham United to Tottenham Hotspur, 1970

£500 000 Kevin Keegan, Liverpool to SV Hamburg, 1977

World records
£6 900 000 Diego Maradona, Barcelona to Napoli, June 1984

£5 500 000 Ruud Gullit, PSV Eindhoven to AC Milan, June 1987

£4 800 000 Diego Maradona, Argentinos Juniors to Barcelona, June 1982

£3 000 000 Karl-Heinz Rummenigge, Bayern Munich to Internazionale, July 1984

£2 800 000 Careca, Sao Paulo to Napoli, May 1987

£2 500 000 Artur Antunes Coimbra (Zico), Flamengo to Udinese, July 1983

£2 330 000 Enzo Scifo, Anderlecht to Internazionale, May 1987

£2 300 000 Rudi Voller, Werder Bremen to AS Roma, June 1987

Scottish League and Cup honours

Championship wins
Rangers 38 (including one shared); Celtic 35; Aberdeen, Heart of Midlothian, Hibernian 4; Dumbarton 2 (including one shared); Dundee, Dundee United, Kilmarnock, Motherwell, Third Lanark 1

Scottish FA Cup
Celtic 28; Rangers 24; Queen's Park 10; Aberdeen 6; Heart of Midlothian 5; Clyde, St Mirren, Vale of Leven 3; Dunfermline Athletic, Falkirk, Hibernian, Kilmarnock, Renton, Third Lanark 2; Airdrieonians, Dumbarton, Dundee, East Fife, Morton, Motherwell, Partick Thistle, St Bernard's 1

Scottish League Skol Cup
Rangers 14; Celtic 9; Heart of Midlothian, Aberdeen 4; Dundee, East Fife 3; Dundee United 2; Hibernian, Motherwell, Partick Thistle 1

David Nish the youngest FA Cup final captain when he played in the 1969 match.

Oldest and youngest players

Youngest players
Football League
Albert Geldard, 15 years 158 days, Bradford Park Avenue v Millwall, Division 2, 16.9.29; and Ken Roberts, 15 years 158 days, Wrexham v Bradford Park Avenue, Division 3N, 1.9.51
Football League scorer
Ronnie Dix, 15 years 180 days, Bristol Rovers v Norwich City, Division 3S, 3.3.28
Division 1
Derek Forster, 15 years 185 days, Sunderland v Leicester City, 22.8.84
Division 1 scorer
Jason Dozzell, 16 years 57 days as substitute Ipswich Town v Coventry City, 4.2.84
FA Cup
Andy Awford, 15 years 88 days as substitute Worcester City v Borehamwood, 3rd Qual. rd, 10.10.87
FA Cup proper
Scott Endersby, 15 years 288 days, Kettering v Tilbury, 1st rd, 26.11.77
FA Cup Final
Paul Allen, 17 years 256 days, West Ham United v Arsenal, 1980
FA Cup Final scorer
Norman Whiteside, 18 years 18 days, Manchester United v Brighton & Hove Albion, 1983
FA Cup Final captain
David Nish, 21 years 212 days, Leicester City v Manchester City, 1969

Internationals
England
Duncan Edwards (Manchester United), 18 years 183 days, v Scotland, 2.4.55
Northern Ireland
Norman Whiteside (Manchester United), 17 years 42 days, v Yugoslavia, 17.6.82
Scotland
Johnny Lambie (Queen's Park), 17 years 92 days, v Ireland, 20.3.1886
Wales
John Charles (Leeds United), 18 years 71 days, v Ireland, 8.3.50
Republic of Ireland
Jimmy Holmes, 17 years 200 days, v Austria, 30.5.71

Oldest players
Football League
Neil McBain, 52 years 4 months, New Brighton v Hartlepools United, Div 3N, 15.3.47 (McBain was New Brighton's manager and had to play in an emergency)
Division 1
Stanley Matthews, 50 years 5 days, Stoke City v Fulham, 6.2.65
FA Cup Final
Walter Hampson, 41 years 8 months, Newcastle United v Aston Villa, 1924
FA Cup
Billy Meredith, 49 years 8 months, Manchester City v Newcastle United, 29.3.24
International debutant
Leslie Compton, 38 years 2 months, England v Wales, 15.11.50
International
Billy Meredith, 45 years 229 days, Wales v England, 15.3.20

Albert Geldard, one of the youngest debutants in the Football League.

Highest attendances

Record
205 000 (199 854 recorded, 173 830 paid) Brazil v Uruguay 1950 World Cup final series, 16.7.50, Maracana, Rio de Janeiro
International
149 547 Scotland v England, Hampden Park, Glasgow, 17.4.37
European Cup
136 505, Celtic v Leeds United semi-final, Hampden Park, Glasgow 15.4.70
FA Cup Final
160 000 (126 047 counted admissions) West Ham United v Bolton Wanderers, Wembley 28.4.23
Scottish Cup Final
146 433, Celtic v Aberdeen, Hampden Park, Glasgow, 24.4.37
Football League
Division 1
83 260, Manchester United v Arsenal, Maine Road, 17.1.48
Division 2
68 029, Aston Villa v Coventry City, Villa Park, 30.10.37
Division 3S
51 621, Cardiff City v Bristol City, Ninian Park, 7.4.47
Division 3N
49 655, Hull City v Rotherham United, Boothferry Park, 25.12.48
Division 3
49 309, Sheffield Wednesday v Sheffield United, Hillsborough, 26.12.79
Division 4
37 774, Crystal Palace v Millwall, Selhurst Park, 31.3.61
Scottish League
118 567, Rangers v Celtic, Ibrox Park, 2.1.39

Non League
FA Amateur Cup Finals
100 000, Pegasus v Harwich and Parkeston, Wembley Stadium, 11.4.53
GM Vauxhall Conference
9432, Lincoln City v Wycombe Wanderers, 2.5.88
Southern League
29 786, Queen's Park Rangers v Plymouth Argyle, Park Royal, 25.12.07

Lowest attendances

British International
2315, Wales v Northern Ireland, Racecourse Ground, Wrexham, 27.5.82
Football League (under 500)
484, Gateshead v Accrington Stanley, Div 3N, 26.3.52; 469, Thames v Luton Town, Div 3S, 6.12.30; and 450, Rochdale v Cambridge United, Div 3, 5.2.74
Division 1
4026, Wimbledon v Norwich City, 18.12.87

NB Although the Stockport County v Leicester City Division 2 game at Old Trafford on 7.5.21 was reported to have had an official attendance of only 13, contemporary reports estimated the crowd at 2000. Similarly, for the FA Cup third round second replay between Bradford City and Norwich City at Lincoln in 1915 the official attendance was nil, but although it was played behind closed doors so as not to interfere with war work in nearby factories, several hundred spectators gained admittance without paying.

Scottish League
80, Meadowbank Thistle v Stenhousemuir, Div 2, 22.12.79 at Meadowbank

World Cup 1930–86

Most appearances in finals: Antonio Carbajal (Mexico) 5 – 1950, 1954, 1958, 1962 and 1966

Most appearances in all matches: 21 Uwe Seeler (West Germany) – 1958, 1962, 1966 and 1970; Wladyslaw Zmuda (Poland) – 1974, 1978, 1982 and 1986

Most appearances in winning teams: Pelé (Brazil) 3 – 1958, 1962* and 1970

Oldest winning medallist: Dino Zoff (Italy) 40 – 1982 (captain)

Youngest finalist: Norman Whiteside (Northern Ireland) 17 – 1982

Winning countries

Year	Winners	P	W	D	L	F	A	Players	Final	Venue	Attendance
1930	Uruguay	4	4	0	0	16	3	15	Uruguay 4 Argentina 2	Montevideo, Uruguay	90 000
1934	Italy	5	4	1	0	12	3	17	Italy 2 Czechoslovakia 1 (aet)	Rome, Italy	50 000
1938	Italy	4	4	0	0	11	5	14	Italy 4 Hungary 2	Paris, France	45 000
1950	Uruguay	4	3	1	0	15	5	14	*Uruguay 2 Brazil 1	Rio de Janeiro, Brazil	199 854
1954	West Germany	6	5	0	1	25	14	18	West Germany 3 Hungary 2	Berne, Switzerland	60 000
1958	Brazil	6	5	1	0	16	4	16	Brazil 5 Sweden 2	Stockholm, Sweden	49 737
1962	Brazil	6	5	1	0	14	5	12	Brazil 3 Czechoslovakia 1	Santiago, Chile	68 679
1966	England	6	5	1	0	11	3	15	England 4 West Germany 2 (aet)	Wembley, England	93 802
1970	Brazil	6	6	0	0	19	7	15	Brazil 4 Italy 1	Mexico City, Mexico	107 412
1974	West Germany	7	6	0	1	13	4	18	West Germany 2 Holland 1	Munich, West Germany	77 833
1978	Argentina	7	5	1	1	15	4	17	Argentina 3 Holland 1 (aet)	Buenos Aires, Argentina	77 000
1982	Italy	7	4	3	0	12	6	15	Italy 3 West Germany 1	Madrid, Spain	90 080
1986	Argentina	7	6	1	0	14	5	18	Argentina 3 West Germany 2	Mexico City, Mexico	114 580

Highest aggregate goalscorer: Gerd Muller (West Germany) 14 – 1970 (10), 1974 (4). Muller scored 19 goals in the 1970 competition including 9 in qualifying games.

Highest scores (finals): Hungary 10 El Salvador 1 (1982); Hungary 9 South Korea 0 (1954); Yugoslavia 9 Zaire 0 (1974)

Highest score (qualifying game): New Zealand 13 Fiji 0 (1981)

First World Cup (finals): Louis Laurent (France v Mexico, 13 July 1930)

Fastest World Cup goal (finals): Bryan Robson (England v France, 16 June 1982)

Hat-trick scorer (Final): Geoff Hurst (England v West Germany, 1966)

Scorers in every match (finals): 13 goals: Just Fontaine (France) 1958; 7 goals: Jairzinho (Brazil) 1970; 4 goals: Alcide Ghiggia (Uruguay) 1950

Highest individual scorers (finals): 4 goals: Gustav Wetterstroem (Sweden v Cuba), Leonidas Da Silva (Brazil v Poland), Ernest Willimowski (Poland v Brazil) 1938; Ademir (Brazil v Sweden), Juan Schiaffino (Uruguay v Bolivia) 1950; Sandor Kocsis (Hungary v West Germany), 1954; Just Fontaine (France v West Germany) 1958; Eusebio (Portugal v North Korea) 1966; Emilio Butragueno (Spain v Denmark) 1986

* Missed Final through injury

Gary Lineker, top scorer in the 1986 World Cup Finals, pictured while on top of the world with Barcelona.

Referee	Aggregate attendances	Average attendance	Matches	Goals	Average	Top scorer	Goals
Langenus, Belgium	434 500	24 139	18	70	3.88	Guillermo Stabile (Argentina)	8
Eklind, Sweden	395 000	23 235	17	70	4.11	Angelo Schiavio (Italy); Oldrich Nejedly (Czechoslovakia); Edmund Cohen (Germany)	4
Capdeville, France	483 000	26 833	18	84	4.66	Leonidas Da Silva (Brazil)	8
Reader, England	1 337 000	60 772	22	88	4.00	Ademir (Brazil)	9
Ling, England	943 000	36 270	26	140	5.38	Sandor Kocsis (Hungary)	11
Guigue, France	868 000	24 800	35	126	3.60	Just Fontaine (France)	13
Latychev, USSR	776 000	24 250	32	89	2.78	Drazen Jerkovic (Yugoslavia)	5
Dienst, Switzerland	614 677	50 458	32	89	2.78	Eusebio (Portugal)	9
Glockner, East Germany	1 673 975	52 312	32	95	2.96	Gerd Muller (West Germany)	10
Taylor, England	1 774 002	46 685	38	97	2.55	Grzegorz Lato (Poland)	7
Gonella, Italy	1 610 215	42 374	38	102	2.68	Mario Kempes (Argentina)	6
Coelho, Brazil	1 766 277	33 967	52	146	2.81	Paolo Rossi (Italy)	6
Filho, Brazil	2 401 480	46 184	52	132	2.53	Gary Lineker (England)	6

* Deciding match

West Germany's second goal in the **1986 World Cup Final**, but Argentina succeed in winning their second trophy in the series by 3–2.

National records in final series 1930–86

Country	P	W	D	L	F	A
Brazil	62	41	11	10	144	63
West Germany*	61	34	13	14	130	85
Italy	47	25	11	11	79	52
Argentina	41	22	6	13	77	55
England	34	15	9	10	47	32
Uruguay	33	14	7	12	59	47
France	34	15	5	14	71	56
USSR	28	14	6	8	49	30
Hungary	32	15	3	14	87	57
Poland	25	13	5	7	39	29
Yugoslavia	28	12	4	12	47	36
Spain	28	11	6	11	37	34
Sweden	28	11	6	11	48	46
Austria	23	11	2	10	38	40
Czechoslovakia	25	8	5	12	34	40
Holland	16	8	3	5	32	19
Mexico	29	6	6	17	27	64
Chile	21	7	3	11	26	32
Belgium	21	5	4	12	27	45
Portugal	9	6	0	3	19	12
Scotland	17	3	6	8	21	32
Switzerland	18	5	2	11	28	44
Northern Ireland	13	3	5	5	13	23
Peru	15	4	3	8	19	31
Paraguay	11	3	4	4	16	25
Denmark	4	3	0	1	10	6
East Germany	6	2	2	2	5	5
USA	7	3	0	4	12	21
Bulgaria	16	0	6	10	11	35
Morocco	7	1	3	3	5	8
Wales	5	1	3	1	4	4
Algeria	6	2	1	3	6	10
Rumania	8	2	1	5	12	17
Tunisia	3	1	1	1	3	2
Cameroon	3	0	3	0	1	1
Cuba	3	1	1	1	5	12
North Korea	4	1	1	2	5	9
Turkey	3	1	0	2	10	11
Honduras	3	0	2	1	2	3
Israel	3	1	0	2	1	3
Kuwait	3	0	1	2	2	6
Australia	3	0	1	2	0	5
Colombia	3	0	1	2	5	11
Iran	3	0	1	2	2	8
South Korea	5	0	1	4	4	23
Norway	1	0	0	1	1	2
Egypt	1	0	0	1	2	4
Dutch East Indies	1	0	0	1	0	6
Iraq	3	0	0	3	1	4
Canada	3	0	0	3	0	5
New Zealand	3	0	0	3	2	12
Haiti	3	0	0	3	2	14
Zaire	3	0	0	3	0	14
Bolivia	3	0	0	3	0	16
El Salvador	6	0	0	6	1	22

Brazil have appeared in all World Cup final tournaments.
* Includes matches as Germany 1930–38.

European Championship

Year	Winners	Runners-up	Venue	Attendance	Referee	Entries	Top scorer (3 or more goals)
1960	**USSR** 2	Yugoslavia 1 (aet)	Paris, France	17 966	Ellis, England	17	—
1964	**Spain** 2	USSR 1	Madrid, Spain	120 000	Holland, England	29	—
1968	**Italy** . . . . 2 (after 1–1 draw)	Yugoslavia 0 (aet)	Rome, Italy	60 000 75 000	Dienst, Switzerland	31	—
1972	**West Germany** . 3	USSR 0	Brussels, Belgium	43 437	Marschall, Austria	32	Gerd Muller (West Germany) 4
1976	**Czechoslovakia** 2 (Czechs won 5–3 on penalties)	West Germany . . 2 (aet)	Belgrade, Yugoslavia	45 000	Gonella, Italy	32	Dieter Muller (West Germany) 4
1980	**West Germany** . 2	Belgium 1	Rome, Italy	*47 864	Rainea, Rumania	32	Klaus Allofs (West Germany) 3
1984	**France** 2	Spain 0	Paris, France	80 000	Christov, Czechoslovakia	33	Michel Platini (France) 8

South American Championship

Year	Venue	Teams	Matches	Goals	Champions	Pts
1916	Buenos Aires, Argentina	4	6	18	URUGUAY	5
1917	Montevideo, Uruguay	4	6	21	URUGUAY	6
1919	Rio de Janeiro, Brazil (1)	4	7	26	BRAZIL	7
1920	Valparaiso, Chile	4	6	16	URUGUAY	5
1921	Buenos Aires, Argentina	4	6	14	ARGENTINA	6
1922	Rio de Janeiro, Brazil (2)	5	11	23	BRAZIL	7
1923	Montevideo, Uruguay	4	6	18	URUGUAY	6
1924	Montevideo, Uruguay	4	6	15	URUGUAY	5
1925	Buenos Aires, Argentina (3)	3	6	26	ARGENTINA	7
1926	Santiago de Chile, Chile	5	10	55	URUGUAY	8
1927	Lima, Peru	4	6	37	ARGENTINA . . .	6
1929	Buenos Aires, Argentina	4	6	23	ARGENTINA . . .	6
1935	Lima, Peru*	4	6	18	URUGUAY	6
1937	Buenos Aires, Argentina (4)	6	16	68	ARGENTINA . . .	10
1939	Lima, Peru	5	10	47	PERU	8
1941	Santiago de Chile, Chile*	5	10	32	ARGENTINA . . .	8
1942	Montevideo, Uruguay (5)	7	21	81	URUGUAY	12
1945	Santiago de Chile, Chile*	7	21	89	ARGENTINA . . .	11
1946	Buenos Aires, Argentina*	6	15	61	ARGENTINA . . .	10
1947	Guayaquil, Ecuador	8	28	102	ARGENTINA . . .	13
1949	Rio de Janeiro, Brazil (6)	8	29	130	BRAZIL	14
1953	Lima, Peru (7)	7	21	67	PARAGUAY	10
1955	Santiago de Chile, Chile	6	15	73	ARGENTINA . . .	9
1956	Montevideo, Uruguay*	6	15	38	URUGUAY	9
1957	Lima, Peru	7	21	101	ARGENTINA . . .	10
1959	Buenos Aires, Argentina	7	21	86	ARGENTINA . . .	11
1959	Guayaquil, Ecuador*	5	20	39	URUGUAY	7
1963	La Paz & Cochabamba, Bolivia	7	21	91	BOLIVIA	11
1967	Montevideo, Uruguay	6	15	49	URUGUAY	9
1975	(Reorganized on home and away basis)	10	25	79	PERU	N/A
1979		10	25	63	PARAGUAY	N/A
1983		10	24	55	URUGUAY	N/A
1987		10	13	33	URUGUAY	N/A

* extraordinary tournaments

(1) play-off; Brazil 1 Uruguay 0
(2) play-off; Brazil 3 Paraguay 1; Uruguay withdrew
(3) two legs were played (home and away)
(4) play-off; Argentina 2 Brazil 0
(5) Chile withdrew
(6) play-off; Brazil 7 Paraguay 0
(7) play-off; Paraguay 3 Brazil 2 (organized by the Paraguayan Football League)

African Nations Cup

Year	Winners	Year	Winners
1957	Egypt	1974	Zaire
1959	Egypt	1976	Morocco
1961	Ethiopia	1978	Ghana
1963	Ghana	1980	Nigeria
1965	Ghana	1982	Ghana
1968	Zaire	1984	Cameroon
1970	Sudan	1986	Egypt
1972	Congo	1988	Cameroon

British International Championship 1883–1984

The final British Championship match between England and Northern Ireland at Wembley in April 1984.

89 tournaments including one not completed (1980–81)
Outright wins
England 34, Scotland 24, Wales 7, Northern Ireland 3
Shared titles
England 20, Scotland 17, Wales and Northern Ireland 5
National record in championships
Goal average or goal difference did not determine the winner until 1978–79. If countries were level on points at the top they shared the title.*

Season ending	*			
1884	Scotland 6	England 4	Wales 2	Ireland 0
1885	Scotland 5	England 4	Ireland 3	Wales 0
1886	Scotland 5	England 5	Wales 2	Ireland 1
1887	Scotland 6	England 4	Ireland 2	Wales 0
1888	England 6	Scotland 4	Wales 2	Ireland 0
1889	Scotland 5	England 4	Ireland 3	Wales 0
1890	Scotland 5	England 5	Wales 2	Ireland 0
1891	England 6	Scotland 4	Ireland 2	Wales 0
1892	England 6	Scotland 4	Ireland 1	Wales 1
1893	England 6	Scotland 4	Ireland 2	Wales 0
1894	Scotland 5	England 4	Wales 2	Ireland 1
1895	England 5	Scotland 3	Wales 2	Ireland 2
1896	Scotland 5	England 4	Wales 2	Ireland 1
1897	Scotland 5	England 4	Ireland 2	Wales 1
1898	England 6	Scotland 4	Ireland 2	Wales 0
1899	England 6	Scotland 4	Ireland 2	Wales 0
1900	Scotland 6	England 3	Wales 3	Ireland 0
1901	England 5	Scotland 4	Wales 3	Ireland 0
1902	Scotland 5	England 4	Ireland 2	Wales 1
1903	Scotland 4	England 4	Ireland 4	Wales 0
1904	England 5	Ireland 3	Scotland 5	Wales 2
1905	England 5	Wales 3	Ireland 2	Scotland 2
1906	England 4	Scotland 4	Wales 3	Ireland 1
1907	Wales 5	England 4	Scotland 3	Ireland 0
1908	England 5	Scotland 5	Ireland 2	Wales 0
1909	England 6	Wales 4	Scotland 2	Ireland 0
1910	Scotland 4	England 3	Ireland 3	Wales 2
1911	England 5	Scotland 4	Wales 3	Ireland 0
1912	England 5	Scotland 5	Ireland 2	Wales 0
1913	England 4	Scotland 3	Wales 3	Ireland 2
1914	Ireland 5	Scotland 4	England 2	Wales 1
1915–19 no competitions				
1920	Wales 4	Scotland 3	England 3	Ireland 2
1921	Scotland 6	Wales 3	England 3	Ireland 0
1922	Scotland 4	Wales 3	England 3	Ireland 2
1923	Scotland 5	England 4	Ireland 2	Wales 1
1924	Wales 6	Scotland 3	Ireland 1	England 1
1925	Scotland 6	England 4	Wales 1	Ireland 1
1926	Scotland 6	Ireland 3	Wales 2	England 1
1927	Scotland 4	England 4	Ireland 2	Wales 2
1928	Wales 5	Ireland 4	Scotland 3	England 0
1929	Scotland 6	England 4	Wales 1	Ireland 1
1930	England 6	Scotland 4	Ireland 2	Wales 0
1931	England 4	Scotland 4	Wales 3	Ireland 1
1932	England 6	Scotland 4	Ireland 2	Wales 0
1933	Wales 5	Scotland 4	England 3	Ireland 0
1934	Wales 5	England 4	Ireland 3	Scotland 0
1935	England 4	Scotland 4	Wales 2	Ireland 2
1936	Scotland 4	England 3	Wales 3	Ireland 2
1937	Wales 6	Scotland 4	England 2	Ireland 0
1938	England 4	Scotland 3	Ireland 3	Wales 2
1939	England 4	Scotland 4	Wales 4	Ireland 0
1940–46 no competitions				
1947	England 5	Ireland 3	Scotland 2	Wales 2
1948	England 5	Wales 4	Ireland 3	Scotland 0
1949	Scotland 6	England 4	Wales 2	Ireland 0
1950	England 6	Scotland 4	Wales 1	Ireland 1
1951	Scotland 6	England 4	Wales 2	Ireland 0
1952	England 5	Wales 5	Scotland 2	Ireland 0
1953	England 4	Scotland 4	Wales 2	Ireland 2
1954	England 6	Scotland 3	Ireland 2	Wales 1
1955	England 6	Scotland 3	Wales 2	Ireland 1
1956	England 3	Scotland 3	Wales 3	Ireland 3
1957	England 5	Scotland 3	Wales 2	Ireland 2
1958	England 4	Ireland 4	Scotland 2	Wales 2
1959	England 4	Ireland 4	Scotland 3	Wales 1
1960	England 4	Scotland 4	Wales 4	Ireland 0
1961	England 6	Wales 4	Scotland 2	Ireland 0
1962	Scotland 6	Wales 3	England 2	Ireland 1
1963	Scotland 6	England 4	Wales 2	Ireland 0
1964	England 4	Scotland 4	Ireland 4	Wales 0

1965	England	5	Wales	4	Scotland	3	Ireland	0
1966	England	5	Ireland	4	Scotland	2	Wales	1
1967	Scotland	5	England	4	Wales	2	Ireland	1
1968	England	5	Scotland	3	Wales	2	Ireland	2
1969	England	6	Scotland	3	Ireland	2	Wales	1
1970	England	4	Scotland	4	Wales	4	Ireland	0
1971	England	5	Scotland	3	Wales	2	Ireland	2
1972	England	4	Scotland	4	Ireland	3	Wales	1
1973	England	6	Ireland	4	Scotland	2	Wales	0
1974	England	4	Scotland	4	Wales	2	Ireland	2
1975	England	4	Scotland	3	Ireland	3	Wales	2
1976	Scotland	6	England	4	Wales	2	Ireland	0
1977	Scotland	5	Wales	4	England	2	Ireland	1
1978	England	6	Wales	3	Scotland	2	Ireland	1
1979	England	5	Wales	4	Scotland	2	Ireland	1
1980	Ireland	5	England	3	Wales	2	Scotland	2
1981 not completed								
1982	England	6	Scotland	3	Wales	2	Ireland	1
1983	England	5	Scotland	3	Ireland	2	Wales	2
1984	Ireland	3	Wales	3	England	3	Scotland	3

Kenny Dalglish, Scotland's most capped international with 102 appearances.

International records

Most capped players in the Home Countries and the Republic of Ireland

Bobby Moore, England's most capped international with 108 appearances.

England
Bobby Moore 108 appearances, 1962–73

Northern Ireland
Pat Jennings, 119 appearances, 1964–86

Scotland
Kenny Dalglish, 102 appearances, 1971–86

Wales
Joey Jones, 72 appearances, 1975–87

Republic of Ireland
Liam Brady, 67 appearances, 1974–

Other most capped players in the world

Hector Chumpitaz (Peru) 150 appearances, 1963–82
Rivelino (Brazil) 120 appearances, 1968–79
Bjorn Nordqvist (Sweden) 115 appearances, 1963–78
Dino Zoff (Italy) 112 appearances, 1968–83
Pelé (Brazil) 111 appearances, 1957–71
(Of the above named players only Nordqvist's and Zoff's totals do not include matches against club sides and other representative selections.)

Highest international goalscorers in the Home Countries and the Republic of Ireland

England
Bobby Charlton 49 goals

Northern Ireland
Billy Gillespie, Joe Bambrick and Gerry Armstrong 12 goals

Scotland
Kenny Dalglish and Denis Law 30 goals

Wales
Ivor Allchurch and Trevor Ford 23 goals

Republic of Ireland
Don Givens 19 goals

Most capped players

With each Football League club

In descending order of appearances, with number of all international appearances in brackets where figures differ.

Bobby Moore	West Ham United	108	England
Bobby Charlton	Manchester United	106	England
Billy Wright	Wolverhampton Wanderers	105	England
Tom Finney	Preston North End	76	England
Pat Jennings	Tottenham Hotspur	75 (119)	Northern Ireland
Kenny Sansom	Arsenal	74 (83)	England
Emlyn Hughes	Liverpool	59 (62)	England
Johnny Haynes	Fulham	56	England
Billy Bremner	Leeds United	54	Scotland
Jimmy McIlroy	Burnley	52 (55)	Northern Ireland
Mal Donaghy	Luton Town	56	Northern Ireland
Colin Bell	Manchester City	48	England
Jimmy Dickinson	Portsmouth	48	England
Allan Hunter	Ipswich Town	47 (53)	Northern Ireland
Mick Channon	Southampton	45 (46)	England
Jimmy Armfield	Blackpool	43	England
Ivor Allchurch	Swansea Town	42 (68)	Wales
Bob Crompton	Blackburn Rovers	41	England
Alf McMichael	Newcastle United	40	Northern Ireland
Alf Sherwood	Cardiff City	39 (41)	Wales
Alan Ball	Everton	39 (72)	England
Gordon Banks	Leicester City	37 (73)	England
Gordon Banks	Stoke City	36 (73)	England
Martin O'Neill	Nottingham Forest	36 (64)	Northern Ireland
Ron Springett	Sheffield Wednesday	33	England
Peter McParland	Aston Villa	33 (34)	Northern Ireland
Martin Harvey	Sunderland	34	Northern Ireland
Nat Lofthouse	Bolton Wanderers	33	England
Stuart Williams	West Bromwich Albion	33 (43)	Wales
Jimmy Nicholson	Huddersfield Town	31 (41)	Northern Ireland
John Barnes	Watford	31 (39)	England
Kenny Jackett	Watford	31	Wales
Rod Thomas	Swindon Town	30 (50)	Wales
Roy McFarland	Derby County	28	England
Malcolm Page	Birmingham City	28	Wales
Dai Davies	Wrexham	28 (51)	Wales
Billy Wedlock	Bristol City	26	England
Wilf Mannion	Middlesbrough	26	England
Don Givens	Queen's Park Rangers	26 (56)	Republic of Ireland
Billy Gillespie	Sheffield United	25	Northern Ireland
Ray Wilkins	Chelsea	24 (84)	England
Eamonn Dunphy	Millwall	22 (23)	Republic of Ireland
Dave Clements	Coventry City	21 (48)	Northern Ireland
Moses Russell	Plymouth Argyle	20 (23)	Wales
John Hewie	Charlton Athletic	19	Scotland
Martin O'Neill	Norwich City	18 (64)	Northern Ireland
Terry Neill	Hull City	15 (59)	Northern Ireland
Mick Kearns	Walsall	15 (17)	Republic of Ireland

Billy Wright (right) with his abundance of trophies and **Tom Finney** (below) in typically ferocious attacking action.

Gerry Ryan	Brighton & Hove Albion	15 (16)	Republic of Ireland
Steve Penney	Brighton & Hove Albion	15	Northern Ireland
Len Graham	Doncaster Rovers	14	Northern Ireland
Paddy Mulligan	Crystal Palace	14 (50)	Republic of Ireland
Peter Nicholas	Crystal Palace	14 (54)	Wales
Ian Walsh	Crystal Palace	14 (18)	Wales
Bill Lewis	Crewe Alexandra	12 (30)	Wales
Lloyd Davies	Northampton Town	12 (16)	Wales
Idris Hopkins	Brentford	12	Wales
Ray Houghton	Oxford United	12 (15)	Republic of Ireland
Bill Gorman	Bury	11 (17)	Republic of Ireland and Northern Ireland
Neil Slatter	Bristol Rovers	10 (16)	Wales
George Mackenzie	Southend United	9	Republic of Ireland

Albert Gray	Oldham Athletic	9 (24)	Wales
Eddie McMorran	Barnsley	9 (15)	Northern Ireland
Harry Hampton	Bradford City	9	Northern Ireland
Tony Millington	Peterborough United	8 (21)	Wales
Harry Cursham	Notts County	8	England
Pat McConnell	Reading	8	Northern Ireland
Tony Grealish	Orient	7 (44)	Republic of Ireland
Tom Finney	Cambridge United	7 (14)	Northern Ireland
Pat Glover	Grimsby Town	7	Wales

Bill Lewis	Chester City	7 (30)	Wales
Peter Scott	York City	7 (10)	Northern Ireland
Sammy Morgan	Port Vale	7 (18)	Northern Ireland
John McClelland	Mansfield Town	6 (47)	Northern Ireland
Colin Clarke	Bournemouth	6 (15)	Northern Ireland
Harold Millership	Rotherham United	6	Wales
Jimmy McLaughlin	Shrewsbury Town	5 (12)	Northern Ireland
Bernard McNally	Shrewsbury Town	5	Northern Ireland
Glyn Hodges	Wimbledon	5 (10)	Wales

Pat Glover, Grimsby Town's most capped international in the 1930s.

Walter McMillen	Chesterfield	4 (7)	Northern Ireland
Eric Welsh	Carlisle United	4	Northern Ireland
Nigel Vaughan	Newport County	3 (10)	Wales
David Pugh	Lincoln City	3 (7)	Wales
Con Moulson	Lincoln City	3	Republic of Ireland
Albert Gray	Tranmere Rovers	3 (24)	Wales
Tony Cascarino	Gillingham	3	Republic of Ireland
Peter Scott	Aldershot	1 (10)	Northern Ireland
Dermot Curtis	Exeter City	1 (17)	Republic of Ireland
Ambrose Fogarty	Hartlepools United	1 (11)	Republic of Ireland
Brian Evans	Hereford United	1 (7)	Wales
Harry Hardy	Stockport County	1	England

Colchester United, Darlington, Halifax Town, Rochdale, Scunthorpe United, Torquay United and Wigan Athletic have not had one of their players capped.

With Scottish League clubs

In descending order of appearances, with number of all international appearances in brackets where figures differ.

Danny McGrain	Celtic	62	Scotland
Willie Miller	Aberdeen	61	Scotland
George Young	Rangers	53	Scotland
Alan Rough	Partick Thistle	51 (53)	Scotland
Lawrie Reilly	Hibernian	38	Scotland
Dave Narey	Dundee United	33	Scotland

Tommy Walker	Heart of Midlothian	29	Scotland
Jimmy Cowan	Morton	25	Scotland
Alec Hamilton	Dundee	24	Scotland
Watty Arnott	Queen's Park	14	Scotland
Alec Parker	Falkirk	14 (15)	Scotland
Tommy Ring	Clyde	12	Scotland
George Stevenson	Motherwell	12	Scotland
Joe Nibloe	Kilmarnock	11	Scotland
Jimmy Crapnell	Airdrieonians	9	Scotland
John Lindsay	Dumbarton	8	Scotland
James McAulay	Dumbarton	8	Scotland
Iain Munro	St Mirren	7	Scotland
Andy Wilson	Dunfermline Athletic	6 (12)	Scotland
Dave Morris	Raith Rovers	6	Scotland
George Aitken	East Fife	5 (8)	Scotland
Humphrey Jones	East Stirlingshire	5	Wales
Sandy McLaren	St Johnstone	5	Scotland
Jim Nisbet	Ayr United	3	Scotland
Jim Paterson	Cowdenbeath	3	Scotland
Billy Houliston	Queen of the South	3	Scotland
Alexander Keillor	Montrose	2 (6)	Scotland
Ned Doig	Arbroath	2 (5)	Scotland
Jimmy King	Hamilton Academicals	2	Scotland
Bobby Howe	Hamilton Academicals	2	Scotland
Jock White	Albion Rovers	1 (2)	Scotland
Jock Hepburn	Alloa	1	Scotland

Berwick Rangers, Brechin City, Clydebank, Forfar Athletic, Meadowbank Thistle, Stenhousemuir, Stirling Albion and Stranraer have not had one of their players capped.

Johnny Haynes (above, left) capped on 56 occasions by England during his distinguished career with Fulham. **Bert Gray** (left) a resolute goalkeeper for Wales and a variety of Football League clubs. **George Young** (above) the stalwart Rangers defender and the Ibrox club's most capped player.

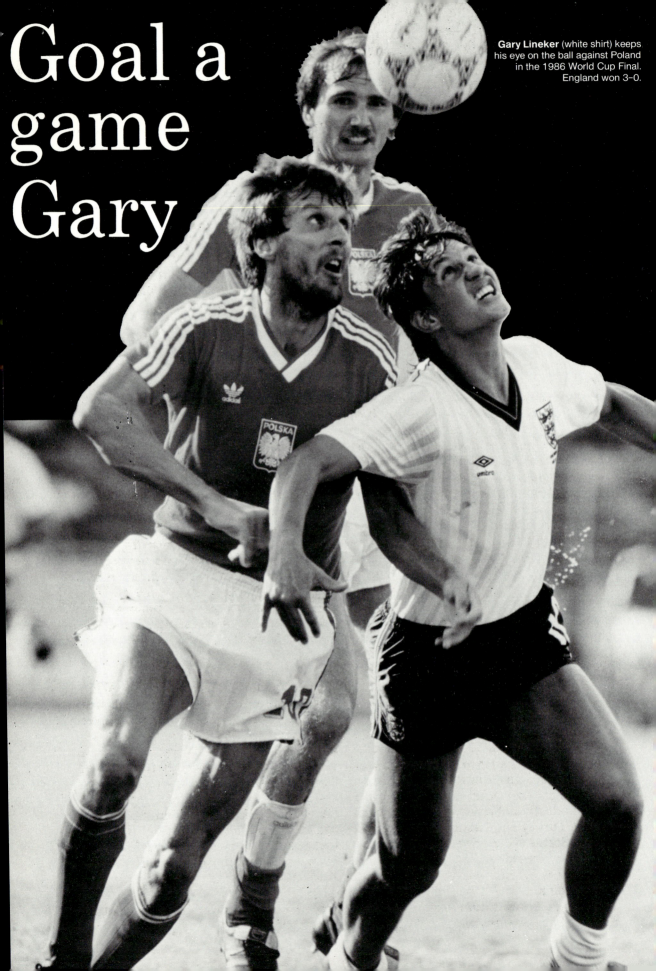

Goal a game Gary

Gary Lineker (white shirt) keeps his eye on the ball against Poland in the 1986 World Cup Final. England won 3–0.

Gary Lineker was the leading scorer in the 1986 World Cup finals in Mexico when he scored six goals in England's five matches. He was promptly signed by Barcelona who paid £2.75 million for his transfer from Everton with whom he had enjoyed his best scoring season with 30 League goals.

35

Born and raised in Leicester, he had been taken on as an apprentice at Filbert Street and was on the short side for a striker in his teenage days, standing barely 5ft 6in. He made his first team debut in the 1978–79 season but did not establish himself as a regular choice until three seasons later.

Once settled in the Leicester attack he became a consistent marksman and in four successive seasons he finished as the club's top scorer. In the summer of 1985 Everton were the successful club who gained his signature after he had rejected a new contract with Leicester. They paid £800 000 for him, though Leicester wanted £1 million and the fee had to be decided by a tribunal. He had scored over 100 League and Cup goals while with them, despite suffering relegation with the club in his early years but helping them back to the First Division when he was a regular.

Lineker's first England honour had come while with City. He came on as substitute against Scotland at Hampden Park in May 1984 but had to wait until the following season before he was given a full outing in England colours.

That came against the Republic of Ireland at Wembley and he celebrated the occasion with a goal. But in his first nine games he scored six times but was the first to admit that the other five goals had been modestly achieved with a hat-trick against Turkey and two more against the United States of America. This prompted critics to consider that his record of scoring was against comparatively weak opposition and with other choices for the England attack was not looked upon as a fixture. Thus he went into the World Cup finals with something to prove not only for England but to himself and his critics. Yet the hallmarks of a goalscorer were already evident in his play.

His directness and speed, allied to an ability to dart into scoring positions in the penalty area, made him a potentially lethal striker and he had the accuracy in finishing to back it up. But he went into the World Cup in Mexico in 1986 still on trial and in the opening two matches was paired up front with Mark Hateley. Nothing went right for Lineker or England. But when changes were forced on the team against Poland and Peter Beardsley was brought into the attack, it all went well.

Lineker responded with a hat-trick and almost overnight became a world-class striker. In reality he had previously been a class player, but had left some people unconvinced. His goal touch was a delight to watch.

Plunged from the international arena into the exacting demands of the Spanish game in Barcelona, he made the transition in fine style. He scored regularly for the Catalan club and though they had to bow to Real Madrid in the Spanish championship, Lineker's marksmanship was acclaimed by the Barcelona supporters. But his finest hour in Spain came that same season while on England duty, when he scored all four goals for them in a 4–2 win which left any remaining doubters sure of his ability.

Lineker's other attribute is a prowess on the snooker table. His friend Willie Thorne, the Leicester snooker professional, is an admirer of his record of making century breaks on several occasions. Perhaps Lineker's dead-eyed accuracy on the football field has been assisted through his potting ability on the green velvet. Oddly enough, although he won a Second Division championship medal with Leicester, most of Lineker's medals had come from snooker, though in 1986 he was elected both Football Writers Association and Professional Footballers Association player of the year and was second in the European Footballer of the Year awards.

Helmut Schoen:

In 14 years in charge of West Germany's national team, Helmut Schoen became the most successful manager in the history of the World Cup and European Championship competitions. He led his country to first, second and third places in the former tournament and to first and second in the latter series.

His background was not one of a footballing family. His father had been a Dresden art dealer and Schoen was given an academic upbringing. Football was more of a hobby at first but did not diminish his enthusiasm for the game. He worked in a bank but developed as an inside-forward with Dresdner FC with whom he won League and Cup honours in the war years. But by then he had already achieved international honours.

He was first capped for Germany in November 1937 scoring twice against Sweden, but after adding further appearances to his credit found that Germany was in the middle of World War Two. The game carried on and Schoen was in Dresdner's team which won the Cup in 1940 and also finished as runners-up in the championship play-offs.

In 1941 they won the Cup again and in 1943 and 1944 they won the championship in successive years. Despite the existence of hostilities, Germany contrived to play international fixtures against other Axis countries, neutrals and satellites. Indeed they managed to play more internationals against other countries than any other nation involved in the war. But Schoen's own last international was oddly enough also against Sweden in October 1941. His best personal performance had been scoring three goals against Yugoslavia in Zagreb in October 1939. In 16 matches he had scored 17 goals.

Yet it was a knee injury which ended his career and after the war he became a foreign correspondent, learning French and English which enabled him to become one of the most fluent and knowledgeable people in his field.

But his interest in soccer had not subsided and he took up coaching in the Wiesbaden area. Later he became regional coach in the Saar and ironically was in charge of the Saarland team which met West Germany in the World Cup qualifying rounds of the 1954 World Cup. A year later he was appointed assistant national team manager in the West Germany hierarchy under Sepp Herberger. In 1964 he took over after Herberger's retirement and was in charge of the National squad in the 1966 World Cup.

West Germany reached the final and though they forced England to extra time, had to be satisfied with runners-up position. Four years later they reached the semi-final but were beaten in the marathon with Italy and had to settle for third place in Mexico.

A stomach operation in 1970 had hindered his health but he was rarely less than courteous, although this was often mistaken as a sign of weakness. But by 1972 and the European Championship, the Germans were at their peak. Schoen's shrewd attitude of giving the players considerable free rein within the system operated, proved of immense benefit to the overall performances, which brought the best out of the players. However, as he himself subsequently admitted, the quality of the players at his disposal at the time was such that it needed the lightest of guiding hands to produce a championship winning team.

Two years later when West Germany

Master manager

West Germany's team manager **Helmut Schoen** hugs Uli Hoeness (left) after the 1974 World Cup triumph.

hosted the World Cup finals, the team was past its peak but Schoen's ingenuity and the experience of the players pulled them through to such an extent that this first place was in many respects a better performance than it had been two years earlier.

In 1976 the Germans just failed to retain their European Championship crown, losing on penalties to Czechoslovakia in the final. But the best was over. The World Cup team of 1978 badly let Schoen down. His frustration led him into arguments with skipper Franz Beckenbauer and his distinguished managerial career ended in an anti-climax after many triumphs.

The Tannadice tangerines

Dundee United's 1987 UEFA Cup Final team (back row, left to right) Redford, Holt, Narey, Thomson, Hegarty, Bannon. Front: Malpas, Kirkwood, McInally, Sturrock, Bowman.

Dundee United celebrated their 75th anniversary in 1984 with the Scottish League title which they won a year earlier for the first time, having consolidated themselves after decades of struggle to a sustained period of challenging for domestic honours and the edge of success in Europe.

It was in the early 1980s that the club finally made the breakthrough with successive wins in the League Cup in 1980 and 1981, a runners-up place the following season, as well as finishing beaten Scottish Cup finalists in 1981.

Previously their achievements had been limited. In 1974 they reached the Scottish Cup Final for the first time but were beaten by Celtic who had just collected their ninth successive championship. But it did give United another chance of playing in Europe, though they had found the second round an insurmountable hurdle in previous entries in the Fairs and UEFA Cups. This was so except in 1966–67 when they reached the third round, though only after a bye in the first.

But the 1981–82 UEFA Cup dramatically changed that situation as Dundee United reached the quarter-finals before losing to Radnicki Nis (Yugoslavia). The following season they again reached the last eight when their conquerors were Bohemians (Czechoslovakia).

United's first honour had been in 1924–25 when they won the Second Division championship. But they stayed in the First Division only two years. Yet two seasons later they were champions again to remain just for one season in the top division. United went up once more as runners-up in 1931 but had to wait almost 30 years before repeating even this modest achievement.

The club's origins had been bound up in the Dundee Hibernians club, formed in 1909. After one season in the Northern League they joined the Second Division of the Scottish League. But during the First World War the Second Division was disbanded, and some of the bigger clubs wanted it to stay that way. So Dundee Hibs joined the Central League in 1920 after war years in the Eastern League.

The situation was resolved the following year and the Second Division reinstated only for Dundee Hibs to lose their place by finishing second from bottom in it. In 1922–23 they played in the Scottish Alliance, only to be restored to the Second Division in 1923–24 at a time when the club was attempting to change its name to Dundee City. However, Dundee, the senior club in the city, objected and so Dundee United came into being instead.

Even so, United were the poor relations if still near neighbours. For many years they made do with their undistinguished wooden stand and cramped dressing-rooms. But in 1956 a successful pools scheme was started to provide much-needed finance.

In the 1960s, Dundee United pioneered the influx of Scandinavian players with recruits from Denmark, Sweden and Norway and in December 1971 the club appointed the dour, thoughtful Jim McLean as manager and the long haul from obscurity began in earnest. They became founder members of the Premier Division in 1975.

Following their achievements in the early 1980s the club were runners-up to Rangers in the Skol Cup in 1985 and Celtic in the Scottish Cup. Moreover for four years in succession to 1986–87 the team finished a creditable third in the Premier Division.

As Scottish champions in 1983, Dundee United undertook their first European Cup venture the next season and shook the continent by reaching the semi-final against AS Roma (Italy), just losing on aggregate by the odd goal in five.

But they went even further in the UEFA Cup in 1986–87 accounting for Lens (France), Universitatea Craiova (Rumania), Hajduk Split (Yugoslavia), Barcelona (Spain) and Borussia Moenchengladbach (West Germany) to reach the two-legged final against IFK Gothenburg (Sweden).

Unfortunately for Dundee United the domestic season was the longest in the history of the Scottish game and four days before the second leg at Tannadice Park and with a single goal deficit to retrieve, they had to play in the Scottish Cup Final against St Mirren, lost 1–0 and wearily could only draw with the Swedes.

Best supported club

In recent years Barcelona have become the best supported team not only in Spain but anywhere in Europe. They have more registered fans than any other club and at the start of the 1987–88 season numbered 108 170 for their Camp Nou ground with its capacity of 115 000.

Barcelona, the No. 1 team in Europe for support, and beating Juventus 1–0 in this European cup quarter-final. Moratalla (dark shirt) beats Juventus substitute Caricola to the ball.

Though they have had their successes on the field at home and abroad they trail behind Real Madrid in the number of League championships won and are second to Athletic Bilbao in the quest for cup honours. Moreover, in Europe they have never been able to match their arch-rivals Real Madrid in the European Cup, a trophy which has always eluded them.

Founded in 1899, they were runners-up in the first Spanish Cup in 1902 and had the distinction of becoming the first Spanish League champions in 1928–29. Barcelona won the Cup in 1910, 1912 and 1913. Runners-up placing in 1919 was the prelude to more successes in the 1920s.

Barcelona won it in 1920, 1922, 1925, 1926 and 1928 but were beaten finalists in 1932 and 1936. Indeed it was not until the 1940s that fortune swung their way again in League and Cup. In 1942 they won the Cup for the ninth time and 1944–45 won only their second championship title.

In successive years 1948 and 1949 they won the League and twice again in 1952 and 1953 when the rivalry with Real Madrid was at its height. There were more triumphs in the Cup which Barcelona won three times in succession from 1951 to 1953. The next year they were runners-up.

The Cup was taken again in 1957 and in 1959 their first League and Cup double was achieved followed by another championship in 1960. By then European football had a firm foothold in Spain thanks chiefly to Real Madrid, but Barcelona were pioneers of success in the Fairs Cup. They won the first competition in 1958, beating a London selection in the two-legged final.

Barcelona kept the Cup the following series which ended in 1960, beating Birmingham City again on aggregate. Yet despite these achievements, they had disappointment in the European Cup.

After five successive years of Real Madrid's domination of the European Champion Clubs Cup, Barcelona managed to reach the final but were beaten 3–2 by Benfica in Berne, Switzerland, in the 1960–61 final. The following season they were runners-up in the Fairs Cup to Valencia but won it in 1965–66 against another Spanish club, Real Zaragoza.

They had the satisfaction of winning the old Fairs Cup outright in a match against Leeds United who were the last winners of that competition. Barcelona won 2–1. But this had come after a Cup Winners' Cup setback in the 1968–69 final against Slovan Bratislava who beat them 3–2 in Basle.

However, there was a happier return to the same Swiss venue for them in the 1978–79 Cup Winners' Cup Final in which they edged out Fortuna Dusseldorf 4–3 after extra time, and in 1981–82 they took full advantage of being at home in the final to beat Standard Liege 2–1 in the same competition.

At home Barcelona won the League in 1973–74 but were beaten Cup finalists the same year, though they had won the Cup twice in 1963 and 1968 and again in 1971.

Further successes came in 1978, 1981 and 1983 plus runners-up in 1984. But the long-awaited Spanish championship revival began with the appointment of Terry Venables in time for the 1984–85 season and ended in triumph when Barcelona won their tenth championship. Competing in the following year's European Cup they managed to reach the final but were beaten 2–0 on penalties in Seville by Steaua Bucharest after the match ended in a goalless draw. It was their second runners-up place as they were also beaten in the Spanish Cup Final, but consolation came in winning the League Cup which they had previously won in 1983.

Bobby Charlton

Bobby Charlton holds three records for Manchester United and one for England which might well stand for all time. He played in more games, scored more goals and was United's most capped player as well as being the highest goalscorer in his country's international history.

But there was far more to Charlton than mere records. When he had established himself with club and country there was no more explosive forward anywhere in the land with the ability to create some-

Bobby Charlton during his early days with Manchester United.

Record breaker

thing positive on the field and excitement off it. It was simply that whenever Charlton had possession, the crowd expected something to happen. He had flair, that rare commodity for an English player. Moreover he was a sportsman first and last, on the pitch and in life.

Born into the famous Milburn footballing family of Ashington he was the younger brother of Jackie Charlton. He signed for Manchester United in 1953 straight from school and in doing so thwarted the aims of 17 other clubs who were chasing this schoolboy starlet.

He played with the other Busby Babes in three FA Youth Cup winning teams for the club from 1954 to 1956 inclusive and was given his first opportunity in the League side on 6 October 1956 as deputy for the injured Tommy Taylor, ironically against Charlton Athletic, and scored two goals on this impressive debut. United won the championship that season. The following term he had won a regular place in the side when the heart of the club was ripped out by the Munich air disaster. Charlton was one of the survivors and assumed a responsibility afterwards which matured and enhanced him as a player and the focal point of the United reconstruction.

He made his debut for England in the immediate post-Munich months and in hindsight his omission from the World Cup side in Sweden was a costly error. After that he was rarely absent on international duty, taking his total of appearances to 106 and a record 49 goals.

Without doubt the peak of his international career came in the 1966 World Cup when he helped England carry off the trophy for the first time. He scored two unforgettable goals against Portugal in the semi-final which set up the final accolade against West Germany. He was elected Footballer of the Year and European Footballer of the Year.

Two years later there was another famous occasion at Wembley when Manchester United won the European Cup beating Benfica 4–1 after extra time. Charlton scored twice including a rare header. The following year he was awarded the OBE.

His other honours included two League championship medals in 1965 and 1967, and FA Cup winners medal in 1963, six Under-23 caps and the CBE in 1974.

Charlton's qualities were power, range and artistry. His distribution with the sweeping crossfield pass could change the point of attack in impressively accurate fashion. He captained United from 1968 to 1973 and also led his country. In April 1973 he left Old Trafford and became player-manager of Preston North End. But like many an outstanding player before and since, his flirtation with the managerial side was not a success and he resigned over a disagreement with the board.

He did have a brief spell as Wigan Athletic caretaker-manager while on that club's board but subsequently became a director of Manchester United and organized a school for youngsters learning soccer skills.

His total number of League appearances for United came to 606 and he scored 199 goals. In League Cup, FA Cup and European games plus his League record he made 754 appearances and scored 247 goals.

Charlton has also become well known on BBC television as an assistant to the commentator on live transmissions on a Sunday afternoon, injecting his own brand of enthusiasm for the game.

Brady: Midfield

Liam Brady is the Republic of Ireland's most capped international. Appropriately, perhaps, he overtook the record of Johnny Giles, one of his idols and another outstanding midfield player from the Emerald Isle, in achieving it. Originally establishing himself in England, he enjoyed a successful period in Italy before returning to continue his career in this country.

Liam Brady who returned to the Football League fold with West Ham after a successful period in Italian football.

maestro

Dublin-born, he came to Arsenal as an apprentice from a footballing family and had to thank a surprise defeat for the club in a League Cup tie at Highbury against Tranmere Rovers for his League debut. This came as substitute in the next League game against Birmingham City in October 1973 when he was 17. His first goal came in the last game of the season against Queen's Park Rangers, also in the No. 12 shirt.

Brady continued to make sporadic appearances that season and the following term established himself in the midfield area quickly to become an influential figure in the Arsenal pattern of play.

Like most naturally gifted left-footed players he became the focus of attention as a cultured exponent of controlled distribution. Only two years after his League debut he was making his first full appearance for the Republic of Ireland against the USSR.

For three successive years in the late 1970s Arsenal reached the FA Cup Final. The first in 1978 brought disappointment when Ipswich Town beat them. In the next it seemed inevitable that the game with Manchester United would go into extra time until Brady launched Graham Rix into a run which produced the winning goal.

The third year was doubly disappointing because Arsenal were also in the Cup Winners' Cup Final and lost both matches. For Brady, who had already made it clear that this was to be his last season at Highbury on the end of his contract, had the misfortune to miss a penalty, ironically along with Rix, in the penalty shoot-out against Valencia.

But Arsenal did not want to lose the services of their most talented Irishman and made him an offer that would have allowed him to become the most highly paid player in the country. Brady declined because he wanted the challenge of fresh fields and was transferred to Juventus who were able to obtain his services for the statutory UEFA and EEC controlled fee of only £600 000.

In all competitions for Arsenal he had made 307 appearances and scored 59 goals, but had more importantly stamped his authority on the Gunners' play.

Brady never hid the admiration he felt for the hallowed halls of Highbury and was soon to learn to respect the awesome organization that was Juventus. Having been pipped for first place in the previous season the Turin club were anxious to win the championship again.

Juventus duly won the title in Brady's first season after a strong challenge from Roma and he proved an integral piece in the club's armoury, missing only two League games. They retained their title in the following 1981–82 season but only by a point from Fiorentina. This time Brady was absent only once.

In 1982–83 Brady moved to Sampdoria for two seasons and had a further two with Internazionale who actually paid £1 168 000 for his signature, before he linked up with Ascoli in 1986–87. But his association with Ascoli was much less than satisfactory. The club was struggling. There was a row over alleged unpaid wages but eventually he agreed to forgo his claim for a transfer to England.

In reality, two of the keenest clubs chasing Brady were the Scottish giants Celtic and Rangers. But in the end Brady decided to accept West Ham United's £100 000 offer, again influenced by their traditions of imaginative and attractive football.

In addition to Giles, Brady's heroes have been George Best, Bobby Charlton and Michel Platini and he has had the talent to stand comparison with all of them.

When Tottenham Hotspur goalkeeper Ray Clemence played at
Wembley in the 1987 FA Cup Final
against Coventry City it was his
42nd appearance on the hallowed

Ray Clemence: Mr Wembley

Ray Clemence prepares to clear the ball upfield.

turf and his second record-breaking achievement of the season. Previously he had reached 1099 first class appearances.

to be considered for further selection if he was merely to be deputy goalkeeper.

Clemence hit his worst injury spell at Tottenham during 1983–84 and it seemed that his senior days were at last over. But during the following summer he trained throughout apart from a holiday break of six days and regained his first team place.

In 1985–86 he made his 1000th first class appearance and in three seasons missed only three League games. Even at the age of 39 he was still turning out for the club, after his personal milestone of his 1099th senior outing on 18 April 1987 against Charlton Athletic. Other highlights of his career have included captaining England against Brazil in 1981, his first FA Cup winners medal in 1974 and the 1977 European Cup Final triumph in Rome against Borussia Moenchengladbach.

His first outing for Liverpool was in a League Cup tie against Swansea City played in atrocious weather with a gale blowing. Clemence had trouble with his goal kicks and one spectator behind his goal told him to give up and leave the field. But Clemence was not beaten in a 2–0 win and this habit of keeping clean sheets became one of his traits. In 1978–79 he conceded only 16 goals in 42 League games for Liverpool which is a record in the First Division.

Clemence began the 1987–88 season with a total of 1106 matches to his credit, comprised of 50 for Scunthorpe, 665 for Liverpool, 324 for Tottenham and 67 in representative matches including internationals.

In June 1987 he was awarded the MBE in the Queen's Birthday Honours List and added a further string to his bow during the early stages of the following campaign when he assisted on the coaching side during a managerial change round at White Hart Lane.

A cool command of his penalty area and beyond made him an additional defender in his Liverpool days. Since then he has matured in all possible aspects of the goalkeeping art.

His record of senior matches at club level would probably have been much higher had it not been for spending nearly three seasons before becoming first choice at Liverpool. But after being on the books of Notts County as a youngster he received his first chance with Scunthorpe United. He made four appearances in his first season with Scunthorpe during 1965–66 and the following term became first choice, missing only two games. A number of clubs became interested in him at the time but it was Liverpool who paid £20 000 for his signature in June 1967.

Senior goalkeeper at Anfield in those days was Tommy Lawrence, and he was as consistent a performer as Clemence was to become himself in later years. So for two years the youngster had to be content with largely Central League football and in 1968–69 let in only 25 goals in 42 reserve outings. But he impressed enough to win an Under-23 cap.

Mid-way through the 1969–70 season he made his League debut and in his first 11 full seasons was absent from League duty on only six occasions. During this period he collected numerous honours including five League championship medals, three European Cups, two UEFA Cups, one FA Cup and one League Cup. In addition to his Under-23 cap for England he added 56 full appearances for the national side.

In 1981 he was transferred to Tottenham Hotspur for £300 000 at the age of 33. But there was no sign of his career taking a nosedive as he added to his list of accomplishments at White Hart Lane. But after winning 61 caps for England at a time when he and Peter Shilton were vying for the No. 1 spot, he said that he did not wish

Forever Everton

Everton captain **Kevin Ratcliffe** (left) just manages to direct his header despite the high-leaping Lee Chapman of Sheffield Wednesday.

Everton have played First Division football for more seasons than any other Football League club. Since they became one of its founder members in 1888, they have spent all but four seasons in the top sphere.

They were not relegated until 1930 but quickly bounced back as champions of the Second Division and did not suffer a similar fate for another 20 years. In 1951 they fell into Division Two for the second time and could only finish seventh. The following term seventh was the highest position they touched all season and their final placing was 16th. But in 1953–54 they were runners-up and regained a First Division status which has been maintained ever since.

The club's origins were wrapped up in the church and cricket. Youngsters connected with St Domingo's Church formed a cricket club and decided to add football to their repertoire in 1878 for the winter months. Thus the St Domingo's Football Club came into being, soon tempting recruits from outside the church and in November 1879 at a meeting in the Queen's Head Hotel, Village Street, the name of the Everton district was chosen.

Everton were among the 12 original League clubs and quietly established themselves after their first season. In 1889–90 they were runners-up to Preston North End and the following season reversed the position to win the championship themselves.

Even after the split in the club in 1892 which saw the separate foundation of Liverpool, Everton continued to enjoy occasional success. In 1893 they were runners-up in the FA Cup and two years later came second in the League race. Then in 1897 they were again beaten finalists in the Cup.

Twice, just after the turn of the century in 1902 and 1905, Everton finished runners-up in the League. The next season they won the FA Cup for the first time and were runners-up in 1907. In 1909 and 1912 Everton finished second in the championship but succeeded in achieving their second title in 1914–15.

The 1920s produced some excellent football without the accompanying honours it deserved. But after narrowly avoiding relegation in 1921 and again in 1927 the club enjoyed a memorable season in 1927–28, winning the championship for the third time and scoring 102 goals in the process.

Even this did not prevent problems arising and after another term of toil they went down in 1931 before scoring a club record 121 goals to win promotion. This time they won the First Division championship the following season and the FA Cup in 1933.

Further indifferent seasons followed until Everton won the 1938–39 First Division championship impressively, never being lower than second place at any time. At the end of the campaign they appointed Theo Kelly as their first manager. It was their fifth championship yet they had to wait until 1963 for the sixth and in between had slumped to the Second Division.

Everton's third FA Cup win came in 1966 and they were runners-up two years later. In 1970 they achieved their seventh championship and the second under their disciplinarian manager Harry Catterick. But it was another seven years before another near honour, runners-up in the League Cup.

However, by the 1980s there were definite signs of a renaissance at Goodison Park under the shrewd managership of Howard Kendall, who had been appointed in 1981.

In 1984 Everton won the FA Cup and were runners-up in the Milk Cup. The next season they came close to a treble but won two: the League championship and the Cup Winners' Cup, and lost in the FA Cup. In 1987 they regained the championship for their ninth title to provide a fitting finale for Kendall, who left to take over Spain's Athletic Bilbao.

The clockwork

Johan Cruyff became the first £1 million player when he joined Barcelona from Ajax in September 1963, the first to win three European Footballer of the Year awards and the inspiration of the enthralling 'total' football which took his Dutch club to three successive European Cup titles.

Johan Cruyff who led Ajax to triumphs on and off the field as player, then manager.

orange

Born in the poor quarter of Amsterdam in 1947, his connections with Ajax were close. In fact his mother worked at the ground as a cleaner. Cruyff joined the club while still a schoolboy and made his senior debut as a 17-year-old in the 1964–65 season.

He scored four League goals that season and the following one as a regular player he scored 16 in the League in helping Ajax to the League and Cup double. In the next seven seasons he took his total to 187 in the League as Ajax won six championships and four Dutch Cup titles.

Between 1971 and 1973 Ajax won three European Cup trophies and in successive years Cruyff was elected Europe's top player. Slightly built, this lanky Dutchman was probably the most outstanding forward produced by the country of his origin and one of Europe's most accomplished. Sharp reactions, excellent control, speed, acceleration and the ability to change direction instantly made him a difficult proposition for defenders to combat.

Though his goalscoring output was not phenomenal, the danger he posed to defenders was enough to create havoc and his final cross or pass was invariably of pin-point accuracy, leaving colleagues with inviting openings.

Cruyff's manager at Ajax had been Rinus Michels who left in 1971 to become boss of Barcelona. Following protracted negotiations he was transferred to the Spanish club for £922 300 with some £400 000 going to Cruyff, who thus became one of the best-paid professional sportsmen in the world at the time.

Cruyff captained Holland in the 1974 World Cup when they finished runners-up and though he helped them qualify for the 1978 finals he said he would retire and not

However, after speculation that his business interests were suffering, he signed for Los Angeles Aztecs in May 1979. Later he played for Washington Diplomats and Levante in Spain. Even so he was not finished with Dutch football and made a further comeback with Ajax's arch-rivals, Feyenoord, before taking up coaching and guiding Ajax once more. In 1987 he led them to the Cup Winners' Cup title, their first European trophy since his own days as a player.

One of the finest players in Europe in the 1970s, Cruyff made 48 appearances for Holland, scoring 33 goals. He had one weakness: a demonstrative temperament which certainly cost him more appearances for his country.

His first full appearance for his country was against Hungary in 1966 at the age of 19. In his second, against Czechoslovakia, he was involved in a stormy argument with the East German referee Rudi Glockner and was sent off for apparently striking the official.

Film of the event made it clear that it had been a gesture rather than a blow, and the Dutch Federation suspended him from the national team for a year, later commuted to six months, though it was ten months before he was restored to the side against, ironically, East Germany.

There were other disappointments, not the least his farewell in the Ajax Stadium on 7 November 1978 in a friendly against Bayern Munich. Ajax lost 8–0 and instead of bouquets, only cushions were thrown onto the pitch by the disappointed crowd.

Cruyff was top scorer in Holland with 33 goals in 1966–67 and again in 1971–72 with 25. With his additional goals for Feyenoord he reached 215 League goals overall in Holland, the third highest total in the country's history.

In the colours of Barcelona he scored 47 League goals and nine in European matches and a further 25 in the North American Soccer League.

Coventry's dynamic duo

When Coventry City won the FA Cup in 1987 it represented their first major honour in 104 years of existence but was achieved with style and good humour, much of which was derived from the unique approach of the management partnership of George Curtis and John Sillett. However, it was not the first trophy which Coventry won in 1987. They had also taken the FA Youth Cup.

Not that Coventry have been slow to produce new ideas. In fact they led the country in bringing football clubs out of the dark ages with many innovations including leisure, refreshment and restaurant facilities which took on an entirely new dimension for football clubs.

Coventry's successful management partnership: **John Sillett** (left) and **George Curtis**, soak up the Wembley atmosphere before the triumph over Spurs.

On the field they could also claim to have survived in the First Division ever since being promoted to it. No other club can boast that record. But it has been a titanic struggle at times for Coventry to retain their membership. Yet it was appropriate that Coventry should enjoy their most rewarding season in 1986–87 as it had been 20 years since they first won a place in Division One at the end of 1966–67.

Naturally, all that was a long way from the embryo days when a group of workers at Singers cycle factory founded Singers FC in 1883. It was not until 1898 that the club changed its name to Coventry City, but it was still some years before they entered the Football League.

It was in 1919 that Coventry became members of the Second Division, by which time they had settled in at Highfield Road. By 1925, however, Coventry had slumped into the Third Division. Because of the overloading of southern-based clubs in the Southern Section that year, City had to be switched to the Northern Section.

But in 1926 they went back to the Southern Section and remained there for 10 years. At the end of that era they had won promotion to the Second Division, thanks to a well-marshalled defence which established a club record of conceding only 45 goals.

That period saw a number of club records established which have remained to the present day. In 1931–32, Coventry scored 108 goals in the League with Clarrie Bourton obtaining 49 of them himself. Actually between 1931 and 1937, Bourton hit an aggregate of 171, which is another Coventry record.

Anyway, Coventry survived in the Second Division until 1952. Once or twice they did more than that. In 1937–38 they missed promotion to the First Division by just two points and finished a highly creditable fourth. Again their defence did well, equalling their record of conceding just 45 goals.

In that season only four teams managed to win at Highfield Road and in 1938–39 the defence again provided the backbone of the team and ironically enough only let in 45 goals. In 1937–38 the then record crowd of 44 930 had crammed into the ground for a match with Aston Villa on 12 March 1938.

But the 1950s were a depressing time for the club. Relegation to the Third Division (South) came in 1952 and worse was to follow. With the formation of the Fourth Division in 1958, City were to find themselves as members of it.

The club had tried the bold, imaginative idea of appointing a top-class coach with continental experience as manager. Jesse Carver, who had made his name in Italy, was the first and his right-hand man was George Raynor who had masterminded Sweden's national side to many triumphs, including runners-up in the 1958 World Cup.

Carver did not stay, neither did Raynor, and eventually Coventry went down but mercifully for just one season and they came back as runners-up in the Fourth Division. But it was not until the appointment of Jimmy Hill in November 1961 that the club really started to take off.

In six years Coventry achieved promotion through the divisions to the top, while off the field the ground was transformed into a modern, compact stadium with plenty of exciting amenities to persuade supporters that the club was leading the way in spectator comfort.

The best season they had was in 1969–70 when they finished sixth, but generally Coventry were scrambling for points at the other end of the table to prevent the drop into the Second Division. But that sixth place gave them a shot at European competition. Alas, this ended in defeat in the Fairs Cup by Bayern Munich.

But when granite George Curtis, who still holds the club record of 486 appearances, and coach jolly John Sillett came together success was finally achieved.

The Dean machine

Dixie Dean (right) shakes hands with the Spanish goalkeeper Ricardo Zamora.

William Ralph 'Dixie' Dean created an individual Football League goal-scoring record in 1927–28 which will probably stand for all time. He scored 60 goals in 39 appearances for Everton, 40 of them with his feet, the other 20 with his head.

He first came to prominence with Tranmere Rovers, making his debut for them in January 1924 as a teenager and had scored 27 goals in 27 matches when Everton paid £3000 for his services in March 1925.

He became an instant goalscoring success at Goodison Park, developing as a powerfully tough, 5ft 10in, 12st 7lb marksman with almost faultless positional sense who scored 32 League goals in his first full season but was then involved in a motor cycle accident which might well have ended his career. It was in June 1926 that he fractured his skull and jaw and it was feared that he might never be able to head the ball again. But he was playing and scoring goals within four months. The following year he had his finest season.

His spirit and determination, as much as his sheer physical presence, made him a formidable opponent for defences. He was especially dangerous in the air and his heading ability was little short of devastating.

His international career was not disrupted by the injury and he made his first appearance for England against Wales in 1927, scoring twice in a 3–3 draw. In fact in his first five internationals he scored 12 goals. He also helped Everton win the FA Cup in 1933, scoring one of the three goals by which his club beat Manchester City.

In 1927–28 his actual total for the season in all matches had been an incredible 82 with three goals from FA Cup ties and 19 in a variety of representative games: six for the Football League, eight in England trials and five in internationals. He quietened the Hampden Roar with two goals to help England beat Scotland there for the first time in 23 years. In the League his 60 included five in a row against Manchester United, a four, plus five hat-tricks and fourteen twos.

Yet after a run of four matches in which they had failed to score, Everton slumped to second place. But Dean rediscovered his dynamic scoring form and finished with 17 goals in the eight successive games in which he played. On the last day of the season, with the title already safe, he scored all three goals in a 3–3 draw with Arsenal to overhaul George Camsell's record of 59 set up the previous season for Second Division Middlesbrough. With only eight minutes remaining Dean headed his third from a corner.

The famous Dean head was again in evidence in the match against Bolton Wanderers to clinch the 1932 championship. It was his 45th League goal and Everton won the title with two matches to spare.

After registering a massive 377 League and Cup goals in 431 matches for Everton, including 349 in 399 League outings alone, he was transferred to Notts County in March 1938.

He ended his Football League career early the following year after 379 League goals in 434 matches. In addition he had scored 27 FA Cup goals and 18 in 16 international appearances for England. Dean joined Sligo Rovers in January 1939 and in less than half a season scored 11 goals in 11 games.

During Army war service he played only a handful of matches for unit and representative sides but was always among the goals and in his one guest appearance for a League club scored for York City.

He disliked the name 'Dixie', preferring friends to call him Bill. His later years were tragic in that he had his right leg amputated in 1976 after a lengthy illness but he had the end he might have wished for himself, dying at Goodison Park in March 1980, minutes after the final whistle of a derby game against Liverpool.

56

Danny McGrain's career might have ended prematurely in 1972, at the age of only 21, after suffering a fractured skull. But he recovered, made more than 600 League and Cup appearances for Celtic and was capped on 62 occasions by Scotland.

Granite

Daniel Fergus McGrain joined the Parkhead club from Mayhill Juniors in 1967–68 season when he was a teenager.

Danny McGrain who was the inspiration of many Celtic teams for more than a decade.

McGrain

Originally he was a wing-half but Celtic converted him with considerable success to full-back, where he developed into a strong-tackling, resourceful pillar of defensive strength.

He had to wait until the 1970–71 season before he made his initial League appearance in the famous green and white hoops and had made only 10 appearances by the time he sustained his serious injury in February 1972 in a match against Falkirk.

But within six months he was completely fit and started the 1972–73 season as Celtic's first choice. A year after his accident he was playing for the Scottish Under-23s against England and the same season made his full international debut against Wales at Wrexham.

McGrain played in eight consecutive games for Scotland and was a regular choice when the team was selected to play in the World Cup finals in West Germany in 1974. He even managed to shake off the effects of a chest injury sustained in the Scottish Cup Final that spring to appear in all three of Scotland's matches in the final stages of the competition.

By the time of the next World Cup he had made 40 appearances for his country but had been further hit by injury problems. An early-season ankle injury kept him on the sidelines for four months in 1977–78 and then news leaked out that he was a diabetic. This condition had been diagnosed shortly after the 1974 World Cup.

In fact McGrain missed the Argentine finals and only came back into senior football reckoning during the 1978–79 season. But by the time the following season came round he had regained his Scotland place.

He made 16 consecutive appearances for the national side in the run-up to the 1982 World Cup finals held in Spain. He began the final series at right-back but missed the defeat against Brazil and was brought back for what turned out to be his last international outing as substitute against the USSR.

But if his career for his country was at an end at the age of 31, his role as club captain continued for Celtic, with whom he had won League and Cup honours. At the end of the 1985–86 season when he was still a regular in the club's defensive formation, McGrain, who had received the MBE, decided to look ahead to his future.

Airdrieonians were looking for a new manager. In fact they wanted McGrain as player-manager. Negotiations reached an advanced stage and all seemed well until changes on the Airdrie board brought about a dramatic change of heart with the result that they did not go ahead with the arrangement.

Having been released by Celtic to take up the appointment, McGrain now had to go back to Parkhead and hope they would be prepared to allow him to stay on. They did and though Celtic boss David Hay considered that McGrain's role, now at the age of 36, might be one of playing in the reserves and only appearing in the senior side in an emergency, he only missed two games in the last half of the season.

McGrain's role had changed little save for the fact that the enormous resources of experience gained over the previous decade and a half were put to good use either on the field coaching the younger players of off it putting the same youngsters through their paces in training spells.

A change of management at Parkhead led to alterations and at the end of the season he was given a free transfer, a decision McGrain described as 'the worst moment of my life'.

But in 1987–88, after coaching and playing in Australia, he was not lost to the game even at the age of 37. He joined only his second Scottish League club when he signed for First Division Hamilton Academical.

Uruguay: South America's enigma

Twice winners of the World Cup in 1930 and 1950 and undoubtedly skilful competitors at the highest level, Uruguay hit rock bottom in the 1986 series with a disgraceful performance of cynicism and indis-cipline which cost them dearly. But they regained some measure of their former stature by winning the South American Championship a year later.

Uruguay's first honours came in the 1924 and 1928 Olympic Games tournament and indeed their success convinced FIFA to take the plunge on organizing a World Cup competition in 1930 with Uruguay as hosts.

The 1986 Uruguay team.

Though Europe could muster only four teams to make the trek to the New World, Uruguay emerged as worthy winners beating their old rivals and neighbours across the River Plate, Argentina, 4–2 in the final.

In 1934 Uruguay declined to defend their title in Italy, piqued that there had been such a poor response from European teams to their tournament four years previously. The same attitude caused them to miss the 1938 finals in France.

After the war, Uruguay competed for only the second time in their history for the 1950 finals in Brazil. Withdrawals at the eleventh hour left them with just one opponent in their group and they demolished Bolivia 8–0.

But it was enough to give them a place in the final round played on a League basis. They started modestly enough, being held to a 2–2 draw by Spain, before edging Sweden out 3–2 in the second game. This brought them to the final match with Brazil, the odds-on favourites, who needed just a draw to win the group and the World Cup itself. But Uruguay proved tenacious opponents and they recovered from being a goal down to beat Brazil 2–1. Four years later they defended their title for the first time and acquitted themselves splendidly.

Indeed their semi-final against Hungary, played in Lausanne in torrential rain, is considered by those fortunate to have witnessed it as one of the most outstanding matches of all time. Uruguay were beaten 4–2 after extra time in a match which showed the varied facets of Uruguay's many qualities of individual control, spirit, application and persistence. But they paid a high price, because in the match for third place they were physically and mentally exhausted.

In 1958 Uruguay did not qualify at all and in 1962 when they did were largely unimpressive. Four years later they held England to a dour 0–0 draw.

They qualified for the quarter-finals where they met West Germany. Denied claims for a penalty when a German defender handled the ball underneath the crossbar, the temperamental Uruguayans lost patience with referee Jim Finney and control of themselves and had two players sent off.

In 1970 Uruguay lost their best player injured in the opening game, but still reached the semi-finals where they did as well as anybody against Brazil for half the game before losing 4–1. In the match for third place their finishing let them down against a disjointed West German side and again they had to settle for fourth place.

In 1974 they did little to instil confidence in the final competition and four years after that they failed to make the finals in nearby Argentina. In 1982 Uruguay were the only one of the previous six World Cup winners who failed to reach the finals in Spain.

Uruguay did qualify for the 1986 finals in Mexico and were among the favourites. They started well enough, holding West Germany to a 1–1 draw but had a player sent off against Denmark and lost 6–1. They had another dismissed against Scotland in the opening minutes but held on for a goalless draw and reached the second round. FIFA fined and threatened them. Inhibited, they lost 1–0 to Argentina.

Interest in Uruguay's domestic game slumped after this, with First Division attendances amounting to little more than a few thousand spectators in a population of under three million. But for the South American Championships a new coach, stringent discipline and a squad based on youth which retained only three World Cup players, retrieved the country's honour by taking the Copa America in Argentina.

Their semi-final win over Argentina in Buenos Aires was their first in that city since 1937. They won the final by a single goal against Chile and despite the fact that four players were sent off, two from each side, for once Uruguay suffered wrongly. Wiser for it, they might have also started on the long road back to success.

Neal's eightsome reel

Phil Neal was a consistent
defender for Liverpool
during their halcyon days as
European Cup protagonists.

Phil Neal established a record in the Football League when he appeared in eight championship winning teams with Liverpool in ten years before joining Bolton as player-manager in December 1985.

Neal had already made 186 League appearances for Northampton when he was given his initial chance by Liverpool and despite his 23 years was already an accomplished professional, even if only in the lower divisions.

During part of this period he missed only one League match in 10 seasons and revealed not only a high standard of fitness but a consistency rarely achieved in the modern game. He was also the only Liverpool player to appear in all the club's European Cup Final wins.

Soon after establishing himself in the first team he became the penalty taker in the 1975–76 season, taking over from Kevin Keegan and celebrating the honour by converting two spot kicks in a 2–2 draw with Arsenal. The same season he was capped by England.

Later he captained Liverpool and displayed a fine attitude to attacking involvement as well as defending with spirit and determination. In his later years, a well-developed positional sense came to his and Liverpool's rescue.

He had originally joined Northampton Town as an apprentice and spent seven years with them as a senior choice after making his debut as a teenager. During his time with the Cobblers he appeared in every position on the field, including goalkeeper for whom he deputized in an emergency.

In November 1974 Liverpool signed him for £65 000 and he was due to play for the reserves at Anfield in the Central League derby on the day of the big Mersey game with Everton's first team at Goodison Park. But first choice full-back Alex Lindsay had an injury problem which was not responding to treatment and a quick call was made on Neal to join the first team squad, just in case. In the event Lindsay failed to pass his test and Neal made his debut in the cauldron of a Mersey derby on their opponents' ground.

Capped by England against Wales at Wrexham in 1976 he made 50 appearances for his country, including the 1982 World Cup in Spain. He also contributed five goals to his England career.

His accuracy from the penalty spot was much in evidence in two of Liverpool's European finals. In 1977 in Rome he scored in the 3–1 win over Borussia Moenchengladbach; while seven years later on the same ground he was responsible for scoring Liverpool's goal in their 1–1 draw with AS Roma, then in extra time converting a spot kick to help his team win on penalty kicks.

After 455 League games and 41 goals in the First Division and in a variety of cup matches, with an impressive overall register of 635 games and 60 goals for the club, he accepted a player-managerial appointment at Bolton. He had turned down a similar position with Grimsby Town.

But there was disappointment for him in his second season when Wanderers were forced into a play-off to preserve their Third Division status. Unfortunately, they were beaten over the two legs by Aldershot and found themselves relegated to Division Four for the first time. After the match at Burnden Park, Neal announced his intention of retiring.

However, the following season he had decided to sign himself on again for emergencies and the 1987–88 season had been in operation but for only a few weeks when he came on as substitute in the Fourth Division. There was an irony in this as in his first season as a senior player at Northampton he had found himself in a team relegated to the same Division Four.

A measure of his value at Anfield was illustrated by the crowd of 23 480 which turned up to provide the attendance for his testimonial game in August 1985.

The quiet

Pat Jennings retired from the game at its height: a World Cup match against Brazil. It was his 119th appearance for Northern Ireland and his 41st birthday. Overall he had made 1098 appearances in first class football.

Born in Newry, County Down, he won his first medal playing for Newry United, the reserve team of Newry Town, in the Irish Junior Cup. He was recommended to Watford by Bill McCracken, the former Irish international defender and ace scout

Pat Jennings retired at the height of his career in the 1986 World Cup finals in Mexico.

Irishman

and eventually signed for them. He made his debut in April 1963 in the unusual surroundings of the White City, where Queen's Park Rangers were experimenting for home matches that season. The game ended in a 2–2 draw.

Jennings was also in the Northern Ireland youth team which reached the final of the European Youth Tournament and played at Wembley in a 4–0 defeat by England. In his first full season for Watford he did not miss a match and won two full caps for his country. Then at the age of 19 he was transferred to Tottenham Hotspur for £20 000.

In his first two seasons at White Hart Lane, Jennings was in and out of the team, but in 1966–67 he became the undisputed first choice and remained as such throughout the next decade. During this period Spurs won the FA Cup, the League Cup twice and the UEFA Cup.

His consistency set up a then club record of 472 League appearances but when Spurs were relegated at the end of the 1976–77 season they sold him to neighbours Arsenal for £45 000. Jennings was 32.

But he slotted in at Highbury with as much ease as he had shown at White Hart Lane and meanwhile his international career had continued to flourish. In the 1975–76 season he had overtaken Terry Neill's record of 59 caps for Northern Ireland and another high spot in his career came in the 1982 World Cup finals for which his country had qualified.

With Arsenal he had also played in three successive FA Cup Finals though the Gunners had lost twice and he received just one winner's medal. In the 1980 Cup Winners' Cup Final he also had to take runners-up honours.

There were more milestones to come, of course. On 26 February 1983 he made his 1000th senior appearance in a match for Arsenal against West Bromwich Albion. It was also his 695th League game.

In the run-up to the 1986 World Cup, Northern Ireland were in an excellent position to qualify again for the finals. They had at least to draw with England at Wembley in November 1985 to achieve this ambition. Jennings had previously said that this was to be his last international, win or lose, as he had by this time been freed by Arsenal and was merely playing for Tottenham again in their reserves.

He kept a clean sheet at Wembley and Northern Ireland accompanied England to the finals in Mexico. Manager Billy Bingham managed to persuade Jennings to postpone his retirement.

But that was not the end of the excitement for Jennings that season. Everton had a goalkeeping crisis with injury to their Welsh international Neville Southall. They decided to sign Jennings as cover before the semi-finals. In the event he was not needed and though it was assumed that Jennings was at the same time available for League games at Spurs and FA Cup ties with Everton, his registration was temporarily cancelled at Tottenham.

So the one-time bobbin boy in the Irish spinning mill who later worked as a labourer in a timber yard duly completed his illustrious career. A gentle giant of a goalkeeper, his huge frame, hands like shovels and the ability to spread himself in front of oncoming forwards, he had always presented a difficult target to beat. Though Brazil put three goals past him in his last match he went out with his reputation and head held high. He was rewarded with the OBE.

Peter The Great

In 1987 Peter Beardsley became the most expensive player in England when he was transferred to Liverpool from Newcastle United for £1.9 million. But he had been rejected by several League clubs in his early career and even spent two spells in Canada when interest in him appeared at a low ebb in his own country. The striker finally established himself as a first class prospect in the 1986 World Cup in Mexico, when he formed a formidable partnership with Gary Lineker in England's attack.

But his early career was fraught with disappointment. Trials with several Football League clubs – Gillingham, Oxford United, Cambridge United and Burnley – came to nothing. He even had an outing with Newcastle's 'A' team. But his discovery by soccer scout Peter Kirkley while working as a labourer and playing for Wallsend Boys' Club was the first move towards breaking into League football.

He was recommended to Carlisle United where former Newcastle United defender Bobby Moncur was manager. Moncur looked after him and even had Beardsley lodge with him and his own family. He cost Carlisle just a set of shirts. It was August 1979 and he was 18 years old. In a little over two years he established himself as a first team player of considerable promise, but despite rave notices, no other club appeared to be prepared to take a gamble on him.

Eventually hard-up Carlisle had to sell him to Vancouver Whitecaps for £250 000 and his prowess grew in North America. Then Manchester United manager Ron

Atkinson brought him to Old Trafford for a two-months trial period. But Beardsley's only senior outing this time was in a League Cup match against Bournemouth on 6 October 1982 and he did not even finish this game, being substituted by Norman Whiteside. Disillusioned, he returned to Vancouver to continue his career. But in September 1983 the club Beardsley wanted to play for, Newcastle United, took a chance where others had been reluctant to do so. They paid a fee of £120 000 for him.

United had Kevin Keegan in their attack and his partnership with Beardsley became an overnight success. The pair scurried through defences at will and were aided by the fast raiding of Chris Waddle. This trio shot Newcastle to promotion in Beardsley's first season in which he contributed 20 goals himself. Then in February 1986 he won a new £2000-a-week contract and celebrated with his 50th League goal in his 100th game for Newcastle.

Quick, with finely-judged control in difficult situations, his reactions in the penalty area were disarming to opposing defences. He scored some spectacular goals and in the arena of the First Division for the first time in his career, he blossomed into a fringe player for England. His first outing was in one of Bobby Robson's build-up matches for the 1986 World Cup finals in Mexico and Beardsley impressed enough against Egypt to warrant inclusion in the final party of 22 players.

England struggled in the opening phase of their group games and Beardsley was just one of the substitutes. But suspension and injury forced a shake-up of the team before the game with Poland and he was paired up front with Lineker. The transformation was remarkable and England qualified for the knock-out stages.

But the season following Mexico was a

disastrous one for Beardsley. He was hit by an achilles tendon injury, then a badly bruised leg and finally a torn hamstring. This restricted his appearances, and in those when he was fit the team was struggling near the bottom of the table and Beardsley was expected to fetch, carry and finish off moves almost single-handed.

For most of the summer months of 1987 he was the subject of speculation for a transfer to Liverpool. Terms were haggled over until finally he was signed at a record fee. Fortunately for him Liverpool were off to a fine start in the championship, which allowed Beardsley time to fit into the unique Anfield scheme of things.

1988 European Championship Roundup

West Germany qualified as hosts

Group 1: Rumania 4 Austria 0; Austria 3 Albania 0; Spain 1 Rumania 0; Albania 1 Spain 2; Rumania 5 Albania 1; Austria 2 Spain 3; Albania 0 Austria 1; Rumania 3 Spain 1; Spain 2 Austria 0; Albania 0 Rumania 1; Spain 5 Albania 0; Austria 0 Rumania 0. **Spain qualified**

Group 2: Sweden 2 Switzerland 0; Portugal 1 Sweden 1; Switzerland 1 Portugal 1; Italy 3 Switzerland 2; Malta 0 Sweden 5; Malta 0 Italy 2; Italy 5 Malta 0; Portugal Italy 1; Portugal 2 Malta 0; Switzerland 4 Malta 1; Sweden 1 Malta 0; Sweden 1 Italy 0; Switzerland 1 Sweden 1; Sweden 0 Portugal 1; Switzerland 0 Italy 0; Portugal 0 Switzerland 0; Italy 2 Sweden 1; Malta 1 Switzerland 1; Italy 3 Portugal 0; Malta 0 Portugal 1. **Italy qualified**

Group 3: Iceland 0 France 0; Iceland 1 USSR 1; Norway 0 E. Germany 0; France 0 USSR 2; USSR 4 Norway 0; E. Germany 2 Iceland 0; E. Germany 0 France 0; France 2 Iceland 0; USSR 2 E. Germany 0; Norway 1 USSR 1; Iceland 0 E. Germany 6; Norway 2 France 0; USSR 1 France 1; Iceland 2 Norway 1; Norway 0 Iceland 1; E. Germany 1 USSR 1; France 1 Norway 1; USSR 2 Iceland 0; E. Germany 3 Norway 1; France 0 E. Germany 1. **USSR qualified**

Group 4: England 3 N. Ireland 0; Yugoslavia 4 Turkey 0; England 2 Yugoslavia 0; Turkey 0 N. Ireland 0; N. Ireland 0 England 2; N. Ireland 1 Yugoslavia 2; Turkey 0 England 0; Yugoslavia 3 N. Ireland 0; England 8 Turkey 0; Yugoslavia 1 England 4; N. Ireland 1 Turkey 0; Turkey 2 Yugoslavia 3. **England qualified**

Group 5: Hungary 0 Holland 1; Poland 2 Greece 1; Greece 2 Hungary 1; Holland 0 Poland 0; Cyprus 2 Greece 4; Cyprus 0 Holland 2; Greece 3 Cyprus 1; Cyprus 0 Hungary 1; Holland 1 Greece 1; Poland 0 Cyprus 0; Greece 1 Poland 0; Holland 2 Hungary 0; Hungary 5 Poland 3; Poland 3 Hungary 2; Hungary 3 Greece 0; Poland 0 Holland 2; Cyprus 0 Poland 1; Hungary 1 Cyprus 0; Holland 4 Cyprus 0; Greece 0 Holland 3. **Holland qualified**

Group 6: Finland 1 Wales 1; Czechoslovakia 3 Finland 0; Denmark 1 Finland 0; Czechoslovakia 0 Denmark 0; Wales 4 Finland 0; Finland 0 Denmark 1; Wales 1 Czechoslovakia 1; Denmark 1 Czechoslovakia 1; Wales 1 Denmark 0; Finland 3 Czechoslovakia 0; Denmark 1 Wales 0; Czechoslovakia 2 Wales 0. **Denmark qualified**

Group 7: Scotland 0 Bulgaria 0; Belgium 2 Rep. Ireland 2; Luxembourg 0 Belgium 6; Rep. Ireland 0 Scotland 0; Scotland 3 Luxembourg 0; Belgium 1 Bulgaria 1; Scotland 0 Rep. Ireland 1; Bulgaria 2 Rep. Ireland 1; Belgium 4 Scotland 1; Rep. Ireland 0 Belgium 0; Luxembourg 1 Bulgaria 4; Bulgaria 3 Luxembourg 0; Luxembourg 0 Rep. Ireland 2; Rep. Ireland 2 Luxembourg 1; Bulgaria 2 Belgium 0; Scotland 2 Belgium 0; Rep. Ireland 2 Bulgaria 0; Belgium 3 Luxembourg 0; Bulgaria 0 Scotland 1; Luxembourg 0 Scotland 0. **Rep. Ireland qualified**

Final tournament in West Germany

Group 1

West Germany (0) **1** (Brehme)
Italy (0) **1** (Mancini)   65 000

Spain (1) **3** (Michel, Butragueno, Gordillo)
Denmark (1) **2** (Laudrup, Poulsen)   60 000

West Germany (1) **2** (Klinsmann, Thon)
Denmark (0) **0**   60 800

Italy (0) **1** (Vialli)
Spain (0) **0**   51 790

West Germany (1) **2** (Voller 2)
Spain (0) **0**   72 308

Italy (0) **2** (Altobelli, De Agostini)
Denmark (0) **0**   60 500

West Germany and Italy qualified

Group 2

Rep. Ireland (1) **1** (Houghton)
England (0) **0**   53 000

USSR (0) **1** (Rats)
Holland (0) **0**   60 500

Holland (1) **3** (Van Basten 3)
England (0) **1** (Robson)   65 000

Rep. Ireland (1) **1** (Whelan)
USSR (0) **1** (Protasov)   45 290

USSR (2) **3** (Aleinikov, Mikhailichenko, Pasulko)
England (1) **1** (Adams)   53 000

Holland (0) **1** (Kieft)
Rep. Ireland (0) **0**   70 800

USSR and Holland qualified

Semi-finals

West Germany (0) **1** (Matthaus (pen))
Holland (0) **2** (Koeman R (pen), Van Basten)
                                            60 000

USSR (0) **2** (Protasov, Litovchenko)
Italy (0) **0**   70 000

Final in Munich, 25 June 1988

Holland (1) **2** (Gullit, Van Basten)
USSR (0) **0**   72 308

Left: **Ruud Gullit** holds the European Championship trophy aloft in triumph after Holland's 2-0 win over the Soviet Union in the final, staged in Munich. The goalscoring hero for the Dutch was Marco Van Basten with five goals in the tournament, including a hat-trick against England and the second against the Russians after Gullit had opened the scoring. Right: The orange-shirted Dutch defenders clear the ball against the USSR watched left by Gullit, the European Footballer of the Year for 1987 and on the right by the white-shirted Igor Belanov, the award winner in 1986.

The moment after Argentina might have imagined that their chances of winning the World Cup for the second time in their history were in the balance. Rudi Voller has scored West Germany's equaliser in the 1986 final in Mexico City and the Argentines kick the ball back into goal. But they persevered and eventually triumphed to the delight of their huge support. Their earlier success had been achieved in 1978 before even more fanatical partisan fans in their capital city, Buenos Aires.

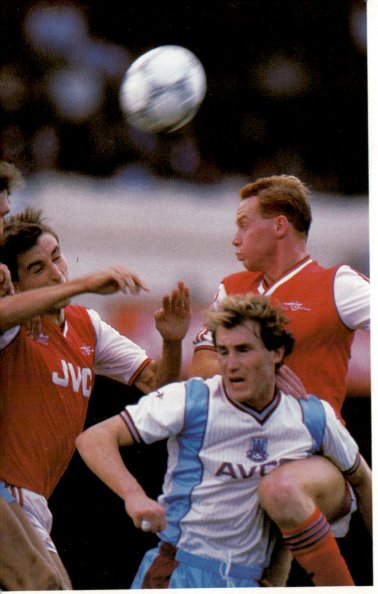

▼ **Brian McClair's** first taste of English football had been with Aston Villa when he was a youth, but he had to wait until returning to Scotland before he was given his League baptism at Motherwell. Subsequently transferred to Celtic, he developed into an outstanding striker and when Manchester United signed him in the 1987 close season, they quickly discovered that his scoring touch was just as spectacular south of the border as it had been north.

▲ Under the tutelage of Manager **George Graham**, Arsenal became renowned as a formidable cup-fighting team and benefited from the signing of players from various sources. Here Alan Smith (red shirt, left), a capture from Leicester City, disputes a high ball with colleague Perry Groves, snapped up from Colchester United, while the unfortunate West Ham United defender is forced to operate on a lower level at Highbury.

▼ **John Barnes** was already established as an England international when Liverpool beat off a number of clubs at home and abroad for his signature at the start of the 1987–88 season. He had been groomed under the tuition of Graham Taylor at Watford and came through their ranks at the most exciting part of that club's rise to the First Division. Playing either as a winger or more of a free-ranging striker, he has earned recognition as one of the most skilful players to have worn an England shirt.

▲ **Dave Watson** (left, dark shirt), was at one time on the books of Liverpool but also found himself having to move elsewhere to gain his initial experience of League football. This came at Norwich City, and England honours were not far away for him as a central defender. Then there was a move back to Merseyside with Everton, the rivals of the Anfield club. Here, his game developed further and he became adept at scoring goals from set pieces where his height was to the fore. In this photograph he battles with Luton's Brian Stein.

Muller: Der

No other player in modern international football has achieved a rate of scoring to equal that of Gerd Muller, who registered 68 goals in 62 appearances for West Germany between 1966 and 1974. His 14 goals in the 1970 and 1974 World Cup finals is a record for the competition.

bomber

His beginnings were humble enough. Born in the Bavarian village of Zinsen in November 1945, there was no proper pitch in the vicinity and he had to travel seven miles on a bus to have a trial with TSV Nordlingen. Muller had to leave school at 15 when his father died and he became an apprentice weaver. But Nordlingen took him on and in his first match on a real pitch and with borrowed boots he scored two goals and was signed.

He had a weight problem and was nicknamed 'Dicker' – Fatty. Even when fully grown he was only 5ft 8in, but this chunky, thick-legged centre-forward had a low centre of gravity, fine balance and an agile sense of anticipation. It helped to make him one of the most dangerous players in the penalty area.

In two seasons for Nordlingen he scored 46 goals and Wilhelm Neudecker, President of Bayern Munich, persuaded his coach Tchik Cajkovski, the former Yugoslavian international, to sign him, though the latter was sceptical, saying: 'Do you want me to put a bear among my racehorses?'

Misfortune struck Muller in his first match for Bayern's reserves when he broke his arm, but eventually he made his senior debut against Freiburger and scored twice in an 11–2 win. He managed 35 goals in the South Regional League and helped Bayern win promotion to the Bundesliga.

In 1965–66 he scored 15 goals in 33 matches and also deputized in goal for the injured Sepp Maier against Hamburg. Muller's marksmanship helped Bayern win the German Cup in 1966 and 1967, the latter year also finishing joint top scorer in the League with 28 goals and helping Bayern win the Cup Winners' Cup. In 1968–69 Bayern won their first Bundesliga title and Muller was their ace striker with 30 goals.

By now he had also established himself in the national team and had scored nine goals in World Cup qualifying matches to help West Germany reach the finals in Mexico where they finished third. Muller scored 10. His scoring for Bayern improved as well and he finished the 1969–70 season with 38 League goals. As a result of his performance for club and country he was voted European Footballer of the Year. An injury sustained against Yugoslavia left him with a bent left arm and he missed national service.

After winning the Cup in 1971, Bayern won three Bundesliga titles in a row and each season Muller was West Germany's leading League scorer with 40, 36 and joint top with 30 goals from 1972 to 1974 inclusive.

In 1974 Bayern won the first of three successive European Cup Finals and Muller also scored the winning goal in the World Cup Final that year when West Germany were the host nation. He retired from international football after that despite being only 29 years old. Though Bayern's domination of European and domestic football was temporarily waning, Muller continued scoring goals and he was joint top for the last time in 1978 with 24.

He had intended retiring completely at the end of the 1978–79 season but differences with the coaching staff resulted in him asking to be released early to take up a lucrative offer with the North American Soccer League club Fort Lauderdale Strikers. In three seasons there he scored 38 goals.

Muller had played 427 Bundesliga matches and scored 365 goals. Overall in Bundesliga, Regional League, West German internationals, Under-23 games, German Cup, League Cup, European Cup, Cup Winners' Cup, Fairs Cup, Super Cup and World Club Championship matches his tally was 628.

Muller's 350th Bundesliga goal came against Werder Bremen on 21 January 1978 and his 600th competitive goal the same season. As a goal poacher he had few equals.

The Anglo connection

Glasgow Rangers won the Scottish Premier Division championship in 1986–87, using an unprecedented number of Anglos in their successful squad. Previously only a handful of English-born players had been associated with Scottish League championship winning teams but Rangers had six.

Graeme Souness directing operations with Sampdoria in Italy prior to his distinguished return to Scottish football with Rangers.

The appointment of Graeme Souness as player-manager and the ability of the Ibrox club to persuade players south of the border that there was entry into Europe denied them by the ban in England were fundamental factors in the influx.

Chris Woods, the English international

goalkeeper, was signed from Norwich City for £600 000, then a record fee for a goalkeeper. Terry Butcher arrived from Ipswich Town and his £750 000 label broke the Scottish transfer record. Colin West, the Watford centre-forward, cost £200 000. Butcher, the incumbent England international centre-back, had actually been born in Singapore, but for the purpose of the argument, counted as an Englishman.

There was also Jimmy Nicholl, the Northern Ireland international full-back, who had been born in Canada. But the season began badly with Souness being sent off after only 37 minutes of his first game against Hibs which Rangers lost.

Still they came over the border. The Doncaster Rovers striker Neil Woods was signed for £100 000 and then the club paid £475 000 for the former England international defender Graham Roberts from Tottenham Hotspur. Before the season ended Jimmy Phillips, the Bolton Wanderers defender, was signed in a £75 000 deal.

The signing of Roberts proved to be a turning point in the fortunes of the Light Blues. He arrived as Rangers were settling down to an unbeaten run which shot them to the top of the table. They lost only one game in the second half of the League campaign, 3–1 away to Celtic.

There were setbacks in the Cup, notably losing to lowly Hamilton Academical, though goalkeeper Woods extended his run of being unbeaten to a record-breaking 1196 minutes.

Rangers' title was clinched on 2 May at Aberdeen when Rangers forced a 1–1 draw with captain Butcher scoring the vital goal. Ironically, Souness was sent off in the match but even this could not sour the first championship win for Rangers since 1978.

Naturally this was not solely an Anglo success. Ally McCoist and Robert Fleck scored 52 League goals between them. McCoist hit 33 and he was the only ever-present in the League, which for the first time in Scottish history had been extended to 44 matches. Ironically, McCoist had been signed in 1983 from Sunderland. Twenty-six different players were used, including David Kirkwood from East Fife who made a solitary appearance as substitute. Another Rangers investment, Lindsay Hamilton from Stenhousemuir, was not called upon. These players cost £50 000.

Souness and Rangers were not content with this and in the close season embarked upon further spending. Avi Cohen, the Israeli international full-back, who had spent part of his early career with Liverpool along with Souness, was signed from Maccabi Tel Aviv for £100 000, and then another Anglo in the shape of striker Mark Falco from Watford for £300 000.

Neil Woods was transferred to Ipswich for £120 000 and Colin West to Sheffield Wednesday for £150 000 to add to other departures during Souness's reign: Iain Ferguson (Dundee United), Bobby Williamson (West Bromwich), Craig Paterson (Motherwell), Doug Bell (Hibernian), Ted McMinn (Seville) and Davie McPherson and Hugh Burns (both to Hearts). Robert Fleck later went to Norwich City.

Still the spending spree continued with Trevor Francis (the first £1 million English player back in 1979) signed from Atalanta for £70 000, Ian McCall from Dunfermline Athletic for £150 000 and then, the prize capture, Richard Gough from Tottenham for a new Scottish record £1.5 million. This took Rangers' spending under Souness to £4 420 000 and selling to £1 245 000.

Mid-way through the 1987–88 season came Ray Wilkins from Paris St Germain at the cost of £250 000, Mark Walters (Aston Villa) for £500 000, Ian Ferguson (St Mirren) for £1 million plus Jan Bartram (Denmark) and John Brown (Dundee) for a further £500 000.

But players moved away from Ibrox just as often. Falco went to Queen's Park Rangers and was later joined by Francis after a short stay.

Mirandinha miracle

Mirandinha became the first Brazilian to play in the Football League for Newcastle United in 1987–88.

Francisco Ernani Lima da Silva, better known as Mirandinha, became the first Brazilian to play in the Football League when the international striker signed for Newcastle United in August 1987 after a relatively inexpensive transfer of £600 000 from Palmeiras.

Newcastle were anxious to secure a reliable goalscorer with the instant spectator appeal of a Hughie Gallacher, Jackie Milburn, Malcolm Macdonald or Kevin Keegan. Ironically Macdonald was one of the behind-the-scenes agents responsible for Mirandinha arriving on Tyneside.

The Brazilian had played for a variety of clubs: Ponte Preta, Botafogo, Nautico, Portuguesa, Cruzeiro, Santos and Palmeiras but maintained a formidable scoring reputation with 232 goals. All this was achieved after he began his working life as a 14-year-old bricklayer's apprentice.

At international level he was a late developer at 28. The Brazilian squad for the 1988 Olympics gave him his first chance in the famous yellow and green shirt of his native country. Brazil qualified for the finals and the nucleus of this team was used to form a tour party for the full national team to tour Europe in the spring of 1987.

At Wembley, Mirandinha revealed the potential which convinced onlookers that he could prove to be a hit in English football. His razor-sharp reflexes in front of goal enabled him to pounce on a goalkeeping fumble and score Brazil's goal in their 1–1 draw against England.

After Brazil's European tour they participated in the South American Championship and failed badly. But Mirandinha had been injured towards the end of the tour and as an absentee escaped the general criticism heaped upon the team and its officials. When fit again he was able to help his club, Palmeiras, in their championship play-offs and this held up his move to Newcastle until they were eliminated from the final stages.

On previous occasions he might have been persuaded to go abroad. In 1982 Internazionale were interested in signing him and in 1987 came a host of clubs showing similar interest including Napoli, two in Spain and even Glasgow Rangers.

After only 12 appearances for his country and five goals he had raised himself to international status but there needed to be protracted negotiations, one flying visit to Newcastle and clearance from the Foreign Office, Customs and Excise, Immigration, Inland Revenue and the Department of Employment before he was finally installed at St James's Park.

In fact he made his Newcastle debut at Norwich, impressing in a 1–1 draw. In less than a week he had been chosen to play for a cosmopolitan Football League representative team against the Irish League as part of the League's centenary celebrations. Again, his goalscoring knack came to the fore and he saved the League's blushes with a late equalizer in a 2–2 draw in front of a meagre crowd. Four days later he was on view before 45 137 highly critical spectators at Old Trafford and scored both Newcastle goals in their draw with Manchester United.

Then he came under the gaze of millions of armchair TV fans at Newcastle in the first live screening of the season, playing almost a lone hand against a rampant Liverpool, but showing enough glimpses of talent to convince the most sceptical Geordie fan of his worth. A week later he promised manager Willie McFaul he would score against Southampton and then did just that as United won for the first time at home in the season.

Compact, muscular and with superb balance, he has the tight control, dribbling ability and acceleration out of difficult situations which are the hallmarks of an outstanding player. To top it he has the appetite to shoot on sight with a proven record as a goalscorer.

The indestructible Pole

In 1986 Wladyslaw Zmuda equalled West German Uwe Seeler's record of appearing in 20 matches in World Cup finals. The Polish defender had made a remarkable comeback from injury to return to the national team at the age of 32.

Wladyslaw Zmuda, the Polish international defender who equalled the record for World Cup final appearances in 1986.

Born in Lublin, he played for the local Motor Lublin club while they were in the Polish Second Division. He stayed with them for three seasons before joining Gwardia Warsaw in 1973. At the same time his international career was also taking shape and he made his debut for Poland in October 1973.

The World Cup finals were held in West Germany in 1974 and Zmuda gained a regular place in the middle of the Polish defence, playing in all seven matches and helping his country to third place.

His performances in the final stages in which he had to face the top strikers in the world like Gerd Muller (West Germany), Jairzinho (Brazil) and Ralf Edstrom (Sweden), made him anxious to leave Eastern Europe and attempt to play in the west.

At the time Polish players were only allowed to go abroad when they reached the age of 30. Zmuda was only 20 and his request was refused. Worse still, he was suspended for six months for even having the audacity to ask to leave.

After two seasons with Gwardia he did get a move but not abroad, only to Slask Wroclaw. Gwardia were relegated while, two years later, Slask won the Polish championship.

He remained with them for four seasons and meanwhile had settled down to become regular choice for the national team, equally able to play as a sweeper or stopper centre-back. In the 1978 World Cup he played in all six games for them and the following year made another move, this time to Widzew Lodz, and also reached a personal milestone with his 50th appearance for Poland.

His third season with Widzew coincided with the next World Cup series in Spain, when Poland again qualified for the finals. Zmuda proved to be a commanding figure once more and appeared in all seven of Poland's games. Their elimination in the semi-finals came at the hands of Italy and it was appropriate since Zmuda had at

last been granted his request to leave for a Western European country.

His destination was the Italian club Verona. As a bonus Poland beat France for third place. Alas, what should have proved to be the most promising period in his history, turned out to be a nightmare. A serious knee injury restricted his performances for Verona. Indeed when he was fit he spent much of the time on the substitutes' bench.

His two League appearances that season were both as a substitute and on each occasion it was but a brief appearance. His debut came on 12 December 1982 against Torino when he was put on for the last six minutes. His only other outing came on 2 January 1983 against Napoli when he was used in the last 13 minutes.

The following season was only slightly better in that he did get on the field on five League occasions, but again they were only as a substitute. In turn they amounted to 13, 7, 17, 16 and 5 minutes.

Naturally during this time he had been lost to the national side completely. But before venturing in the summer months of 1984 to New York to play for the Cosmos, before coming back to Italy to play for Cremonese, Zmuda returned to the Polish team after an absence of two years in a goalless draw with the Republic of Ireland in Dublin.

Although he managed a dozen games and even scored his first goal in Italian League football, Cremonese were relegated from the First Division. Still he had edged his way back to national recognition and after his second season with Cremonese when he was virtually a regular in the team, he was selected for the World Cup squad in Mexico. He had already won 91 caps for Poland.

Though this tall, calm and resolute figure and an excellent reader of the game had slowed noticeably, his experience was considered of importance. Despite the fact that he did not make the first team, he was given his 20th World Cup outing as a substitute late in the game against Brazil.

Just the goal merchant

Just Fontaine was the leading scorer in the 1958 World Cup finals with 13 goals, a figure never achieved before or since in that competition. He scored in every one of France's six matches.

Born in Marrakesh, Morocco, in August 1933, he developed as a goalscoring inside-forward with USM Casablanca before moving to France where he turned professional with OGC Nice. In 1953–54 he scored 17 League goals when they finished eighth in the championship.

But it was the French Cup that provided him with his first honour as Nice won the trophy beating Marseille 2–1 in the final.

In January 1961 **Just Fontaine** fractured his leg for the second time, in a match for Reims against Limoges. Here he scans his x-ray.

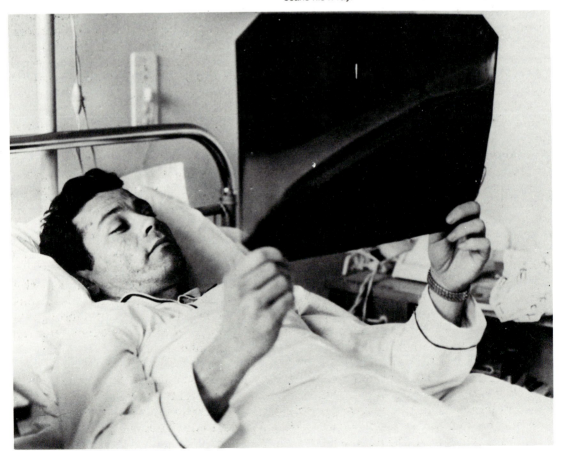

And though the team slipped to ninth in the League the following season, Fontaine increased his personal tally finishing with 20 goals. However, in 1955–56 Nice became French champions and Fontaine was transferred to Reims where he enjoyed his best scoring season with 30 goals which put him second among the scorers in France.

He had already achieved his first international recognition, being selected for what was a French Under-23 XI against Luxembourg, and though it was a World Cup qualifying match, was not counted as a full international by the French! Fontaine scored three goals in an 8–0 win.

He did not succeed in gaining a place in the 1954 World Cup final selection, and it was not until October 1956 that he reappeared in a full international shirt, in a 2–1 defeat against Hungary in the Colombes Stadium in Paris. And it was another year before he was chosen again for the return with the Hungarians in Budapest. Again the French were beaten, this time by two clear goals and Fontaine was axed once more until recalled for a friendly at the Parc des Princes against Spain in the following March.

This time Fontaine scored in a 2–2 draw and was retained for the following goalless draw with Switzerland. With France having qualified for the 1958 World Cup finals in Sweden, his next game was in Norrkoping against Paraguay in the opening match of the series.

Fontaine scored three times in a 7–3 win, followed it with both goals in the 3–2 defeat against Yugoslavia and then one in the 2–1 success over Scotland. He also hit two in the 4–0 win over Northern Ireland and one of the goals in the 5–2 defeat by Brazil. In the 6–3 win over West Germany for third place he joined a select band of World Cup players who have scored as many as four times in one game.

It had certainly been Fontaine's year. In the championship, Reims had finished seven points clear of the nearest opposition and he had been top scorer with 34 goals. Reims managed the double beating

Nimes 3–1 in the Cup final, Fontaine scoring once.

In 1958–59 Fontaine scored 24 League goals but there was disappointment on the European front as Reims lost 2–0 in the final of the Champions Cup to Real Madrid.

The next season Fontaine scored 28 goals and Reims won their second championship. But it was not a happy season for him as he suffered a double fracture of his leg at Sochaux. His international career had been continuing impressively. He had scored two hat-tricks in succession against Austria and Spain, followed by a couple of goals against Chile.

Then after a painful time recovering and returning to fitness he made his international comeback in a World Cup qualifying match against Bulgaria in December 1960. But before he could carry on he had the misfortune to break his leg again and this effectively ended his career. He was only 28.

Fontaine had superb control, was mobile, intelligent in his awareness of situations and had supreme confidence in his own ability. But above all he was a lethal marksman which was simply confirmed by his goalscoring record.

He had played in eight World Cup games, two Nations Cup matches and friendly internationals. Yet in this modest total of 21 internationals he had hit 30 goals, including 16 in the World Cup and five in the Nations Cup.

Fontaine had also scored 10 goals in the European Cup for Reims and had amassed 163 goals in League games for Nice and Reims. His partnership with Raymond Kopa for the national team was certainly one of the most outstanding features ever presented by a French pair on international duty.

On retiring, Fontaine became a sports writer and later took over as national team manager for two matches before resuming as coach to the Toulouse youth team.

The cannonball kid

Peter Lorimer whose sharp-shooting helped Leeds United to many honours and earned himself some scoring records.

Peter Patrick Lorimer scored more goals in European club football than any other British player and also established an aggregate scoring record for Leeds United. Lethally accurate with his right foot, the ferocity of his shot was such that it was timed at 90 mph.

He found his shooting boots early and in one season at Stobswell School in his native Dundee he registered 176 goals. Not surprisingly there were a host of clubs chasing him and at one stage no fewer than 26 different ones took an interest in him.

Leeds United succeeded in beating their rivals to his door and so keen was manager Don Revie to sign Lorimer that he was stopped for speeding on his way north.

One day, while sweeping the terraces as a groundstaff boy, Lorimer was told that he was to be given his Football League debut on 29 September 1962 against Southampton at Elland Road. Lorimer was only 15 years 289 days old and as such was the youngest debutant in the history of the club. The match ended in a 1–1 draw. In 1963–64 he also played in the League Cup against Swansea.

But there was a serious setback for Lorimer as he broke a leg in the Northern Intermediate League Cup Final against Sheffield United, and in fact did not make another League appearance until 20 April 1965 when he played against Sheffield Wednesday. This time United won 2–0.

Lorimer's own first senior goal arrived the following season when he started to establish himself as a senior player. It came in a home game against Nottingham Forest in a 2–1 win on 4 September 1965.

He had signed professional forms when he was 17, following an apprenticeship which had started in December 1963. As a youngster he had also picked up Scottish amateur international honours, having previously won them at schoolboy level.

However, it was an even more exciting time on the domestic scene. Leeds United were in danger of being tagged as the 'nearly' team, but were never far away from major honours.

In 1965–66 they were runners-up in the championship and the following season reached the FA Cup semi-final. In 1967–68 they did win the League Cup but were again denied in the FA Cup semi-final.

Lorimer's goalscoring talents had also graced the European scene by then. His first goal in the Fairs Cup had been scored

in East Germany in November 1965 against Lokomotive Leipzig and Leeds went to the semi-final that season.

The following season they reached the final, losing to Dynamo Zagreb. But in 1967–68 they won the final held over until the start of the following season, beating Ferencvaros of Hungary. Earlier in the competition, Lorimer had hit a personal best four goals against Spora Luxembourg. Then in 1968–69 the many championship failures were dispelled at Elland Road as United won the First Division title.

In 1969–70 Leeds had to be satisfied with runners-up in League and FA Cup as well as the semi-final stage of the European Cup. Still, for Lorimer there were Scottish Under-23 honours and his first taste of full international football with a substitute's outing against Austria in November 1969.

Yet it was in 1970–71 that Lorimer achieved his highest total of 23 League goals. Again, United were runners-up but had the consolation of winning the Fairs Cup in the final year of that competition.

In 1971–72 Leeds won the FA Cup but had to settle for second place in the championship yet again. The following season Leeds were beaten FA Cup finalists.

But there was to be more satisfaction in 1972–73 when Leeds pulled off the championship. So it was back into the European Cup but once more United fell at the final hurdle.

Meanwhile, Lorimer's personal scoring achievements were mounting. But just when it seemed that he was close to overhauling John Charles's record for the club, he left in March 1979 for Toronto Blizzards. In the next September he played for York City before moving to Vancouver Whitecaps, but in March 1984 returned to Elland Road to complete 256 League games and record 168 goals for an overall total of 701 appearances and 237 goals. He was also capped 21 times for Scotland. He then played briefly for Whitby before going to play in Israel.

Club by club record League appearances

Highest aggregate of League appearances for each Football League club, in descending order

Games	Player	Club	Years
770	John Trollope	Swindon Town	1960-80
764	Jimmy Dickinson	Portsmouth	1946-65
761	Roy Sproson	Port Vale	1950-72
713	Terry Paine	Southampton	1956-74
663	Billy Bonds	West Ham United	1967-88
655	Steve Perryman	Tottenham Hotspur	1969-86
655	Ron Harris	Chelsea	1962-80
640	Ian Callaghan	Liverpool	1960-78
629	Joe Shaw	Sheffield United	1948-66
629	Jack Charlton	Leeds United	1953-73
614	Bob McKinlay	Nottingham Forest	1951-70
613	Micky Cook	Colchester United	1969-84
613	Dave Blakey	Chesterfield	1948-67
606	Bobby Charlton	Manchester United	1956-73
597	John Atyeo	Bristol City	1951-66
596	Derek Fazackerley	Blackburn Rovers	1970-86
595	Harold Bell	Tranmere Rovers	1946-64
595	Jack Brownsword	Scunthorpe United	1950-65
594	Johnny Haynes	Fulham	1952-70
592	Arfon Griffiths	Wrexham	1959-61 and 1962-79
592	Ron Ashman	Norwich City	1947-64
591	Mick Mills	Ipswich Town	1966-82
585	Wilfred Milne	Swansea Town	1919-37
583	Sam Bartram	Charlton Athletic	1934-56
574	Tony Brown	West Bromwich Albion	1963-80
571	Jim Cannon	Crystal Palace	1973-88
571	John Simpson	Gillingham	1957-72
568	Jimmy Armfield	Blackpool	1952-71
565	Alan Oakes	Manchester City	1959-76
564	Albert Iremonger	Notts County	1904-26
561	Tim Williamson	Middlesbrough	1902-23
560	Charlie Aitken	Aston Villa	1961-76
545	Stuart Taylor	Bristol Rovers	1966-80
537	Jim Montgomery	Sunderland	1962-77
530	Jerry Dawson	Burnley	1906-29
528	Adam Black	Leicester City	1920-35
525	Ian Wood	Oldham Athletic	1966-80
524	Len Weare	Newport County	1955-70
523	Barry Kitchener	Millwall	1967-82
521	Tommy Fowler	Northampton Town	1946-61
520	Billy Smith	Huddersfield Town	1914-34
519	Eddie Hopkinson	Bolton Wanderers	1956-70
519	Tony Ingham	Queen's Park Rangers	1950-63
514	Barry Murphy	Barnsley	1962-78
513	Ken Coote	Brentford	1949-64
511	Andy Davidson	Hull City	1952-67
509	Tug Wilson	Brighton & Hove Albion	1922-36
506	Norman Bullock	Bury	1920-35
506	Eric Skeels	Stoke City	1958-76
502	Cec Podd	Bradford City	1970-84
501	Andy Wilson	Sheffield Wednesday	1900-20
501	Derek Parkin	Wolverhampton Wanderers	1967-82
500	George Armstrong	Arsenal	1960-77
495	Arnold Mitchell	Exeter City	1952-66
494	Bob Morton	Luton Town	1948-64
486	Kevin Hector	Derby County	1966-78 and 1980-82
486	Gil Merrick	Birmingham City	1946-60
486	George Curtis	Coventry City	1956-70
482	Tommy Robson	Peterborough United	1968-81
481	Barry Jackson	York City	1958-70
480	John Shuker	Oxford United	1962-77
471	Steve Death	Reading	1969-82
471	Phil Dwyer	Cardiff City	1972-85
470	Sammy Black	Plymouth Argyle	1924-38
467	Colin Harrison	Walsall	1964-82
466	Alan Ross	Carlisle United	1963-79
465	Bob Murray	Stockport County	1952-63
465	Ted Sagar	Everton	1929-53
461	Murray Brodie	Aldershot	1970-83
459	Danny Williams	Rotherham United	1946-62
451	Sandy Anderson	Southend United	1950-63
448	Wattie Moore	Hartlepools United	1948-64
448	Keith Jobling	Grimsby Town	1953-69
447	Alan Kelly	Preston North End	1961-75
443	Dennis Lewis	Torquay United	1947-59
442	Ron Greener	Darlington	1955-68
440	Rod Arnold	Mansfield Town	1970-83
436	Tommy Lowry	Crewe Alexandra	1966-78
432	Jim Lawrence	Newcastle United	1904-22
431	Peter Allen	Orient	1965-78
416	Steve Spriggs	Cambridge United	1975-87
414	Ray Bumstead	Bournemouth	1958-70
411	Duncan Welbourne	Watford	1963-74
408	Ray Gill	Chester City	1951-62
406	Fred Emery	Doncaster Rovers	1925-36
402	Tony Emery	Lincoln City	1946-59
370	Ken Mulhearn	Shrewsbury Town	1971-80
367	John Pickering	Halifax Town	1965-74
330	Chris Price	Hereford United	1976-86
330	Alan Cork	Wimbledon	1978-88
317	Graham Smith	Rochdale	1966-74
296	Colin Methven	Wigan Athletic	1979-86

Club records in European cup competitions

In ties decided on away goals or penalty kicks, results are as at full-time or after extra time.

Football League

	P	W	D	L	F	A
Arsenal						
European	6	4	0	2	13	4
Cup Winners	9	4	5+	0	13	5
Fairs	24	12	5	7	46	19
UEFA	12	6	1	5	19	15
Aston Villa						
European	15	9	3	3	24	10
UEFA	14	5	4	5	24	16
Super	2	1	0	1	3	1
Birmingham City						
Fairs	25	14	6	5	51	38
Burnley						
European	4	2	0	2	8	8
Fairs	8	4	3	1	16	5
Cardiff City						
Cup Winners	41	15	12	14	58	44

Paul Sturrock chasing the striped shirt Gothenburg player in the 1987 UEFA Cup Final with Dundee United.

Chelsea

Cup Winners	14	9	4	1	39	7
Fairs	20	10	5	5	33	24

Coventry City

Fairs	4	3	0	1	9	8

Derby County

European	12	6	3	3	18	11
UEFA	10	5	2	3	32	17

Everton

European	8	2	5	1	12	6
Cup Winners	13	9	3	1	19	5
Fairs	12	7	2	3	22	15
UEFA	8	3	1	4	12	5

Ipswich Town

European	4	3	0	1	16	5
Cup Winners	6	3	2	1	6	3
UEFA	40	23	10	7	78	43

Leeds United

European	17	12	1	4	42	11
Cup Winners	9	5	3	1	13	3
*Fairs	53	28	17	8	91	38
UEFA	12	5	3	4	18	13

* Includes match for final possession of trophy

Leicester City

Cup Winners	4	2	1	1	8	5

Liverpool

European	77	48	13	16	159	64
Cup Winners	17	8	4	5	29	12
Fairs	22	12	4	6	46	15
UEFA	24	16	5	3	44	15
Super	5	2	1	2	10	7

Manchester City

European	2	0	1	1	1	2
Cup Winners	18	11	2	5	32	13
UEFA	14	4	6	4	21	19

Manchester United

	P	W	D	L	F	A
European	41	26	7	8	100	45
Cup Winners	18	8	5	5	35	27
Fairs	11	6	3	2	29	10
UEFA	16	7	5	4	18	14

Newcastle United

	P	W	D	L	F	A
Fairs	24	13	6	5	37	21
UEFA	4	1	1	2	6	5

Newport County

	P	W	D	L	F	A
Cup Winners	6	2	3	1	12	3

Nottingham Forest

	P	W	D	L	F	A
European	20	12	4	4	32	14
Fairs	6	3	0	3	8	9
UEFA	12	7	3	2	12	7
Super	4	2	1	1	4	3

Queen's Park Rangers

	P	W	D	L	F	A
UEFA	12	8	1	3	39	20

Sheffield Wednesday

	P	W	D	L	F	A
Fairs	10	5	0	5	25	18

Southampton

	P	W	D	L	F	A
Cup Winners	6	4	0	2	16	8
Fairs	6	2	3	1	11	6
UEFA	10	2	5	3	10	12

Stoke City

	P	W	D	L	F	A
UEFA	4	1	2	1	4	6

Sunderland

	P	W	D	L	F	A
Cup Winners	4	3	0	1	5	3

Swansea City

	P	W	D	L	F	A
Cup Winners	14	3	3	8	26	21

Tottenham Hotspur

	P	W	D	L	F	A
European	8	4	1	3	21	13
Cup Winners	25	16	3	6	58	31
UEFA	54	33	12	9	129	41

Watford

	P	W	D	L	F	A
UEFA	6	2	1	3	10	12

West Bromwich Albion

	P	W	D	L	F	A
Cup Winners	6	2	2	2	8	5
Fairs	4	1	1	2	7	9
UEFA	12	5	2	5	15	13

West Ham United

	P	W	D	L	F	A
Cup Winners	30	15	6	9	58	42

Wolverhampton Wanderers

	P	W	D	L	F	A
European	8	2	2	4	12	16
Cup Winners	4	1	1	2	6	5
UEFA	20	13	3	4	41	23

Wrexham

	P	W	D	L	F	A
Cup Winners	22	9	6	7	33	29

Billy Bonds, the stalwart West Ham United defender.

Scottish League

Aberdeen

	P	W	D	L	F	A
European	12	5	4	3	14	12
Cup Winners	31	18	4	9	64	32
Fairs	4	2	1	1	4	4
UEFA	24	9	7	8	36	34
Super	2	1	1	0	2	0

Celtic

	P	W	D	L	F	A
European	74	41	14	19	139	71
Cup Winners	32	18	4	10	62	25
Fairs	6	1	3	2	9	10
UEFA	10	4	2	4	15	12

Dundee

	P	W	D	L	F	A
European	8	5	0	3	20	14
Cup Winners	2	0	1	1	3	4
Fairs	8	5	1	2	14	7
UEFA	10	4	0	6	17	21

Dundee United

	P	W	D	L	F	A
European	8	5	1	2	14	5
Cup Winners	4	1	1	2	3	3
Fairs	10	5	1	4	11	12
UEFA	60	25	19	16	92	55

Dunfermline Athletic

	P	W	D	L	F	A
Cup Winners	14	7	2	5	34	14
Fairs	28	16	3	9	49	31

Heart of Midlothian

	P	W	D	L	F	A
European	4	1	0	3	4	11
Cup Winners	4	1	0	3	8	11
Fairs	12	4	4	4	20	20
UEFA	4	1	1	2	5	9

Hibernian

	P	W	D	L	F	A
European	6	3	1	2	9	5
Cup Winners	6	3	1	2	19	10
Fairs	36	18	5	13	66	60
UEFA	18	8	5	5	27	23

Kilmarnock

	P	W	D	L	F	A
European	4	1	2	1	4	7
Fairs	20	8	3	9	34	32

Ted Ditchburn, the Tottenham Hotspur goalkeeper in the years immediately after the Second World War.

Morton						
Fairs	2	0	0	2	3	9
Partick						
Fairs	4	3	0	1	10	7
UEFA	2	0	0	2	0	4
Rangers						
European	49	23	6	20	80	83
Cup Winners	54	27	11	16	100	62
Fairs	18	8	4	6	27	17
UEFA	16	8	3	5	20	19
Super	2	0	0	2	3	6
St Johnstone						
UEFA	6	3	0	3	8	8
St Mirren						
Cup Winners	4	1	2	1	1	2
UEFA	10	2	3	5	9	12

Irish League

Ards						
European	2	0	0	2	3	10
Cup Winners	4	0	1	3	2	17
UEFA	2	1	0	1	4	8
Ballymena United						
Cup Winners	6	0	0	6	1	15
UEFA	2	1	0	1	2	4
Carrick Rangers						
Cup Winners	4	1	0	3	7	12
Cliftonville						
Cup Winners	2	0	0	2	0	8
Coleraine						
European	2	0	0	2	1	11
Cup Winners	8	0	1	7	7	34
Fairs	8	2	1	5	15	23
UEFA	8	0	3	5	4	17

Crusaders						
European	4	0	0	4	0	19
Cup Winners	6	0	2	4	5	18
Derry City						
European	3	1	0	2	8	15
Cup Winners	2	0	0	2	0	5
Distillery						
European	2	0	1	1	3	8
Cup Winners	2	0	0	2	1	7
Glenavon						
European	2	0	1	1	0	3
Cup Winners	2	0	0	2	2	7
UEFA	4	0	0	4	2	13
Glentoran						
European	16	3	5	8	17	26
Cup Winners	16	3	6	7	15	27
Fairs	8	1	1	6	7	22
UEFA	12	1	3	8	8	34
Linfield						
European	37	4	11	22	42	80
Cup Winners	4	2	0	2	5	6
Fairs	4	1	0	3	3	11
UEFA	2	0	0	2	0	8
Portadown						
Cup Winners	2	1	0	1	4	7
UEFA	4	1	2	1	3	7

League of Ireland

Athlone Town						
European	4	0	2	2	7	14
UEFA	4	1	2	1	4	4
Bohemians						
European	6	1	2	3	4	13
Cup Winners	6	2	1	3	6	9
UEFA	12	1	3	8	8	23

The FA Cup

Club / Competition	P	W	D	L	F	A
Cork Celtic						
European	2	0	0	2	1	7
Cup Winners	2	0	1	1	1	3
Cork Hibs						
European	2	0	0	2	1	7
Cup Winners	6	2	1	3	7	8
Fairs	2	0	0	2	1	6
Drogheda						
UEFA	2	0	0	2	0	14
Drumcondra						
European	6	1	0	5	3	25
Fairs	6	2	0	4	8	19
Dundalk						
European	14	3	3	8	12	30
Cup Winners	8	2	1	5	7	14
Fairs	6	1	1	4	4	25
UEFA	2	0	1	1	0	1
Finn Harps						
Cup Winners	2	0	1	1	2	4
UEFA	6	0	0	6	3	33
Galway United						
Cup Winners	2	0	0	2	2	4
UEFA	2	0	0	2	2	8
Home Farm						
Cup Winners	2	0	1	1	1	7
Limerick						
European	4	0	0	4	4	16
Cup Winners	6	0	1	5	2	11
UEFA	2	0	1	1	1	4
Shamrock Rovers						
European	14	0	4	10	7	28
Cup Winners	16	5	2	9	19	27
Fairs	4	0	2	2	4	6
UEFA	4	2	0	2	7	5
Shelbourne						
European	2	0	0	2	1	7
Cup Winners	2	0	0	2	1	5
Fairs	5	1	2	2	3	4
UEFA	2	0	1	1	1	2
Sligo Rovers						
Cup Winners	2	0	0	2	0	4
St Patrick's Athletic						
Cup Winners	2	0	0	2	1	8
Fairs	2	0	0	2	4	9
University College, Dublin						
Cup Winners	2	0	1	1	0	1
Waterford						
European	14	3	0	11	15	46
Cup Winners	8	1	1	6	6	14

Welsh Non-League clubs

Club / Competition	P	W	D	L	F	A
Bangor City						
Cup Winners	7	1	2	4	5	9
Borough United						
Cup Winners	4	1	1	2	2	4
Merthyr Tydfil						
Cup Winners	2	1	0	1	2	3

Representative teams

Team / Competition	P	W	D	L	F	A
London						
Fairs	8	4	1	3	14	13

Year	Date	Winners		Runners-up		Venue	Attendance	Referee	Entries
1872	16 March	Wanderers	1	Royal Engineers	0	Oval	2 000	A. Stair	15
1873	29 March	Wanderers	2	Oxford University	0	Lillie Bridge	3 000	A. Stair	16
1874	14 March	Oxford University	2	Royal Engineers	0	Oval	2 000	A. Stair	28
1875	13 March	Royal Engineers	1	Old Etonians	1*	Oval	3 000	C. W. Alcock	29
Replay	16 March	Royal Engineers	2	Old Etonians	0	Oval	3 000	C. W. Alcock	
1876	11 March	Wanderers	1	Old Etonians	1	Oval	3 000	W. S. Rawson	32
Replay	18 March	Wanderers	3	Old Etonians	0	Oval	3 500	W. S. Rawson	
1877	24 March	Wanderers	2	Oxford University	1*	Oval	3 000	S. H. Wright	37
1878	23 March	Wanderers	3	Royal Engineers	1	Oval	4 500	S. R. Bastard	43
1879	29 March	Old Etonians	1	Clapham Rovers	0	Oval	5 000	C. W. Alcock	43
1880	10 April	Clapham Rovers	1	Oxford University	0	Oval	6 000	Major Marindin	54
1881	9 April	Old Carthusians	3	Old Etonians	0	Oval	4 500	W. Pierce Dix	63
1882	25 March	Old Etonians	1	Blackburn Rovers	0	Oval	6 500	J. C. Clegg	73
1883	31 March	Blackburn Olympic	2	Old Etonians	1*	Oval	8 000	C. Crump	84
1884	29 March	Blackburn Rovers	2	Queen's Park	1	Oval	4 000	Major Marindin	100
1885	4 April	Blackburn Rovers	2	Queen's Park	0	Oval	12 500	Major Marindin	116
1886	3 April	Blackburn Rovers	0	West Bromwich Albion	0	Oval	15 000	Major Marindin	130
Replay	10 April	Blackburn Rovers	2	West Bromwich Albion	0	Baseball Ground	12 000	Major Marindin	
1887	2 April	Aston Villa	2	West Bromwich Albion	0	Oval	15 500	Major Marindin	126
1888	24 March	West Bromwich Albion	2	Preston North End	1	Oval	19 000	Major Marindin	149
1889	30 March	Preston North End	3	Wolverhampton Wanderers	0	Oval	22 000	Major Marindin	149
1890	29 March	Blackburn Rovers	6	Sheffield Wednesday	1	Oval	20 000	Major Marindin	132
1891	25 March	Blackburn Rovers	3	Notts County	1	Oval	23 000	C. J. Hughes	161
1892	19 March	West Bromwich Albion	3	Aston Villa	0	Oval	25 000	J. C. Clegg	163
1893	26 March	Wolverhampton Wanderers	1	Everton	0	Fallowfield	45 000	C. J. Hughes	183
1894	31 March	Notts County	4	Bolton Wanderers	1	Goodison Park	37 000	C. J. Hughes	155
1895	20 April	Aston Villa	1	West Bromwich Albion	0	Crystal Palace	42 560	J. Lewis	179
1896	18 April	Sheffield Wednesday	2	Wolverhampton Wanderers	1	Crystal Palace	48 836	Capt. W. Simpson	210
1897	10 April	Aston Villa	3	Everton	2	Crystal Palace	65 891	J. Lewis	244
1898	16 April	Nottingham Forest	3	Derby County	1	Crystal Palace	62 017	J. Lewis	213
1899	15 April	Sheffield United	4	Derby County	1	Crystal Palace	73 833	A. Scragg	235
1900	21 April	Bury	4	Southampton	0	Crystal Palace	68 945	A. G. Kingscott	242
1901	20 April	Tottenham Hotspur	2	Sheffield United	2	Crystal Palace	110 820	A. G. Kingscott	220
Replay	27 April	Tottenham Hotspur	3	Sheffield United	1	Burnden Park	20 470	A. G. Kingscott	
1902	19 April	Sheffield United	1	Southampton	1	Crystal Palace	76 914	T. Kirkham	226
Replay	26 April	Sheffield United	2	Southampton	1	Crystal Palace	33 068	T. Kirkham	
1903	18 April	Bury	6	Derby County	0	Crystal Palace	63 102	J. Adams	223
1904	23 April	Manchester City	1	Bolton Wanderers	0	Crystal Palace	61 374	A. J. Barker	252
1905	15 April	Aston Villa	2	Newcastle United	0	Crystal Palace	101 117	P. R. Harrower	274
1906	21 April	Everton	1	Aston Villa	0	Crystal Palace	75 609	T. Kirkham	280
1907	20 April	Sheffield Wednesday	2	Everton	1	Crystal Palace	84 584	N. Whittaker	305
1908	25 April	Wolverhampton Wanderers	3	Newcastle United	1	Crystal Palace	74 967	T. P. Campbell	348
1909	26 April	Manchester United	1	Bristol City	0	Crystal Palace	71 401	J. Mason	361
1910	23 April	Newcastle United	1	Barnsley	1	Crystal Palace	77 747	J. T. Ibbotson	424
Replay	28 April	Newcastle United	2	Barnsley	0	Goodison Park	69 000	J. T. Ibbotson	
1911	22 April	Bradford City	0	Newcastle United	0	Crystal Palace	69 098	J. H. Pearson	403
Replay	26 April	Bradford City	1	Newcastle United	0	Old Trafford	58 000	J. H. Pearson	
1912	20 April	Barnsley	0	West Bromwich Albion	0	Crystal Palace	54 556	J. R. Schumacher	410
Replay	24 April	Barnsley	1	West Bromwich Albion	0*	Bramall Lane	38 555	J. R. Schumacher	
1913	19 April	Aston Villa	1	Sunderland	0	Crystal Palace	120 081	A. Adams	457
1914	25 April	Burnley	1	Liverpool	0	Crystal Palace	72 778	H. S. Bamlett	476
1915	24 April	Sheffield United	3	Chelsea	0	Old Trafford	49 557	H. H. Taylor	454
1920	24 April	Aston Villa	1	Huddersfield Town	0*	Stamford Bridge	50 018	J. T. Howcroft	445
1921	23 April	Tottenham Hotspur	1	Wolverhampton Wanderers	0	Stamford Bridge	72 805	J. Davies	674
1922	29 April	Huddersfield Town	1	Preston North End	0	Stamford Bridge	53 000	J. W. D. Fowler	656
1923	28 April	Bolton Wanderers	2	West Ham United	0	Wembley	126 047	D. H. Asson	548
1924	26 April	Newcastle United	2	Aston Villa	0	Wembley	91 695	W. E. Russell	555
1925	25 April	Sheffield United	1	Cardiff City	0	Wembley	91 763	G. N. Watson	548
1926	24 April	Bolton Wanderers	1	Manchester City	0	Wembley	91 447	I. Baker	570
1927	23 April	Cardiff City	1	Arsenal	0	Wembley	91 206	W. F. Bunnell	552
1928	21 April	Blackburn Rovers	3	Huddersfield Town	1	Wembley	92 041	T. G. Bryan	544
1929	27 April	Bolton Wanderers	2	Portsmouth	0	Wembley	92 576	A. Josephs	520
1930	26 April	Arsenal	2	Huddersfield Town	0	Wembley	92 488	T. Crew	525

Above: Commemorative plaque depicting **Newcastle United**'s successful FA Cup season of 1909–10. Dark-shirted **West Ham United** players (right) in action against Bolton Wanderers in the 1923 FA Cup Final. **Spurs** Ricky Villa (below, right, white shirt) has the Manchester City defence in tatters in the 1981 FA Cup Final – the 100th in the series.

Year	Date	Winner		Runner-up		Venue	Attendance	Referee	
1931	25 April	West Bromwich Albion	2	Birmingham	1	Wembley	92 406	A. H. Kingscott	526
1932	23 April	Newcastle United	2	Arsenal	1	Wembley	92 298	W. P. Harper	529
1933	29 April	Everton	3	Manchester City	0	Wembley	92 950	E. Wood	543
1934	28 April	Manchester City	2	Portsmouth	1	Wembley	93 258	S. F. Rous	554
1935	27 April	Sheffield Wednesday	4	West Bromwich Albion	2	Wembley	93 204	A. E. Fogg	573
1936	25 April	Arsenal	1	Sheffield United	0	Wembley	93 384	H. Nattrass	571
1937	1 May	Sunderland	3	Preston North End	1	Wembley	93 495	R. G. Rudd	563
1938	30 April	Preston North End	1	Huddersfield Town	0*	Wembley	93 497	A. J. Jewell	574
1939	29 April	Portsmouth	4	Wolverhampton Wanderers	1	Wembley	99 370	T. Thompson	556
1946	27 April	Derby County	4	Charlton Athletic	1*	Wembley	98 000	E. D. Smith	294
1947	26 April	Charlton Athletic	1	Burnley	0*	Wembley	99 000	J. M. Wiltshire	438
1948	24 April	Manchester United	4	Blackpool	2	Wembley	99 000	C. J. Barrick	510
1949	30 April	Wolverhampton Wanderers	3	Leicester City	1	Wembley	99 500	R. A. Mortimer	617
1950	29 April	Arsenal	2	Liverpool	0	Wembley`	100 000	H. Pearce	617
1951	28 April	Newcastle United	2	Blackpool	0	Wembley	100 000	W. Ling	615
1952	3 May	Newcastle United	1	Arsenal	0	Wembley	100 000	A. Ellis	478
1953	2 May	Blackpool	4	Bolton Wanderers	3	Wembley	100 000	M. Griffiths	477
1954	1 May	West Bromwich Albion	3	Preston North End	2	Wembley	100 000	A. Luty	460
1955	7 May	Newcastle United	3	Manchester City	1	Wembley	100 000	R. Leafe	504
1956	5 May	Manchester City	3	Birmingham City	1	Wembley	100 000	A. Bond	460
1957	4 May	Aston Villa	2	Manchester United	1	Wembley	100 000	F. Coultas	438
1958	3 May	Bolton Wanderers	2	Manchester United	0	Wembley	100 000	J. Sherlock	442
1959	2 May	Nottingham Forest	2	Luton Town	1	Wembley	100 000	J. Clough	447
1960	7 May	Wolverhampton Wanderers	3	Blackburn Rovers	0	Wembley	100 000	K. Howley	462
1961	6 May	Tottenham Hotspur	2	Leicester City	0	Wembley	100 000	J. Kelly	433
1962	5 May	Tottenham Hotspur	3	Burnley	1	Wembley	100 000	J. Finney	414
1963	25 May	Manchester United	3	Leicester City	1	Wembley	100 000	K. Aston	411
1964	2 May	West Ham United	3	Preston North End	2	Wembley	100 000	A. Holland	400
1965	1 May	Liverpool	2	Leeds United	1*	Wembley	100 000	W. Clements	395
1966	14 May	Everton	3	Sheffield Wednesday	2	Wembley	100 000	J. K. Taylor	403

Year	Date					Venue	Attendance	Referee	
1967	20 May	Tottenham Hotspur	2	Chelsea	1	Wembley	100 000	K. Dagnall	406
1968	18 May	West Bromwich Albion	1	Everton	0*	Wembley	100 000	L. Callaghan	429
1969	26 April	Manchester City	1	Leicester City	0	Wembley	100 000	G. McCabe	438
1970	11 April	Chelsea	2	Leeds United	2*	Wembley	100 000	E. Jennings	451
Replay	29 April	Chelsea	2	Leeds United	1*	Old Trafford	62 078	E. Jennings	
1971	8 May	Arsenal	2	Liverpool	1	Wembley	100 000	N. Burten-shaw	464
1972	6 May	Leeds United	1	Arsenal	0	Wembley	100 000	D. W. Smith	471
1973	5 May	Sunderland	1	Leeds United	0	Wembley	100 000	K. Burns	471
1974	4 May	Liverpool	3	Newcastle United	0	Wembley	100 000	G. C. Kew	468
1975	3 May	West Ham United	2	Fulham	0	Wembley	100 000	P. Partridge	453
1976	1 May	Southampton	1	Manchester United	0	Wembley	100 000	C. Thomas	441
1977	21 May	Manchester United	2	Liverpool	1	Wembley	100 000	R. Matthewson	454
1978	6 May	Ipswich Town	1	Arsenal	0	Wembley	100 000	D. R. G. Nippard	469
1979	12 May	Arsenal	3	Manchester United	2	Wembley	100 000	R. Challis	466
1980	10 May	West Ham United	1	Arsenal	0	Wembley	100 000	G. Courtney	475
1981	9 May	Tottenham Hotspur	1	Manchester City	1*	Wembley	100 000	K. Hackett	480
Replay	14 May	Tottenham Hotspur	3	Manchester City	2	Wembley	100 000	K. Hackett	
1982	22 May	Tottenham Hotspur	1	Queen's Park Rangers	1*	Wembley	100 000	C. White	486
Replay	27 May	Tottenham Hotspur	1	Queen's Park Rangers	0	Wembley	100 000	C. White	
1983	21 May	Manchester United	2	Brighton & H.A.	2*	Wembley	100 000	A. Grey	479
Replay	26 May	Manchester United	4	Brighton & H.A.	0	Wembley	100 000	A. Grey	
1984	19 May	Everton	2	Watford	0	Wembley	100 000	J. Hunting	487
1985	18 May	Manchester United	1	Everton	0*	Wembley	100 000	P. Willis	494
1986	10 May	Liverpool	3	Everton	1	Wembley	98 000	A. Robinson	496
1987	16 May	Coventry City	3	Tottenham Hotspur	2*	Wembley	98 000	N. Midgley	504
1988	14 May	Wimbledon	1	Liverpool	0	Wembley	98 000	B. Hill	516

* after extra time

The Giant-Killers

Since the reorganization of the FA Cup in 1925 the following non-League clubs have reached the 3rd round

1925-26
Chilton Colliery, lost 0-3 South Shields (A); Clapton, lost 2-3 Swindon Town (H); *Corinthians, lost 0-4 Manchester City (A) after 3-3 (H); Boston, lost 1-8 Sunderland (A).

1926-27
Rhyl Athletic, lost 1-2 Darlington (A); Carlisle United, lost 0-2 Wolverhampton Wanderers (H); Poole, lost 1-3 Everton (A); *Corinthians, beat Walsall 4-0 (A), 4th round, lost 1-3 Newcastle United (H).

1927-28
*Corinthians, lost 1-2 New Brighton (A); Peterborough United, lost 3-4 Birmingham City (A); London Caledonians, lost 2-3 Crewe Alexandra (H).

1928-29
*Corinthians, beat Norwich City 5-0 (A); 4th round, lost 0-3 West Ham United (A); Mansfield Town, beat Wolverhampton Wanderers 1-0 (A), 4th round, lost 0-2 Arsenal (A).

1929-30
*Corinthians, lost 1-5 Millwall (at Chelsea) after 2-2 (H), 1-1 (A) aet.

1930-31
*Corinthians, lost 1-3 Port Vale (H); Scarborough, lost 1-2 Grimsby Town (H); Aldershot Town, lost 0-1 Bradford City (H).

1931-32
Darwen, lost 1-11 Arsenal (A); *Corinthians, lost 1-2 Sheffield United (A); Bath City, lost 0-2 Brentford (A); Burton Town, lost 0-4 Blackburn Rovers (H); Crook Town, lost 0-7 Leicester City (A).

1932-33
*Corinthians, lost 0-2 West Ham United (H); Folkestone, lost 0-2 Huddersfield Town (A).
*Corinthians exempted to 3rd round.

1933-34
Workington Town, beat Gateshead 4-1 (H), 4th round, lost 1-2 Preston North End (H); Cheltenham Town, lost 1-3 Blackpool (H).

1934-35
Bath City, lost 0-2 Norwich City (A); Wigan Athletic, lost 1-4 Millwall (H); Yeovil and Petters, lost 2-6 Liverpool (H).

1935-36
Southall, lost 1-4 Watford (H); Margate, lost 1-3 Blackpool (A); Dartford, lost 2-3 Derby County (A).

1936-37
Spennymoor United, lost 1-7 West Bromwich Albion (A); Dartford, lost 0-1 Darlington (H).

1937-38
Yeovil and Petters, lost 0-3 Manchester United (A); Scarborough, lost 1-5 Luton Town (A), after 1-1 (H).

1938-39
Runcorn, lost 2-4 Preston North End (H); Chelmsford City, beat Southampton 4-1 (H), 4th round, lost 0-6 Birmingham (A); Yeovil and Petters, lost 1-2 Sheffield Wednesday (H), after 1-1 (A).

1945-46
Lovell's Athletic, lost on aggregate Wolverhampton Wanderers 2-4 (H), 1-8 (A).

1946-47
Gillingham, lost 1-4 Swansea Town (A).

1947-48
Colchester United, beat Huddersfield Town 1-0 (H), 4th round, beat Bradford 3-2 (H), 5th round, lost 0-5 Blackpool (A); Gillingham, lost 1-3 Queen's Park Rangers (A) after 1-1 aet (H).

1948-49
Yeovil Town, beat Bury 3-1 (H), 4th round, beat Sunderland 2-1 (H) aet, 5th round, lost 0-8 Manchester United (A).

1949-50
Yeovil Town, lost 1-3 Chesterfield (A); Weymouth, lost 0-4 Manchester United (A); Nuneaton Borough, lost 0-3 Exeter City (A).

1950-51
None.

1951-52
Stockton, lost 0-4 Notts County (A); Buxton, lost 0-2 Doncaster Rovers (A).

1952-53
Finchley, lost 0-2 Shrewsbury Town (A); Walthamstow Avenue, beat Stockport County 2-1 (H), 4th round, lost 2-5 Manchester United (H) after 1-1 (A).

1953-54
Wigan Athletic, lost 2-3 Newcastle United (H) after 2-2 (A); Peterborough United, lost 1-3 Cardiff City (A); Hastings United, lost 0-3 Norwich City (A) after 3-3 (H); Headington United, beat Stockport County 1-0 (H) after 0-0 (A), 4th round, lost 2-4 Bolton Wanderers (H).

1954-55
Bishop Auckland, beat Ipswich Town 3-0 (H) after 2-2 (A), 4th round, lost 1-3 York City (H); Hastings United, lost 1-2 Sheffield Wednesday (A).

1955-56
Bedford Town, lost 1-2 Arsenal (H) after 2-2 (A); Burton Albion, lost 0-7 Charlton Athletic (A); Worksop Town, lost 0-1 Swindon Town (A); Boston United, lost 0-4 Tottenham Hotspur (A).

1956-57
Rhyl, beat Notts County 3-1 (A), 4th round, lost 0-3 Bristol City (A); New Brighton, beat Torquay United 2-1 (H), 4th round, lost 0-9 Burnley (A); Peterborough United, beat Lincoln City 5-4 (A) after 2-2 (H), 4th round, lost 1-3 Huddersfield Town (A); Goole Town, lost 0-6 Nottingham Forest (A).

1957-58
Hereford United, lost 0-3 Sheffield Wednesday (H); Yeovil Town, lost 0-4 Fulham (A).

1958-59
Worcester City, beat Liverpool 2-1 (H), 4th round, lost 0-2 Sheffield United (H); Peterborough United, lost 0-1 Fulham (H) after 0-0 (A); Tooting and Mitcham United, lost 0-3 Nottingham Forest (A) after 2-2 (H).

1959-60
Peterborough United, beat Ipswich Town 3-2 (A), 4th round, lost 0-2 Sheffield Wednesday (A); Bath City, lost 0-1 Brighton & Hove Albion (H).

1960-61
Oxford United, lost 1-3 Leicester City (A).

1961-62
King's Lynn, lost 0-4 Everton (A); Morecambe, lost 0-1 Weymouth (H); Weymouth, beat Morecambe 1-0 (A), 4th round, lost 0-2 Preston North End (A).

1962-63
Gravesend and Northfleet, beat Carlisle United 1-0 (A), 4th round, lost 2-5 Sunderland (A) after 1-1 (H).

1963-64
Yeovil, lost 0-2 Bury (H); Bedford Town, beat Newcastle United 2-1 (A), 4th round, lost 0-3 Carlisle United (H); Bath City, lost 0-3 Bolton Wanderers (A) after 1-1 (H).

1964-65
Barnet, lost 2-3 Preston North End (H).

Terry Bly who sparked Peterborough United in several memorable FA Cup ties.

1965-66
Bedford Town, beat Hereford United 2-1 (H), 4th round, lost 0-3 Everton (H); Folkestone Town, lost 1-5 Crewe Alexandra (H); Altrincham, lost 0-5 Wolverhampton Wanderers (A); Corby Town, lost 0-6 Plymouth Argyle (A).

1966-67
Bedford Town, lost 2-6 Peterborough United (H); Nuneaton Borough, lost 0-1 Rotherham United (A) after 1-1 (H).

1967-68
Macclesfield, lost 2-4 Fulham (A).

1968-69
Kettering Town, lost 1-2 Bristol Rovers (H) after 1-1 (A).

1969-70
South Shields, lost 1-4 Queen's Park Rangers (A); Brentwood Town, lost 0-1 Northampton Town (A); Hillingdon Borough, lost 1-4 Sutton United (A) after 0-0 (H). Sutton United, beat Hillingdon Borough 4-1 (H) after 0-0 (A), 4th round, lost 0-6 Leeds United (H).

1970-71
Yeovil Town, lost 0-3 Arsenal (H); Wigan Athletic, lost 0-1 Manchester City (A); Barnet, lost 0-1 Colchester United (H); Rhyl, lost 1-6 Swansea City (A).

1971-72
Boston United, lost 0-1 Portsmouth (H); Hereford United, beat Newcastle United 2-1 (H) after 2-2 (A), 4th round, lost 1-3 West Ham United (A) after 0-0 (H); Blyth Spartans, lost 1-6 Reading (A) after 2-2 (H).

1972-73
Chelmsford, lost 1-3 Ipswich Town (H); Margate, lost 0-6 Tottenham Hotspur (H); Barnet, lost 0-3 Queen's Park Rangers (H) after 0-0 (A).

1973-74
Boston United, lost 1-6 Derby County (H) after 0-0 (A); Alvechurch, lost 2-4 Bradford City (A); Grantham, lost 0-2 Middlesbrough (H); Hendon, lost 0-4 Newcastle United (H) after 1-1 (A).

1974-75
Leatherhead, beat Brighton 1-0 (A), 4th round, lost 2-3 Leicester City (A); Wimbledon, beat Burnley 1-0 (A), 4th round, lost 0-1 Leeds United (H) after 0-0 (A); Stafford Rangers, beat Rotherham United 2-0 (A) after 0-0 (H), 4th round, lost 1-2 Peterborough United (H); Wycombe Wanderers, lost 0-1 Middlesbrough (A) after 0-0 (H); Altrincham, lost 0-2 Everton (H) after 1-1 (A).

1975-76
Tooting and Mitcham United, beat Swindon Town 2-1 (H) after 2-2 (A), 4th round lost, 1-3 Bradford City (A); Scarborough, lost 1-2 Crystal Palace (H).

1976-77
Kettering Town, lost 2-3 Colchester United (H); Wimbledon, lost 0-1 Middlesbrough (A) after 0-0 (H); Northwich Victoria, beat Watford 3-2 (H), 4th round, lost 1-3 Oldham Athletic (H); Matlock Town, lost 1-5 Carlisle United (A).

1977-78
Scarborough, lost 0-3 Brighton (A); Wigan Athletic, lost 0-4 Birmingham City (A); Wealdstone, lost 0-4 Queen's Park Rangers (A); Tilbury, lost 0-4 Stoke City (A); Blyth Spartans, beat Enfield 1-0 (H), 4th round, beat Stoke City 3-2 (A), 5th round, lost Wrexham 1-2 (H) after 1-1 (A).

1978-79
Maidstone United, lost 1-2 Charlton Athletic (H) after 1-1 (A); Altrincham, lost 0-3 Tottenham Hotspur (H) after 1-1 (A).

1979-80
Yeovil Town, lost 0-3 Norwich City (H); Harlow Town, beat Leicester City 1-0 (H) after 1-1 (A), 4th round, lost 3-4 Watford (A); Chesham United, lost 0-2 Cambridge United (H); Altrincham, lost 1-2 Orient (A) after 1-1 (H).

1980-81
Altrincham, lost 1-4 Liverpool (A); Maidstone United, lost 2-4 Exeter City (H); Enfield, beat Port Vale 3-0 (H) after 1-1 (A), 4th round, lost 0-3 Barnsley (H) after 1-1 (A).

1981-82
Altrincham, lost 1-6 Burnley (A); Barnet, lost 1-3 Brighton (A) after 0-0 (H).

1982-83
Bishop's Stortford, lost 1-2 Middlesbrough (H) after 2-2 (A); Weymouth, lost 0-1 Cambridge United (A); Worcester City, lost 1-3 Coventry City (A).

1983-84
Maidstone United, lost 1-4 Darlington (A); Telford United, beat Rochdale 4-1 (A); 4th round, lost 2-3 Derby County (A).

1984-85
Burton Albion, lost 1-6 Leicester City (H); Dagenham, lost 0-1 Carlisle United (A); Telford United, beat Bradford City 2-1 (H), 4th round, beat Darlington 3-0 (H) after 1-1 draw (A); 5th round, lost 0-3 Everton (A).

1985-86
Altrincham, beat Birmingham City 2-1 (A), 4th round, lost 0-2 York City (A); Frickley Athletic, lost 1-3 Rotherham United (H); Wycombe Wanderers, lost 0-2 York City (A).

1986-87
Caernarfon, lost 0-1 Barnsley (A) after 0-0 draw (H); Maidstone United, lost 1-3 Watford (A); Telford United, lost 1-2 Leeds United (N).

1987-88
Sutton United, lost 0-1 Middlesbrough (A) after 1-1 draw (H); Yeovil Town, lost 0-3 Queen's Park Rangers (H); Maidstone United, lost 0-1 Sheffield United (A); Bath City, lost 0-4 Mansfield Town (A); Macclesfield, lost 0-1 Port Vale (A).

FA Cup attendances from 1966-67 to 1986-87

Season	1st Rd	2nd Rd	3rd Rd	4th Rd	5th Rd	6th Rd	S F+F	Total	Matches	Average
1966-67	390 292	295 112	1 288 341	921 303	602 111	252 672	217 378	3 967 209	169	23 475
1967-68	322 121	236 195	1 229 519	771 284	563 779	240 095	223 831	3 586 824	160	22 418
1968-69	331 858	252 710	1 094 043	883 675	464 915	188 121	216 232	3 431 554	157	21 857
1969-70	345 229	195 102	925 930	651 374	319 893	198 537	390 700	3 026 765	170	17 805
1970-71	329 687	230 942	956 683	757 852	360 687	304 937	279 644	3 220 432	162	19 879
1971-72	277 726	236 127	986 094	711 399	468 378	230 292	248 546	3 158 562	160	19 741
1972-73	259 432	169 114	938 741	735 825	357 386	241 934	226 543	2 928 975	160	18 306
1973-74	214 236	125 295	840 142	747 909	346 012	233 307	273 051	2 779 952	167	16 646
1974-75	283 956	170 466	914 994	646 434	393 323	268 361	291 369	2 968 903	172	17 261
1975-76	255 533	178 099	867 880	573 843	471 925	206 851	205 810	2 759 941	161	17 142
1976-77	379 230	192 159	942 523	631 265	373 330	205 379	258 216	2 982 102	174	17 139
1977-78	258 248	178 930	881 406	540 164	400 751	137 059	198 020	2 594 578	160	16 216
1978-79	243 773	185 343	880 345	537 748	243 683	263 213	249 897	2 604 002	166	15 687
1979-80	267 121	204 759	804 701	507 725	364 039	157 530	355 541	2 661 416	163	16 328
1980-81	246 824	194 502	832 578	534 402	320 530	288 714	339 250	2 756 800	169	16 312
1981-82	236 220	127 300	513 185	356 987	203 334	124 308	279 621	1 840 955	160	11 506
1982-83	191 312	150 046	670 503	452 688	260 069	193 845	291 162	2 209 625	159	13 897
1983-84	192 276	151 647	625 965	417 298	181 832	185 382	187 000	1 941 400	166	11 695
1984-85	174 604	137 078	616 229	320 772	269 232	148 690	242 754	1 909 359	157	12 162
1985-86	171 142	130 034	486 838	495 526	311 833	184 262	192 316	1 971 951	168	11 738
1986-87	209 290	146 769	593 520	349 342	263 550	119 396	195 533	1 877 400	165	11 378

Scottish Cup Finals

	Year	Date	Winners		Runners-up		Venue	Attendance
	1874	21 March	Queen's Park	2	Clydesdale	0	First Hampden	3 500
	1875	10 April	Queen's Park	3	Renton	0	First Hampden	7 000
	1876	11 March	Queen's Park	1	3rd Lanark Rifles	1	Hamilton Crescent	10 000
Replay		18 March	Queen's Park	2	3rd Lanark Rifles	0	Hamilton Crescent	6 000
	1877	17 March	Vale of Leven	1	Rangers	1	Hamilton Crescent	10 000
Replay		7 April	Vale of Leven	1	Rangers	1	Hamilton Crescent	15 000
2nd Replay		13 April	Vale of Leven	3	Rangers	2	First Hampden	12 000
	1878	30 March	Vale of Leven	1	3rd Lanark Rifles	0	First Hampden	5 000
(1)	1879	19 April	Vale of Leven	1	Rangers	1	First Hampden	9 000
	1880	21 February	Queen's Park	3	Thornliebank	0	First Cathkin	4 000
	1881	26 March	Queen's Park	2	Dumbarton	1	Kinning Park	15 000
(2) Replay		9 April	Queen's Park	3	Dumbarton	1	Kinning Park	7 000
	1882	18 March	Queen's Park	2	Dumbarton	2	First Cathkin	12 500
Replay		1 April	Queen's Park	4	Dumbarton	1	First Cathkin	14 000
	1883	31 March	Dumbarton	2	Vale of Leven	2	First Hampden	9 000
Replay		7 April	Dumbarton	2	Vale of Leven	1	First Hampden	12 000
(3)	1884		Queen's Park	W.O.	Vale of Leven Scr.			
	1885	21 February	Renton	0	Vale of Leven	0	Second Hampden	2 500
Replay		28 February	Renton	3	Vale of Leven	1	Second Hampden	3 500
	1886	13 February	Queen's Park	3	Renton	1	First Cathkin	7 000
	1887	12 February	Hibernian	2	Dumbarton	1	Second Hampden	12 000
	1888	4 February	Renton	6	Cambuslang	1	Second Hampden	11 000
	1889	2 February	Third Lanark	3	Celtic	0	Second Hampden	18 000
(4) Replay		9 February	Third Lanark	2	Celtic	1	Second Hampden	13 000
	1890	15 February	Queen's Park	1	Vale of Leven	1	Ibrox	11 000
Replay		22 February	Queen's Park	2	Vale of Leven	1	Ibrox	14 000
	1891	7 February	Heart of Midlothian	1	Dumbarton	0	Second Hampden	10 836
	1892	12 March	Celtic	1	Queen's Park	0	Ibrox	40 000
(5) Replay		9 April	Celtic	5	Queen's Park	1	Ibrox	26 000
	†1893	25 February	Queen's Park	0	Celtic	1	Ibrox*	18 771
Replay		11 March	Queen's Park	2	Celtic	1	Ibrox	13 239
	1894	17 February	Rangers	3	Celtic	1	Second Hampden	17 000
	1895	20 April	St Bernard's	2	Renton	1	Ibrox	15 000
	1896	14 March	Heart of Midlothian	3	Hibernian	1	Logie Green	17 034
	1897	20 March	Rangers	5	Dumbarton	1	Second Hampden	14 000
	1898	26 March	Rangers	2	Kilmarnock	0	Second Hampden	13 000
	1899	22 April	Celtic	2	Rangers	0	Second Hampden	25 000
	1900	14 April	Celtic	4	Queen's Park	3	Ibrox	15 000
	1901	6 April	Heart of Midlothian	4	Celtic	3	Ibrox	12 000
	1902	26 April	Hibernian	1	Celtic	0	Celtic Park	16 000
	1903	11 April	Rangers	1	Heart of Midlothian	1	Celtic Park	40 000
Replay		18 April	Rangers	0	Heart of Midlothian	0	Celtic Park	35 000
2nd Replay		25 April	Rangers	2	Heart of Midlothian	0	Celtic Park	32 000
	1904	16 April	Celtic	3	Rangers	2	Hampden Park	65 000
	1905	8 April	Third Lanark	0	Rangers	0	Hampden Park	54 000
Replay		15 April	Third Lanark	3	Rangers	1	Hampden Park	55 000
	1906	28 April	Heart of Midlothian	1	Third Lanark	0	Ibrox	25 000
	1907	20 April	Celtic	3	Heart of Midlothian	0	Hampden Park	50 000
	1908	18 April	Celtic	5	St Mirren	1	Hampden Park	55 000
(6)	1909	10 April	Celtic	2	Rangers	2	Hampden Park	70,000
Replay		17 April	Celtic	1	Rangers	1	Hampden Park	61 000
	1910	9 April	Dundee	2	Clyde	2	Ibrox	62 300
Replay		16 April	Dundee	0	Clyde	0	Ibrox	24 500
2nd Replay		20 April	Dundee	2	Clyde	1	Ibrox	25 400
	1911	8 April	Celtic	0	Hamilton Acad.	0	Ibrox	45 000
Replay		15 April	Celtic	2	Hamilton Acad.	0	Ibrox	24 700
	1912	6 April	Celtic	2	Clyde	0	Ibrox	46 000
	1913	12 April	Falkirk	2	Raith Rovers	0	Celtic Park	45 000
	1914	11 April	Celtic	0	Hibernian	0	Ibrox	56 000
Replay		16 April	Celtic	4	Hibernian	1	Ibrox	40 000
	1920	17 April	Kilmarnock	3	Albion Rovers	2	Hampden Park	95 000
	1921	16 April	Partick Thistle	1	Rangers	0	Celtic Park	28 300
	1922	15 April	Morton	1	Rangers	0	Hampden Park	75 000
	1923	31 March	Celtic	1	Hibernian	0	Hampden Park	80 100
	1924	19 April	Airdrieonians	2	Hibernian	0	Ibrox	59 218
	1925	11 April	Celtic	2	Dundee	1	Hampden Park	75 137
	1926	10 April	St Mirren	2	Celtic	0	Hampden Park	98 620
	1927	16 April	Celtic	3	East Fife	1	Hampden Park	80 070
	1928	14 April	Rangers	4	Celtic	0	Hampden Park	118 115
	1929	6 April	Kilmarnock	2	Rangers	0	Hampden Park	114 708
	1930	12 April	Rangers	0	Partick Thistle	0	Hampden Park	107 475
Replay		16 April	Rangers	2	Partick Thistle	1	Hampden Park	103 686
	1931	11 April	Celtic	2	Motherwell	2	Hampden Park	105 000

	Date	Team	Score	Team	Score	Venue	Attendance
Replay	15 April	Celtic	4	Motherwell	2	Hampden Park	98 579
1932	16 April	Rangers	1	Kilmarnock	1	Hampden Park	111 982
Replay	2 April	Rangers	3	Kilmarnock	0	Hampden Park	104 965
1933	15 April	Celtic	1	Motherwell	0	Hampden Park	102 339
1934	21 April	Rangers	5	St Mirren	0	Hampden Park	113 403
1935	20 April	Rangers	2	Hamilton Acad.	1	Hampden Park	87 286
1936	18 April	Rangers	1	Third Lanark	0	Hampden Park	88 859
1937	24 April	Celtic	2	Aberdeen	1	Hampden Park	147 365
1938	23 April	East Fife	1	Kilmarnock	1	Hampden Park	80 091
Replay	27 April	East Fife	4	Kilmarnock	2	Hampden Park	92 716
1939	22 April	Clyde	4	Motherwell	0	Hampden Park	94 799
1947	19 April	Aberdeen	2	Hibernian	1	Hampden Park	82 140
1948	17 April	Rangers	1	Morton	1	Hampden Park	129 176
Replay	21 April	Rangers	1	Morton	0	Hampden Park	133 570
1949	23 April	Rangers	4	Clyde	1	Hampden Park	108 435
1950	22 April	Rangers	3	East Fife	0	Hampden Park	118 262
1951	21 April	Celtic	1	Motherwell	0	Hampden Park	131 943
1952	19 April	Motherwell	4	Dundee	0	Hampden Park	136 274
1953	25 April	Rangers	1	Aberdeen	1	Hampden Park	129 681
Replay	29 April	Rangers	1	Aberdeen	0	Hampden Park	112 619
1954	24 April	Celtic	2	Aberdeen	1	Hampden Park	129 926
1955	23 April	Clyde	1	Celtic	1	Hampden Park	106 111
Replay	27 April	Clyde	1	Celtic	0	Hampden Park	68 735
1956	21 April	Heart of Midlothian	3	Celtic	1	Hampden Park	133 339
1957	20 April	Falkirk	1	Kilmarnock	1	Hampden Park	83 000
Replay	24 April	Falkirk	2	Kilmarnock	1	Hampden Park	79 785
1958	26 April	Clyde	1	Hibernian	0	Hampden Park	95 124
1959	25 April	St Mirren	3	Aberdeen	1	Hampden Park	108 591
1960	23 April	Rangers	2	Kilmarnock	0	Hampden Park	108 017
1961	22 April	Dunfermline Athletic	0	Celtic	0	Hampden Park	113 618
Replay	26 April	Dunfermline Athletic	2	Celtic	0	Hampden Park	87 866
1962	21 April	Rangers	2	St Mirren	0	Hampden Park	126 930
1963	4 May	Rangers	1	Celtic	1	Hampden Park	129 527
Replay	15 May	Rangers	3	Celtic	0	Hampden Park	120 263
1964	25 April	Rangers	3	Dundee	1	Hampden Park	120 982
1965	24 April	Celtic	3	Dunfermline Athletic	2	Hampden Park	108 800
1966	23 April	Rangers	0	Celtic	0	Hampden Park	126 552
Replay	27 April	Rangers	1	Celtic	0	Hampden Park	98 202
1967	29 April	Celtic	2	Aberdeen	0	Hampden Park	127 117
1968	27 April	Dunfermline Athletic	3	Heart of Midlothian	1	Hampden Park	56 366
1969	26 April	Celtic	4	Rangers	0	Hampden Park	132 874
1970	11 April	Aberdeen	3	Celtic	1	Hampden Park	108 434
1971	9 May	Celtic	1	Rangers	1	Hampden Park	120 092
Replay	12 May	Celtic	2	Rangers	1	Hampden Park	103 332
1972	6 May	Celtic	6	Hibernian	1	Hampden Park	106 102
1973	5 May	Rangers	3	Celtic	2	Hampden Park	122 714
1974	4 May	Celtic	3	Dundee United	0	Hampden Park	75 959
1975	3 May	Celtic	3	Airdrieonians	1	Hampden Park	75 457
1976	1 May	Rangers	3	Heart of Midlothian	1	Hampden Park	85 354
1977	7 May	Celtic	1	Rangers	0	Hampden Park	54 252
1978	6 May	Rangers	2	Aberdeen	1	Hampden Park	61 563
1979	12 May	Rangers	0	Hibernian	0	Hampden Park	50 610
Replay	16 May	Rangers	0	Hibernian	0	Hampden Park	33 506
2nd Replay	28 May	Rangers	3	Hibernian	2	Hampden Park	30 602
1980	10 May	Celtic	1	Rangers	0	Hampden Park	70 303
1981	9 May	Rangers	0	Dundee United	0	Hampden Park	55 000
Replay	12 May	Rangers	4	Dundee United	1	Hampden Park	43 009
1982	22 May	Aberdeen	4	Rangers	1	Hampden Park	53 788
1983	21 May	Aberdeen	1	Rangers	0	Hampden Park	62 979
1984	19 May	Aberdeen	2	Celtic	1	Hampden Park	58 900
1985	18 May	Celtic	2	Dundee United	1	Hampden Park	60 346
1986	10 May	Aberdeen	3	Heart of Midlothian	0	Hampden Park	62 841
1987	16 May	St Mirren	1	Dundee United	0	Hampden Park	51 782
1988	14 May	Celtic	2	Dundee United	1	Hampden Park	74 000

(1) Vale of Leven awarded cup; Rangers failed to appear for replay after 1–1 draw
(2) After Dumbarton protested the first game, which Queen's Park won 2–1
(3) Queen's Park awarded cup, Vale of Leven failing to appear
(4) Replay by order of Scottish FA because of playing conditions in first match, won 3–0 by Third Lanark
(5) After mutually protested first game which Celtic won 1–0
(6) Owing to riot, the cup was withheld after two drawn games
* Declared a friendly due to fog and frost

Managerial Magic

Since the 1946–47 season there have been 19 managers who have won three or more competitions in one or other of the principal tournaments, excluding the Charity Shield and European Super Cup, both of which are one-off games.

Bob Paisley of Liverpool with 13 such achievements between season 1975–76 and 1982–83 established a lengthy lead over all others.

Alf Ramsey has been the only one who has managed a club which won the championships of the First, Second and Third Divisions.

Bob Paisley (below right), Liverpool manager. Right: **Howard Kendall**, Everton player and subsequently manager.

Matt Busby.

	Divisions				FA Cup	Milk League Cup	World Cup	European Cup	Cup Winners' Cup	UEFA/ Fairs Cup	Total
	1	2	3	4							
Bob Paisley	6					3		3		1	13
Matt Busby	5				2			1			8
Bill Nicholson	1				3	2			1	1	8
Brian Clough	2	1				2		2			7
Joe Mercer	1	2			1	2			1		7
Don Revie	2	1			1	1				2	7
Bill Shankly	3	1			2					1	7
Stan Cullis	3				2						5
Howard Kendall	2				1				1		4
Harry Catterick	2	1			1						4
Alf Ramsey	1	1	1				1				4
Ron Saunders	1	1				2					4
Keith Burkinshaw					2					1	3
Tommy Docherty		1			1	1					3
Joe Fagan	1					1		1			3
John Lyall		1			2						3
Lawrie McMenemy			2		1						3
Bertie Mee	1				1					1	3
Alec Stock		2			1						3

Individual scoring feats

Record individual scoring feats – for and against – of all clubs in Football League matches

This table shows the best individual goalscoring performance for each Football League club in one game and also the highest number of goals scored by an opponent against that same team. Only Football League matches are included and feats of four or more goals shown.

	For				Against			
	Player	Gls	Against		Player	Club	Gls	
Aldershot	C. Mortimore	5	Orient	25.2.50	P. Simpson	Palace	4	18.11.33
					T. Cheetham	Q.P.R.	4	14.9.35
	D. Banton	5	Halifax	7.5.83	T. Cheetham	Q.P.R.	4	12.11.38
					M. Tadman	Plymouth	4	14.10.50
					R. Smith	Peterborough	4	4.3.61
Arsenal	E. J. Drake	7	Aston Villa	14.12.35	S. Bloomer	Middlesbrough	4	5.1.07
					A. Turnbull	Manchester U.	4	23.11.07
					W. Walker	Aston Villa	4	28.8.20
					F. Morris	West Brom.	4	14.10.22
					N. Harris	Notts C.	4	26.12.25
					H. Johnson	Sheffield U.	4	7.1.28
Aston Villa	H. Hampton	5	Sheffield W.	5.10.12	E. J. Drake	Arsenal	7	14.12.35
	H. J. Halse	5	Derby C.	19.10.12				
	L. Capewell	5	Burnley	29.8.25				
	G. Brown	5	Leicester	2.1.32				
	G. Hitchens	5	Charlton	14.11.59				
Barnsley	F. Eaton	5	Sth Shields	9.4.27	A. Chandler	Leicester	5	26.2.25
	P. Cunningham	5	Darlington	4.2.33	T. Phillipson	Wolves	5	26.4.26
	B. Asquith	5	Darlington	12.12.38	B. R. Mills	Notts C.	5	19.12.27
	C. McCormack	5	Luton	9.9.50	J. Hallows	Bradford C.	5	2.1.32
					W. R. Scott	Brentford	5	15.12.34
					K. Hector	Bradford PA	5	20.11.65
Birmingham	W. Abbott	5	Darwen	26.11.1898	L. A. Page	Burnley	6	10.4.26
	J. McMillan	5	Blackpool	2.3.01				
	J. Windridge	5	Glossop	23.1.15				
Blackburn	T. Briggs	7	Bristol R.	5.2.55	G. Henson	Bradford PA	6	29.1.38
Blackpool	J. Hampson	5	Reading	10.11.28	J. Cookson	West Brom.	6	17.9.27
	J. McIntosh	5	Preston	1.5.48				
Bolton W.	T. Caldwell	5	Walsall	10.9.83	R. Gurney	Sunderland	5	7.12.35
Bournemouth	J. Russell	4	Orient	7.1.33	C. Bourton	Coventry	5	17.10.31
	J. Russell	4	Bristol C.	28.1.33				
	H. Mardon	4	Southend	1.1.38				
	J. McDonald	4	Torquay	8.11.47				
Bradford C.	A. Whitehurst	7	Tranmere	6.3.29	T. Phillipson	Wolves	5	25.12.26
Brentford	W. R. Scott	5	Barnsley	15.12.34	G. Whitworth	Northampton	4	2.4.21
	P. McKennan	5	Bury	19.2.49	L. Thompson	Swansea	4	8.11.24
					W. Arblaster	Merthyr	4	17.4.26
					F. White	Birmingham	4	10.12.38
					S. Cooper	Newport	4	26.1.85
Brighton	J. Doran	5	Northampton	5.11.21	J. Riley	Bristol C.	5	7.2.34
	A. Thorne	5	Watford	30.4.58	R. Blackman	Reading	5	11.11.50
					B. Clough	Middlesbrough	5	23.8.58
Bristol C.	T. Walsh	6	Gillingham	15.1.27	K. McDonald	Hull C.	5	17.11.26
Bristol R.	R. A. Leigh	4	Exeter	2.5.21	J. Payne	Luton	10	13.4.36
	J. Wilcox	4	Bournemouth	26.12.25				
	W. Culley	4	Q.P.R.	5.3.27				
Burnley	L. A. Page	6	Birmingham	10.4.26	R. Jardine	Notts C.	5	27.10.1888
					L. Capewell	Aston Villa	5	29.8.25
					T. Browell	Manchester C.	5	24.10.25
					H. Ferguson	Cardiff	5	5.9.28

	For				Against			
	Player	Gls	Against		Player	Club	Gls	
Bury	E. Quigley	5	Millwall	15.2.47	P. McKennan	Brentford	5	19.2.49
	R. Pointer	5	Rotherham U.	2.10.65				
Cambridge	B. Greenhalgh	4	Darlington	18.9.71	J. Howarth	Aldershot	4	13.4.74
Cardiff	H. Ferguson	5	Burnley	5.9.28	A. G. Dawes	Palace	5	1.9.34
	W. Robbins	5	Thames	6.2.32				
	W. Henderson	5	Northampton	22.4.33				
Carlisle	H. Mills	5	Halifax	11.9.37	T. Bamford	Wrexham	5	17.3.34
	J. Whitehouse	5	Scunthorpe	25.12.52	G. Alsop	Walsall	5	2.2.35
Charlton	W. Lennox	5	Exeter	2.2.29	J. Fowler	Swansea	5	27.9.24
	E. Firmani	5	Aston Villa	5.2.55	W. Carter	Plymouth	5	27.12.60
	J. Summers	5	Huddersfield T.	21.12.57	G. Hitchens	Aston Villa	5	14.11.59
	J. Summers	5	Portsmouth	1.10.60				
Chelsea	G. Hilsdon	5	Glossop	1.9.06	W. R. Dean	Everton	5	14.12.31
	J. Greaves	5	Wolves	30.8.58	A. Lochhead	Burnley	5	24.4.65
	J. Greaves	5	Preston	19.12.59				
	J. Greaves	5	West Brom.	3.12.60				
	R. Tambling	5	Aston Villa	17.9.66				
Chester	T. Jennings	5	Walsall	30.1.32	E. Gemmell	Oldham	7	19.1.52
	B. Jepson	5	York	8.2.58				
Chesterfield	J. Cookson	4	Accrington	16.1.26	S. Littlewood	Port Vale	6	24.9.32
	J. Cookson	4	Ashington	1.5.26				
	J. Cookson	4	Wigan	4.9.26				
	T. Lyon	4	Southampton	3.12.38				
Colchester	R. R. Hunt	4	Bradford C.	30.12.61	D. Pacey	Orient	4	30.4.53
	M. King	4	Bradford C.	30.12.61	R. Poole	Chesterfield	4	3.3.61
	R. R. Hunt	4	Doncaster	30.4.62	I. Towers	Oldham	4	4.2.67
Coventry	C. Bourton	5	Bournemouth	17.10.31	T. Hunt	Norwich	5	15.3.30
	A. Bacon	5	Gillingham	30.12.33				
Crewe A.	W. Caulfield	4	Stalybe	28.1.22	A. Graver	Lincoln	6	29.9.51
	A. Rice	4	York	27.12.38				
Crystal P.	P. P. Simpson	6	Exeter	4.10.30	J. Moore	Derby	5	25.12.22
					R. V. Hoten	Northampton	5	27.10.28
Darlington	T. Ruddy	5	Sth Shields	23.4.27	P. Cunningham	Barnsley	5	4.2.33
	M. Wellock	5	Rotherham	15.2.30	B. Asquith	Barnsley	5	12.11.38
Derby C.	S. Bloomer	5	Sheffield W.	21.1.1899	H. J. Halse	Aston Villa	5	19.10.12
					D. Mangnall	Huddersfield T.	5	21.11.31
					F. Steele	Stoke	5	11.9.37
					S. Garner	Blackburn	5	10.9.83
Doncaster	T. Keetley	6	Ashington	16.2.29	T. Eglington	Everton	5	27.9.52
					J. Hill	Fulham	5	15.3.58
Everton	J. Southworth	6	West Brom.	30.12.1893	T. Johnson	Manchester C.	5	15.9.28
					D. Kevan	West Brom.	5	19.3.60
Exeter C.	H. Kirk	4	Portsmouth	3.3.23	P. Simpson	Palace	6	4.10.30
	F. Dent	4	Bristol R.	5.11.27				
	F. Whitlow	4	Watford	29.10.32				
Fulham	F. Harrison	5	Stockport	5.9.08	H. Leonard	Derby	4	4.11.11
	B. Jezzard	5	Hull	8.10.55	G. Camsell	Middlesbrough	4	20.11.26
	J. Hill	5	Doncaster	15.3.58	W. Kirkham	Port Vale	4	2.4.27
	S. Earle	5	Halifax	16.9.69	T. Keetley	Notts C.	4	6.9.30
Gillingham	F. Cheesemuir	6	Merthyr	26.4.30	T. Walsh	Bristol C.	6	15.1.27
Grimsby	T. McCairns	6	Leicester	11.4.1896	J. W. Glover	Southport	6	22.10.21
Halifax	W. Chambers	5	Hartlepools	7.4.34	F. Keetley	Lincoln	6	16.1.32
	A. Valentine	5	New Brighton	9.3.35				
Hartlepool	H. Simmons	5	Wigan B.	1.1.31	E. Harston	Mansfield	7	23.1.37
	D. Folland	5	Oldham	15.4.61				
Hereford	R. McNeil	4	Chester	10.3.76	M. Sanford	Aldershot	4	26.12.80
Huddersfield	D. Mangnall	5	Derby C.	21.11.31	J. Summers	Charlton	5	21.12.57
	A. Lythgoe	5	Blackburn	13.4.35				

	For				Against			
	Player	Gls	Against		Player	Club	Gls	
Hull City	K. McDonald	5	Bristol C.	17.11.28	W. McLeod	Leeds City	5	16.1.15
	S. Raleigh	5	Halifax	26.12.30	B. Jezzard	Fulham	5	8.10.55
Ipswich	A. Brazil	5	Southampton	16.2.81	T. Lawton	Notts C.	4	9.9.48
Leeds United	G. Hodgson	5	Leicester	1.10.38	V. Watson	West Ham	6	9.2.29
Leicester	J. Duncan	6	Port Vale	25.12.24	T. McCairns	Grimsby	6	11.4.1896
	A. Chandler	6	Portsmouth	20.10.28				
Lincoln C.	F. Keetley	6	Halifax	16.1.32	N. Coleman	Stoke	7	23.2.57
	A. Graver	6	Crewe	29.9.51				
Liverpool	A. McGuigan	5	Stoke	4.1.02	C. M. Buchan	Sunderland	5	7.12.12
	J. Evans	5	Bristol R.	15.9.54				
	I. Rush	5	Luton	29.10.83				
Luton Town	J. Payne	10	Bristol R.	13.4.36	C. McCormack	Barnsley	5	9.9.50
					B. Thomas	Scunthorpe	5	24.4.65
					R. Davies	Derby C.	5	29.3.75
					I. Rush	Liverpool	5	29.10.83
Manchester C.	F. Williams	5	Darwen	18.2.1899	G. Camsell	Middlesbrough	5	25.12.26
	T. Browell	5	Burnley	24.10.25				
	T. Johnson	5	Everton	15.9.28				
	G. Smith	5	Newport	14.6.47				
Manchester U.	A. Turnbull	4	Arsenal	23.11.07	W. R. Dean	Everton	5	8.10.27
	J. Spence	4	West Ham	1.2.30				
	J. Rowley	4	Charlton	30.8.47				
	C. Mitten	4	Aston Villa	8.3.50				
Mansfield	E. Harston	7	Hartlepools	23.1.37	W. Evans	Walsall	5	5.10.35
					W. McNaughton	Stockport	5	14.12.35
					K. East	Swindon	5	20.11.65
Middlesbrough	A. Wilson	5	Forest	6.10.23	J. Cantrell	Spurs	4	13.2.15
	G. Camsell	5	Manchester C.	25.12.26	E. J. Drake	Arsenal	4	19.4.35
	B. Clough	5	Brighton	23.8.58	W. Richardson	West Brom.	4	26.12.35
					T. Lawton	Everton	4	11.3.39
					E. J. Dodds	Blackpool	4	15.4.39
Millwall	R. Parker	5	Norwich	28.8.26	E. Quigley	Bury	5	15.2.47
Newcastle	L. Shackleton	6	Newport	6.10.46	E. C. Harper	Blackburn	5	9.9.25
Newport C.	T. J. Martin	5	Merthyr	10.4.30	L. Shackleton	Newcastle	6	5.10.46
Northampton	R. V. Hoten	5	Palace	7.10.28	J. Doran	Brighton	5	5.11.21
					W. Henderson	Cardiff	5	22.4.33
Norwich	T. Hunt	5	Coventry	15.3.30	D. A. Hunt	Sheffield W.	6	19.11.38
	R. Hollis	5	Walsall	29.12.51				
Nottingham F.	T. Peacock	4	Port Vale	23.12.33	A. Wilson	Middlesbrough	5	6.10.23
	T. Peacock	4	Barnsley	9.11.35	J. Robson	Burnley	5	21.11.59
	T. Peacock	4	Port Vale	23.11.35				
	T. Peacock	4	Doncaster	26.12.35				
	T. Capel	4	Gillingham	18.11.50				
Notts C.	R. Jardine	5	Burnley	27.10.1888	F. Morris	West Brom.	5	25.10.19
	D. Bruce	5	Port Vale	26.2.1895	W. Hartill	Wolves	5	12.10.29
	B. R. Mills	5	Barnsley	19.11.27	D. Dooley	Sheffield W.	5	3.11.51
Oldham	E. Gemmell	7	Chester	19.1.52	R. C. Bell	Tranmere	9	26.12.35
Orient	W. Leigh	4	Bradford C.	13.4.06	W. Boyd	Luton	5	28.12.35
	A. A. Pape	4	Oldham	1.9.24	C. Mortimore	Aldershot	5	25.2.50
	P. Kitchen	4	Millwall	21.4.84				
Oxford	A. Jones	4	Newport	22.9.62	R. Jenkins	Watford	4	23.9.78
Peterborough	T. Bly	4	Darlington	24.12.61	W. Best	Southend	4	28.3.70
	T. Bly	4	Chester	13.3.61				
	R. Smith	4	Aldershot	4.3.61				
	J. Hall	4	Oldham	26.11.69				
Plymouth	W. Carter	5	Charlton	27.12.60	W. R. Dean	Everton	4	27.12.30
					J. Stein	Everton	4	27.12.30
					B. Clough	Middlesbrough	4	5.9.59
Portsmouth	A. H. Strange	5	Gillingham	27.1.22	A. Chandler	Leicester	6	20.10.28
	P. Harris	5	Villa	3.9.58				

	For				Against			
	Player	Gls	Against		Player	Club	Gls	
Port Vale	S. Littlewood	6	Chesterfield	24.9.32	J. Duncan	Leicester	6	25.12.24
Preston	J. Ross	7	Stoke	6.10.1888	J. McIntosh	Blackpool	5	1.5.48
					J. Greaves	Chelsea	5	19.12.59
Q.P.R.	G. Goddard	4	Merthyr	9.3.29	D. H. Morris	Swindon	5	18.12.26
	G. Goddard	4	Swindon	12.4.30				
	G. Goddard	4	Exeter	20.12.30				
	G. Goddard	4	Watford	19.9.31				
	T. Cheetham	4	Aldershot	14.9.35				
	T. Cheetham	4	Aldershot	12.11.38				
Reading	A. Bacon	6	Stoke	3.4.31	J. Hampson	Blackpool	5	10.11.28
					E. C. Harper	Tottenham	5	30.8.30
Rochdale	T. Tippett	6	Hartlepools	21.4.30	F. Watts	Tranmere	5	25.12.31
					E. Harston	Mansfield	5	9.9.36
					J. Campbell	Lincoln	5	21.11.36
Rotherham	R. Bastow	4	York	9.11.35	M. Wellock	Darlington	5	15.2.30
	R. Bastow	4	Rochdale	7.3.36	F. Watkin	Port Vale	5	22.2.30
	W. Ardron	4	Crewe	5.10.46	H. Gallacher	Gateshead	5	17.9.38
	W. Ardron	4	Carlisle	13.9.47	A. Patrick	York	5	20.11.48
	W. Ardron	4	Hartlepools	13.10.48	R. Pointer	Bury	5	2.10.65
Scarborough	Never more than 3 goals				Never more than 3 goals			
Scunthorpe	B. Thomas	5	Luton	24.4.65	J. Whitehouse	Carlisle	5	25.12.52
Sheffield U.	H. Hammond	5	Bootle	26.12.1892	J. Lambert	Arsenal	5	24.12.32
	H. Johnson	5	West Ham	26.12.27				
Sheffield W.	D. A. Hunt	6	Norwich	19.11.38	S. Bloomer	Derby C.	6	21.1.1899
Shrewsbury	A. Wood	5	Blackburn	2.10.71	J. Gilfillan	Southend	4	4.4.64
					J. Atyeo	Bristol C.	4	19.4.65
					G. Yardley	Transmere	4	8.9.67
Southampton	C. Wayman	5	Leicester	23.10.48	A. Brazil	Ipswich	5	16.2.82
Southend	J. Shankly	5	Merthyr	1.3.30	R. Blackman	Reading	5	14.8.51
Stockport	J. Smith	5	Southport	7.1.28	F. Harrison	Fulham	5	5.9.08
	J. Smith	5	Lincoln	15.9.28	J. Trotter	Sheffield W.	5	21.9.25
	F. Newton	5	Nelson	19.9.29				
	A. Lythgoe	5	Southport	25.8.34				
	W. McNaughton	5	Mansfield	14.12.35				
	J. Connor	5	Workington	8.11.52				
	J. Connor	5	Southport	7.4.56				
Stoke	N. Coleman	7	Lincoln	23.2.57	J. Ross	Preston	7	6.10.88
Sunderland	C. M. Buchan	5	Liverpool	7.12.12	G. Hurst	West Ham	6	19.10.68
	R. Gurney	5	Bolton	7.12.35				
	D. Sharkey	5	Norwich	20.3.63				
Swansea	J. Fowler	5	Charlton	17.9.24	G. Camsell	Middlesbrough	4	18.12.26
					T. Glidden	West Brom.	4	26.10.29
Swindon	D. H. Morris	5	Q.P.R.	18.12.26	T. Tait	Luton	5	16.4.32
	D. H. Morris	5	Norwich	26.4.30				
	K. East	5	Mansfield	20.11.65				
Torquay	R. Stubbs	5	Newport C.	19.10.63	J. Devlin	Walsall	5	1.9.49
Tottenham	E. C. Harper	5	Reading	30.8.30	F. Pagnum	Liverpool	4	31.10.14
	A. Stokes	5	Birmingham	18.9.57	J. H. Carter	West Brom.	4	8.12.23
	R. Smith	5	Aston Villa	29.3.58	J. W. Bowers	Derby C.	4	7.4.34
					E. J. Drake	Arsenal	4	20.10.34
Tranmere	R. C. Bell	9	Oldham	26.12.35	A. Whitehurst	Bradford	7	6.3.29
Walsall	G. Alsop	5	Carlisle	2.2.35	Adrian Capes	Burton W.	5	12.1.1895
	W. Evans	5	Mansfield	5.10.35	T. Jennings	Chester	5	30.1.32
	J. Devlin	5	Torquay	1.9.49	R. Hollis	Norwich	5	29.12.51
Watford	A. Mummery	5	Newport	5.1.24	J. C. Martin	Aberdare	5	2.1.26
					A. Thorne	Brighton	5	30.4.58
West Brom.	J. Cookson	6	Blackpool	17.9.27	J. Southworth	Everton	6	30.12.1893

	For				Against			
	Player	Gls	Against		Player	Club	Gls	
West Ham	W. Watson	6	Leeds	9.2.29	H. Johnson	Sheffield U.	5	26.12.27
	G. Hurst	6	Sunderland	19.10.68				
Wigan A.	Never more than three goals				Never more than three goals			
Wimbledon	A. Cork	4	Torquay	28.2.79	Never more than three goals			
Wolves	J. H. Butcher	5	Accrington	19.11.1892	J. McMillan	Derby C.	5	10.1.1891
	T. Phillipson	5	Barnsley	26.4.26	J. Greaves	Chelsea	5	30.8.58
	T. Phillipson	5	Bradford C.	25.12.26				
	W. Hartill	5	Notts C.	12.10.29				
	W. Hartill	5	Aston Villa	3.9.34				
Wrexham	T. H. Lewis	5	Crewe	20.9.30	B. Twell	Southport	5	18.4.30
	T. Bamford	5	Carlisle	17.3.34				
York City	A. Patrick	5	Rotherham	20.11.48	B. Jepson	Chester	5	15.2.58

Littlewoods Cup (Milk Cup) (League Cup)

The 1987 Littlewoods Cup Final in which Ian Rush (left, white shirt) lost his record of scoring and keeping Liverpool unbeaten. Arsenal won 2–1.

Year	Winners	Runners-up	Venue	Attendance	Referee	Aggregate attendances
1961	Aston Villa 3	† Rotherham United 2	home/away	12 226	K. A. Collinge	1 204 580
				31 202	C. W. Kingston	
1962	Norwich City 4	† Rochdale 0	home/away	11 123	A. Holland	1 030 534
				19 708	R. H. Mann	
1963†	Birmingham City 3	Aston Villa 1	home/away	31 850	E. Crawford	1 029 893
				37 920	A. W. Starling	
1964	Leicester City 4	† Stoke City 3	home/away	22 309	W. Clements	945 265
				25 372	A. Jobling	
1965†	Chelsea 3	Leicester City 2	home/away	20 690	J. Finney	962 802
				26 958	K. Howley	
1966	West Bromwich Albion 5	† West Ham United 3	home/away	28 341	D. W. Smith	1 205 876
				31 925	J. Mitchell	
1967	Queen's Park Rangers 3	West Bromwich Albion 2	Wembley	97 952	W. Crossley	1 394 553

Year	Winners	Runners-up	Venue	Attendance	Referee	Aggregate attendances
1968	Leeds United 1	Arsenal 0*	Wembley	97 887	L. Hamer	1 671 326
1969	Swindon Town 3	Arsenal 1*	Wembley	98 189	W. Handley	2 064 647
1970	Manchester City 2	West Bromwich Albion 1	Wembley	97 963	J. James	2 299 819
1971	Tottenham Hotspur 2	Aston Villa 0	Wembley	100 000	J. Finney	2 038 809
1972	Stoke City 2	Chelsea 1	Wembley	100 000	N. C. Burtenshaw	2 397 154
1973	Tottenham Hotspur 1	Norwich City 0	Wembley	100 000	D. W. Smith	1 935 474
1974	Wolverhampton Wanderers 2	Manchester City 1	Wembley	100 000	E. D. Wallace	1 722 629
1975	Aston Villa 1	Norwich City 0	Wembley	100 000	G. W. Hill	1 901 094
1976	Manchester City 2	Newcastle United 1	Wembley	100 000	J. K. Taylor	1 841 735
1977	Aston Villa 3 (after first replay 1–1*) (after 0–0)	Everton 2*	Old Trafford Hillsborough Wembley	54 749 55 000 100 000	G. C. Kew G. C. Kew G. C. Kew	2 236 636
1978	Nottingham Forest 1 (after 0–0*)	Liverpool 0	Old Trafford Wembley	54 375 100 000	P. Partridge P. Partridge	2 038 295
1979	Nottingham Forest 3	Southampton 2	Wembley	100 000	P. G. Reeves	1 827 464
1980	Wolverhampton Wanderers 1	Nottingham Forest 0	Wembley	100 000	D. Richardson	2 322 866
1981	Liverpool 2 (after 1–1*)	West Ham United 1	Villa Park Wembley	36 693 100 000	C. Thomas C. Thomas	2 051 576
1982	Liverpool 3	Tottenham Hotspur 1*	Wembley	100 000	P. M. Willis	1 880 682
1983	Liverpool 2	Manchester United 1	Wembley	100 000	G. Courtney	1 679 756
1984	Liverpool 1 (after 0–0*)	Everton 0	Maine Road	52 089	A. Robinson A. Robinson	1 900 491
1985	Norwich City 1	Sunderland 0	Wembley	¹100 000	N. Midgley	1 876 429
1986	Oxford United 3	Queen's Park Rangers 0	Wembley	90 396	K. Hackett	1 579 243
1987	Arsenal 2	Liverpool 1	Wembley	96 000	L. Shapter	1 534 547
1988	Luton Town 3	Arsenal 2	Wembley	95 732	J. Worrall	¹1 541 786

* after extra time   † home team in first leg   ¹unofficial figures

Leading scorers

Year	Games	Average attendance	Entries	Top Scorer	
1961	112	10 755	87	Gerry Hitchens (Aston Villa)	11
1962	104	9 909	82	Ray Charnley (Blackpool)	6
1963†	102	10 097	80	Ken Leek (Birmingham City)	8
1964	104	9 089	82	John Ritchie (Stoke City)	10
1965†	98	9 825	82	Tony Hateley (Aston Villa)	10
1966	106	11 376	83	Tony Brown (West Bromwich Albion) Geoff Hurst (West Ham United) }	11
1967	118	11 818	90	Rodney Marsh (Queen's Park Rangers)	11
1968	110	15 194	90	John O'Hare (Derby County) Jim Fryatt (Torquay United) }	6
1969	118	17 497	91	Don Rogers (Swindon Town)	7
1970	122	18 851	92	Jeff Astle (West Bromwich Albion) John Byrom (Bolton Wanderers) Francis Lee (Manchester City) Rodney Marsh (Queen's Park Rangers) }	5
1971	117	17 425	91	Martin Chivers (Tottenham Hotspur)	7
1972	123	19 489	92	Martin Chivers (Tottenham Hotspur)	7
1973	120	16 129	92	Kevin Keegan (Liverpool) Graham Paddon (Norwich City) Martin Peters (Tottenham Hotspur) }	5
1974	132	13 050	92	Francis Lee (Manchester City)	8
1975	127	14 969	92	Lou Macari (Manchester United)	7
1976	140	13 155	92	Dennis Tueart (Manchester City)	8
1977	147	15 215	92	Brian Little (Aston Villa)	10
1978	148	13 722	92	Kenny Dalglish (Liverpool) Ian Bowyer (Nottingham Forest) }	6
1979	139	13 148	92	Garry Birtles (Nottingham Forest) Bob Latchford (Everton) }	6
1980	169	13 745	92	Alan Mayes (Swindon Town)	6

	Games	Average attendance	Entries	Top Scorer	
1981	161	12 743	92	Kenny Dalglish (Liverpool)	7
1982	161	11 681	92	Ian Rush (Liverpool)	8
1983	160	10 498	92	Steve Coppell (Manchester United)	6
1984	168	11 312	92	Ian Rush (Liverpool)	8
1985	167	11 236	92	Kerry Dixon (Chelsea)	8
1986	163	9 688	92	Simon Stainrod (Aston Villa)	9
1987	157	9 774	92	Clive Allen (Tottenham Hotspur)	12
1988	158	¹9 758	92	Jimmy Quinn (Swindon Town)	8

Freight Rover/ Sherpa Van Trophy

Year	Final	Attendance
*1984	Bournemouth 2 Hull City 1	6 514
1985	Wigan Athletic 3 Brentford 1	34 932
1986	Bristol City 3 Bolton Wanderers 0	55 330
1987	Mansfield Town 1 Bristol City 1	60 050
	(Mansfield Town won 5–4 on penalties)	
1988	Wolverhampton Wanderers 2 Burnley 0	80 841

*Associate Members Cup

Full Members Cup/Simod Cup

Year	Final	Attendance
1986	Chelsea 5 Manchester City 4	68 000
1987	Blackburn Rovers 1 Charlton Athletic 0	40 000
1988	Reading 4 Luton Town 1	61 740

Attendances
Freight Rover/Sherpa Van Trophy

Year	Overall	Average	Matches
1983–84	135 813	2663	51
1984–85	210 279	2804	75
1985–86	212 114	3166	67
1986–87	279 594	3452	81

Full Members/Simod Cup

Year	Overall	Average	Matches
1985–86	180 401	6443	28
1986–87	218 506	6243	35
1987–88	293 834	7534	39

Mick Harford, Luton Town's leading scorer in the 1988 Littlewoods Cup.

European Champion

Season	Winners		Runners-up		Venue	Attendance at final
1955–56	Real Madrid	4	Stade de Reims	3	Paris, France	38 000
1956–57	Real Madrid	2	Fiorentina	0	Madrid, Spain	124 000
1957–58	Real Madrid	3	AC Milan	2	Brussels, Belgium	67 000
1958–59	Real Madrid	2	Stade de Reims	0	Stuttgart, West Germany	80 000
1959–60	Real Madrid	7	Eintracht Frankfurt	3	Glasgow, Scotland	135 000
1960–61	Benfica	3	Barcelona	2	Berne, Switzerland	28 000
1961–62	Benfica	5	Real Madrid	3	Amsterdam, Holland	65 000
1962–63	AC Milan	2	Benfica	1	Wembley, England	45 000
1963–64	Internazionale	3	Real Madrid	1	Vienna, Austria	74 000
1964–65	Internazionale	1	Benfica	0	Milan, Italy	80 000
1965–66	Real Madrid	2	Partizan Belgrade	1	Brussels, Belgium	55 000
1966–67	Celtic	2	Internazionale	1	Lisbon, Portugal	56 000
1967–68	Manchester United	4	Benfica	1	Wembley, England	100 000
1968–69	AC Milan	4	Ajax	1	Madrid, Spain	50 000
1969–70	Feyenoord	2	Celtic	1	Milan, Italy	50 000
1970–71	Ajax	2	Panathinaikos	0	Wembley, England	90 000
1971–72	Ajax	2	Internazionale	0	Rotterdam, Holland	67 000
1972–73	Ajax	1	Juventus	0	Belgrade, Yugoslavia	93 500
1973–74	Bayern Munich	1	Atletico Madrid	1	Brussels, Belgium	65 000
Replay	Bayern Munich	4	Atletico Madrid	0	Brussels, Belgium	65 000
1974–75	Bayern Munich	2	Leeds United	0	Paris, France	50 000
1975–76	Bayern Munich	1	St Etienne	0	Glasgow, Scotland	54 864
1976–77	Liverpool	3	Borussia Moenchengladbach	1	Rome, Italy	57 000
1977–78	Liverpool	1	FC Bruges	0	Wembley, England	92 000
1978–79	Nottingham Forest	1	Malmo	0	Munich, West Germany	57 500
1979–80	Nottingham Forest	1	Hamburg	0	Madrid, Spain	50 000
1980–81	Liverpool	1	Real Madrid	0	Paris, France	48 360
1981–82	Aston Villa	1	Bayern Munich	0	Rotterdam, Holland	46 000
1982–83	Hamburg	1	Juventus	0	Athens, Greece	75 000
1983–84	Liverpool	1	Roma	1	Rome, Italy	69 693
	(aet; Liverpool won 4–2 on penalties)					
1984–85	Juventus	1	Liverpool	0	Brussels, Belgium	58 000
1985–86	Steaua Bucharest	0	Barcelona	0	Seville, Spain	70 000
	(aet; Steaua won 2–0 on penalties)					
1986–87	Porto	2	Bayern Munich	1	Vienna, Austria	59 000
1987–88	PSV Eindhoven	0	Benfica	0	Stuttgart, West Germany	70 000
	(aet; PSV won 6–5 on penalties)					

Clubs Cup

Referee	Total games played	Total goals scored	Attendances Overall	Average	Top scorer	Goals
Ellis (England)	29	127	912 000	31 450	Milutinovic (Partizan Belgrade)	7
Horn (Holland)	44	170	1 786 000	40 590	Viollet (Manchester United)	9
Alsteen (Belgium)	48	189	1 790 000	37 290	Di Stefano (Real Madrid)	10
Dutsch (West Germany)	55	199	2 010 000	36 545	Fontaine (Stade de Reims)	10
Mowat (Scotland)	52	218	2 780 000	50 545	Puskas (Real Madrid)	12
Dienst (Switzerland)	51	166	1 850 000	36 274	Aguas (Benfica)	10
Horn (Holland)	55	221	2 135 000	45 727	Di Stefano, Puskas and Tejada (Real Madrid)	7
Holland (England)	59	214	2 158 000	36 593	Altafini (AC Milan)	14
Stoll (Austria)	61	212	2 180 000	35 737	Mazzola (Internazionale)	7
Dienst (Switzerland)	62	215	2 577 000	41 564	Eusebio and Torres (Benfica)	9
Kreitlein (West Germany)	58	234	2 112 000	36 431	Albert (Ferencvaros) and Eusebio (Benfica)	7
Tschenscher (West Germany)	65	211	2 248 000	34 584	Van Himst (Anderlecht)	6
Lo Bello (Italy)	60	162	2 544 000	42 500	Eusebio (Benfica)	6
Ortiz de Mendibil (Spain)	52	176	2 056 000	39 540	Law (Manchester United)	9
Lo Bello (Italy)	63	202	2 345 000	37 222	Jones (Leeds United)	8
Taylor (England)	63	210	2 124 000	33 714	Antoniadis (Panathinaikos)	10
Helies (France)	64	175	2 066 976	32 280	Cruyff (Ajax), Macari (Celtic), Takac (Standard)	5
Guglovic (Yugoslavia)	58	160	1 712 277	30 000	Muller (Bayern Munich)	11
Loraux (Belgium) Delcourt (Belgium)	60	180	1 586 852	26 448	Muller (Bayern Munich)	9
Kitabdjian (France)	55	174	1 380 254	25 096	Almquist (Atvidaberg), Kreuz (Feyenoord), Markarov (Ararat), Muller (Bayern Munich), Zungul (Hajduk)	5
Palotai (Hungary)	61	202	1 736 087	28 460	Heynckes (Moenchengladbach), Santillana (Real Madrid)	6
Wurtz (France)	61	155	2 010 000	34 325	Cucinotta (Zurich), Muller (Bayern Munich)	5
Corver (Holland)	59	172	1 509 471	25 584	Simonsen (Moenchengladbach)	5
Linemayr (Austria)	63	185	1 511 291	23 988	Sulser (Grasshoppers)	11
Garrido (Portugal)	63	185	1 729 415	27 451	Lerby (Ajax)	10
Palotai (Hungary)	63	166	1 166 593	26 374	Rummenigge (Bayern Munich), McDermott and Souness (Liverpool)	6
Konrath (France)	63	170	1 530 082	24 287	Hoeness (Bayern Munich), Geurts (Anderlecht)	7
Rainea (Rumania)	61	180	1 718 075	28 165	Rossi (Juventus)	6
Fredriksson (Sweden)	59	165	1 601 065	27 137	Sokol (Dynamo Minsk)	6
Daina (Switzerland)	61	186	1 475 740	24 192	Platini (Juventus), Nilsson (Gothenburg)	7
Vautrot (France)	59	167	1 493 117	25 307	Nilsson (Gothenburg)	6
Ponnet (Belgium)	57	163	1 829 442	32 095	Cvetkovic (Red Star Belgrade)	7
Agnolin (Italy)	60	140	N/A	N/A	N/A	N/A

Season	Winners		Runners-up		Venue	Attendance
1960–61	Fiorentina (First Leg)	2	Rangers	0	Glasgow, Scotland	80 000
	Fiorentina (Second Leg)	2	Rangers	1	Florence, Italy	50 000
1961–62	Atletico Madrid	1	Fiorentina	1	Glasgow, Scotland	27 389
Replay	Atletico Madrid	3	Fiorentina	0	Stuttgart, West Germany	45 000
1962–63	Tottenham Hotspur	5	Atletico Madrid	1	Rotterdam, Holland	25 000
1963–64	Sporting Lisbon	3	MTK Budapest	3	Brussels, Belgium	9 000
Replay	Sporting Lisbon	1	MTK Budapest	0	Antwerp, Belgium	18 000
1964–65	West Ham United	2	Munich 1860	0	Wembley, England	100 000
1965–66	Borussia Dortmund (aet)	2	Liverpool	1	Glasgow, Scotland	41 657
1966–67	Bayern Munich (aet)	1	Rangers	0	Nuremberg, West Germany	69 480
1967–68	AC Milan	2	Hamburg	0	Rotterdam, Holland	60 000
1968–69	Slovan Bratislava	3	Barcelona	2	Basle, Switzerland	40 000
1969–70	Manchester City	2	Gornik Zabrze	1	Vienna, Austria	10 000
1970–71	Chelsea	1	Real Madrid	1	Athens, Greece	42 000
Replay	Chelsea	2	Real Madrid	1	Athens, Greece	24 000
1971–72	Rangers	3	Moscow Dynamo	2	Barcelona, Spain	35 000
1972–73	AC Milan	1	Leeds United	0	Salonika, Greece	45 000
1973–74	Magdeburg	2	AC Milan	0	Rotterdam, Holland	5 000
1974–75	Dynamo Kiev	3	Ferencvaros	0	Basle, Switzerland	13 000
1975–76	Anderlecht	4	West Ham United	2	Brussels, Belgium	58 000
1976–77	Hamburg	2	Anderlecht	0	Amsterdam, Holland	65 000
1977–78	Anderlecht	4	Austria/WAC	0	Amsterdam, Holland	48 679
1978–79	Barcelona (aet)	4	Fortuna Dusseldorf	3	Basle, Switzerland	58 000
1979–80	Valencia (aet: Valencia won 5–4 on penalties)	0	Arsenal	0	Brussels, Belgium	40 000
1980–81	Dynamo Tbilisi	2	Carl Zeiss Jena	1	Dusseldorf, West Germany	9 000
1981–82	Barcelona	2	Standard Liege	1	Barcelona, Spain	100 000
1982–83	Aberdeen (aet)	2	Real Madrid	1	Gothenburg, Sweden	17 804
1983–84	Juventus	2	Porto	1	Basle, Switzerland	60 000
1984–85	Everton	3	Rapid Vienna	1	Rotterdam, Holland	30 000
1985–86	Dynamo Kiev	3	Atletico Madrid	0	Lyon, France	39 300
1986–87	Ajax	1	Lokomotive Leipzig	0	Athens, Greece	35 000
1987–88	Mechelen	1	Ajax	0	Strasbourg, France	39 446

Referee	Total games played	Total goals scored	Attendances Overall	Attendances Average	Top scorer	Goals
Steiner (Austria)	18	60	290 000	16 111		
Hernadi (Hungary)						
Wharton (Scotland)	44	174	650 000	14 733		
Tschenscher (West Germany)						
Van Leuwen (Holland)	48	169	1 100 000	22 916		
Van Nuffel (Belgium)	62	202	1 300 000	20 967		
Versyp (Belgium)						
Szolt (Hungary)	61	163	1 100 000	18 032		
Schwinte (France)	59	188	1 546 000	26 203	Emmerich (Dortmund)	14
Lo Bello (Italy)	61	170	1 556 000	25 508	Muller (Bayern Munich)	9
Ortiz de Mendibil (Spain)	64	200	1 683 000	26 269	Seeler (Hamburg)	6
Van Ravens (Holland)	51	157	957 000	18 765	Ruhl (Cologne)	6
Schiller (Austria)	64	179	1 675 000	25 890	Lubanski (Gornik)	8
Scheurer (Switzerland)	67	203	1 570 000	23 582	Lubanski (Gornik)	8
Bucheli (Switzerland)						
Ortiz de Mendibil (Spain)	65	186	1 145 211	17 615	Osgood (Chelsea)	8
Mihas (Greece)	61	174	908 564	15 000	Chiarugi (AC Milan)	7
Van Gemert (Holland)	61	169	1 105 494	18 123	Heynckes (Moenchengladbach)	10
Davidson (Scotland)	59	177	1 298 850	22 014	Onishenko (Dynamo Kiev)	7
Wurtz (France)	61	189	1 128 962	18 508	Rensenbrink (Anderlecht)	8
Partridge (England)	63	198	1 537 000	24 400	Milanov (Levski)	13
Adlinger (West Germany)	63	179	1 161 383	18 434	Gritter (Twente)	7
Palotai (Hungary)	59	160	1 041 135	17 646	Altobelli (Internazionale)	7
Christov (Czechoslovakia)	63	176	1 193 682	18 947	Kempes (Valencia)	9
Lattanzi (Italy)	65	176	1 239 795	19 074	Cross (West Ham United)	6
Eschweiler (West Germany)	63	176	1 504 023	23 873	Shengelia (Tbilisi), Voordeckers (Standard)	6
Menegali (Italy)	65	198	1 424 104	21 909	Santillana (Real Madrid)	8
Prokop (East Germany)	63	198	1 451 136	23 034	McGhee (Aberdeen)	5
Casarin (Italy)	62	156	1 152 605	18 590	Gazayev (Dynamo Moscow), Panenka (Rapid), Gray (Everton)	5
Wohrer (Austria)	59	191	1 330 286	22 547	Yaremchuk (Dynamo Kiev), Funkel (Bayer Uerdingen)	6
Agnolin (Italy)	61	172	1 139 609	18 682	Bosman (Ajax)	8
Pauly (West Germany)	63	126	N/A	N/A	N/A	N/A

UEFA Cup

Season	Winners		Runners-up		Venue	Attendance
1955–58	BARCELONA (First Leg)	2	LONDON	2	Stamford Bridge, England	45 466
	BARCELONA (Second Leg)	6	LONDON	0	Barcelona, Spain	62 000
1958–60	BARCELONA (First Leg)	0	BIRMINGHAM CITY	0	Birmingham, England	40 500
	BARCELONA (Second Leg)	4	BIRMINGHAM CITY	1	Barcelona, Spain	70 000
1960–61	ROMA (First Leg)	2	BIRMINGHAM CITY	2	Birmingham, England	21 005
	ROMA (Second Leg)	2	BIRMINGHAM CITY	0	Rome, Italy	60 000
1961–62	VALENCIA (First Leg)	6	BARCELONA	2	Valencia, Spain	65 000
	VALENCIA (Second Leg)	1	BARCELONA	1	Barcelona, Spain	60 000
1962–63	VALENCIA (First Leg)	2	DYNAMO ZAGREB	1	Zagreb, Yugoslavia	40 000
	VALENCIA (Second Leg)	2	DYNAMO ZAGREB	0	Valencia, Spain	55 000
1963–64	ZARAGOZA	2	VALENCIA	1	Barcelona, Spain	50 000
1964–65	FERENCVAROS	1	JUVENTUS	0	Turin, Italy	25 000
1965–66	BARCELONA (First Leg)	0	ZARAGOZA	1	Barcelona, Spain	70 000
	BARCELONA (Second Leg)	4	ZARAGOZA	2	Zaragoza, Spain	70 000
1966–67	DYNAMO ZAGREB (First Leg)	2	LEEDS UNITED	0	Zagreb, Yugoslavia	40 000
	DYNAMO ZAGREB (Second Leg)	0	LEEDS UNITED	0	Leeds, England	35 604
1967–68	LEEDS UNITED (First Leg)	1	FERENCVAROS	0	Leeds, England	25 368
	LEEDS UNITED (Second Leg)	0	FERENCVAROS	0	Budapest, Hungary	70 000
1968–69	NEWCASTLE UNITED (First Leg)	3	UJPEST DOZSA	0	Newcastle, England	60 000
	NEWCASTLE UNITED (Second Leg)	3	UJPEST DOZSA	2	Budapest, Hungary	37 000
1969–70	ARSENAL (First Leg)	1	ANDERLECHT	3	Brussels, Belgium	37 000
	ARSENAL (Second Leg)	3	ANDERLECHT	0	Highbury, England	51 612
1970–71	LEEDS UNITED (Abandoned 51 minutes)	0	JUVENTUS	0	Turin, Italy	65 000
	LEEDS UNITED (First Leg)	2	JUVENTUS	2	Turin, Italy	65 000
	LEEDS UNITED (Second Leg)	1	JUVENTUS (Leeds won on away goals)	1	Leeds, England	42 483
1971–72	TOTTENHAM HOTSPUR (First Leg)	2	WOLVERHAMPTON WANDERERS	1	Wolverhampton, England	45 000
	TOTTENHAM HOTSPUR (Second Leg)	1	WOLVERHAMPTON WANDERERS	1	White Hart Lane, England	48 000
1972–73	LIVERPOOL (First Leg)	3	MOENCHENGLADBACH	0	Anfield, England	41 169
	LIVERPOOL (Second Leg)	2	MOENCHENGLADBACH	0	Moenchengladbach, West Germany	35 000
1973–74	FEYENOORD (First Leg)	2	TOTTENHAM HOTSPUR	2	White Hart Lane, England	46 281
	FEYENOORD (Second Leg)	2	TOTTENHAM HOTSPUR	0	Rotterdam, Holland	68 000
1974–75	MOENCHENGLADBACH (First Leg)	0	TWENTE	0	Dusseldorf, West Germany	45 000
	MOENCHENGLADBACH (Second Leg)	5	TWENTE	1	Enschede, Holland	24 500
1975–76	LIVERPOOL (First Leg)	3	FC BRUGES	2	Anfield, England	56 000
	LIVERPOOL (Second Leg)	1	FC BRUGES	1	Bruges, Belgium	32 000

Season	Winners		Runners-up		Venue	Attendance
1976–77	JUVENTUS (First Leg)	1	ATHLETIC BILBAO	0	Turin, Italy	75 000
	JUVENTUS (Second Leg)	1	ATHLETIC BILBAO	2	Bilbao, Spain	43 000
1977–78	PSV EINDHOVEN (First Leg)	0	BASTIA	0	Bastia, Corsica	15 000
	PSV EINDHOVEN (Second Leg)	3	BASTIA	0	Eindhoven, Holland	27 000
1978–79	MOENCHENGLADBACH (First Leg)	1	RED STAR BELGRADE	1	Belgrade, Yugoslavia	87 500
	MOENCHENGLADBACH (Second Leg)	1	RED STAR BELGRADE	0	Dusseldorf, West Germany	45 000
1979–80	EINTRACHT FRANKFURT (First Leg)	2	MOENCHENGLADBACH	3	Moenchengladbach, West Germany	25 000
	EINTRACHT FRANKFURT (Second Leg)	1	MOENCHENGLADBACH (Eintracht won on away goals)	0	Frankfurt, West Germany	60 000
1980–81	IPSWICH TOWN (First Leg)	3	AZ '67	0	Ipswich, England	27 532
	IPSWICH TOWN (Second Leg)	2	AZ '67	4	Amsterdam, Holland	28 500
1981–82	GOTHENBURG (First Leg)	1	HAMBURG	0	Gothenburg, Sweden	42 548
	GOTHENBURG (Second Leg)	3	HAMBURG	0	Hamburg, West Germany	60 000
1982–83	ANDERLECHT (First Leg)	1	BENFICA	0	Brussels, Belgium	45 000
	ANDERLECHT (Second Leg)	1	BENFICA	1	Lisbon, Portugal	80 000
1983–84	TOTTENHAM HOTSPUR (First Leg)	1	ANDERLECHT	1	Brussels, Belgium	40 000
	TOTTENHAM HOTSPUR (Second Leg)	1	ANDERLECHT (Tottenham won 4–3 on penalties)	1	White Hart Lane, England	46 258
1984–85	VIDEOTON (First Leg)	0	REAL MADRID	3	Szekesfehervar	30 000
	REAL MADRID (Second Leg)	0	VIDEOTON	1	Madrid, Spain	98 300
1985–86	REAL MADRID (First Leg)	5	COLOGNE	1	Madrid, Spain	80 000
	REAL MADRID (Second Leg)	0	COLOGNE	2	West Berlin, West Germany	15 000
1986–87	GOTHENBURG (First Leg)	1	DUNDEE UNITED	0	Gothenburg. Sweden	50 023
	GOTHENBURG (Second Leg)	1	DUNDEE UNITED	1	Tannadice Park, Scotland	20 911
1987–88	BAYER LEVERKUSEN (First Leg)	0	ESPANOL	3	Barcelona, Spain	42 000
	BAYER LEVERKUSEN (Second Leg)	3	ESPANOL (Leverkusen won 3–2 on penalties)	0	Leverkusen, West Germany	22 000

European Super Cup

Year	Winners	Runners-up	Scores	Year	Winners	Runners-up	Scores
1973	Ajax	Rangers	3-1, 3-2	1981	Not Contested		
1974	Ajax	AC Milan	0-1, 6-0	1982	Aston Villa	Barcelona	0-1, 3-0
1975	Dynamo Kiev	Bayern Munich	1-0, 2-0	1983	Aberdeen	Hamburg	0-0, 2-0
1976	Anderlecht	Bayern Munich	4-1, 1-2	1984	Juventus	Liverpool	2-0 (in Turin)
1977	Liverpool	Hamburg	1-1, 6-0	1985	Not Contested		
1978	Anderlecht	Liverpool	3-1, 1-2	1986	Steaua Bucharest	Dynamo Kiev	1-0 (in Monaco)
1979	Nottingham Forest	Barcelona	1-0, 1-1	1987	Porto	Ajax	1-0, 1-0
1980	Valencia	Nottingham Forest	1-2, 1-0 (on away goals)				

South American Cup (Copa Libertadores)

Year	Winner	Entries	Matches	Goals	Year	Winner	Entries	Matches	Goals
1960	Penarol	8	13	39	1974	Independiente	21	76	178
1961	Penarol	9	16	52	1975	Independiente	21	76	208
1962	Santos	10	25	101	1976	Cruzeiro	21	77	211
1963	Santos	9	19	63	1977	Boca Juniors	21	75	152
1964	Independiente	10	25	89	1978	Boca Juniors	21	75	181
1965	Independiente	10	27	72	1979	Olimpia	21	74	211
1966	Penarol	17	94	218	1980	Nacional	21	75	160
1967	Racing	19	114	355	1981	Flamengo	21	77	220
1968	Estudiantes	21	93	232	1982	Penarol	21	73	163
1969	Estudiantes	17	74	211	1983	Gremio	21	74	179
1970	Estudiantes	19	88	253	1984	Independiente	21	75	206
1971	Nacional	21	73	196	1985	Argentinos Juniors	21	71	181
1972	Independiente	20	69	176	1986	River Plate	19	64	166
1973	Independiente	19	66	190	1987	Penarol	21	76	207

World Club Championship

Year	Winners	Runners-up	Scores	Venue	First Leg Attendance
1960	Real Madrid	Penarol	0-0, 5-1	Montevideo	75 000
1961	Penarol	Benfica	0-1, 5-0, 2-1	Lisbon	55 000
1962	Santos	Benfica	3-2, 5-2	Rio de Janeiro	90 000
1963	Santos	AC Milan	2-4, 4-2, 1-0	Milan	80 000
1964	Internazionale	Independiente	0-1, 2-0, 1-0	Buenos Aires	70 000
1965	Internazionale	Independiente	3-0, 0-0	Milan	70 000
1966	Penarol	Real Madrid	2-0, 2-0	Montevideo	70 000
1967	Racing	Celtic	0-1, 2-1, 1-0	Hampden Park	103 000
1968	Estudiantes	Manchester United	1-0, 1-1	Buenos Aires	65 000
1969	AC Milan	Estudiantes	3-0, 1-2	Milan	80 000
1970	Feyenoord	Estudiantes	2-2, 1-0	Buenos Aires	65 000
1971	Nacional	Panathinaikos	1-1, 2-1	Athens	60 000
1972	Ajax	Independiente	1-1, 3-0	Buenos Aires	65 000
1973	Independiente	Juventus	1-0	Rome	35 000
1974	Atletico Madrid	Independiente	0-1, 2-0	Buenos Aires	60 000
1975	Independiente and Bayern Munich could not agree on dates to play				
1976	Bayern Munich	Cruzeiro	2-0, 0-0	Munich	22 000
1977	Boca Juniors	Borussia Moenchengladbach	2-2, 3-0	Buenos Aires	50 000
1978	Not contested; Liverpool declined to play				
1979	Olimpia	Malmo	1-0, 2-1	Malmo	4 811
1980	Nacional	Nottingham Forest	1-0	Tokyo	62 000
1981	Flamengo	Liverpool	3-0	Tokyo	62 000
1982	Penarol	Aston Villa	2-0	Tokyo	62 000
1983	Gremio	Hamburg	2-1	Tokyo	62 000
1984	Independiente	Liverpool	1-0	Tokyo	62 000
1985	Juventus	Argentinos Juniors	2-2	Tokyo	62 000
	(aet; Juventus won 4-2 on penalties)				
1986	River Plate	Steaua Bucharest	1-0	Tokyo	62 000
1987	Porto	Penarol	2-1 (aet)	Tokyo	45 000

Bill Foulkes (dark shirt) is given off-side after scoring for Manchester United against Estudiantes in the 1968 World Club Championship.

First Leg or Final Referee	Venue	Second Leg Attendance	Referee	Venue	Play-off Attendance	Referee
Praddaude (Argentina)	Madrid	125 000	Aston (England)			
Ebert (Switzerland)	Montevideo	57 358	Nay Foino (Argentina)	Montevideo	62 300	Praddaude (Argentina)
Ramirez (Paraguay)	Lisbon	75 000	Schwinte (France)			
Harbseliner (Austria)	Rio de Janeiro	150 000	Brozzi (Argentina)	Rio de Janeiro	121 000	Brozzi (Argentina)
Armando Marques (Brazil)	Milan	70 000	Geroe (Hungary)	Madrid	45 000	De Mendibil (Spain)
Kreitlein West Germany)	Buenos Aires	70 000	Yamasaki (peru)			
Vicuna (Chile)	Madrid	70 000	Lo Bello (Italy)			
Gardeazabal (Spain)	Buenos Aires	80 000	Esteban Marino (Spain)	Montevideo	65 172	Osorio (Paraguay)
Miranda (Paraguay)	Old Trafford	60 000				
Machin (France)	Buenos Aires	65 000	Massaro (Chile)			
Glockner (East Germany)	Rotterdam	70 000	Tejada (Peru)			
	Montevideo	70 000				
Bakhramov (USSR)	Amsterdam	65 000	Romey (Paraguay)			
Belcourt (Belgium)						
Corver (Holland)	Madrid	45 000	Robles (Chile)			
Pestarino (Argentina)	Belo Horizonte	114 000	Partridge (England)			
Doudine (Bulgaria)	Karlsruhe	21 500	Cerullo (Uruguay)			
Partridge (England)	Ascuncion	35 000	Cardellino (Uruguay)			
Klein (Israel)						
Vasquez (Mexico)						
Siles (Costa Rica)						
Vautrot (France)						
Filho (Brazil)						
Roth (West Germany)						
Bazan (Uruguay)						
Wohrer (Austria)						

Football League title wins

Division 1

Liverpool 17; Everton 9; Arsenal 8; Manchester United, Aston Villa 7; Sunderland 6; Newcastle United, Sheffield Wednesday 4; Huddersfield Town, Wolverhampton Wanderers 3; Blackburn Rovers, Portsmouth, Preston North End, Burnley, Manchester City, Tottenham Hotspur, Leeds United, Derby County 2; Chelsea, Sheffield United, West Bromwich Albion, Ipswich Town, Nottingham Forest 1.

Division 2

Leicester City, Manchester City 6; Sheffield Wednesday 5; Birmingham City, Derby County, Liverpool 4; Notts County, Preston North End, Middlesbrough 3; Grimsby Town, Nottingham Forest, Tottenham Hotspur, West Bromwich Albion, Aston Villa, Stoke City, Leeds United, Ipswich Town, Burnley, Manchester United, West Ham United, Wolverhampton Wanderers, Bolton Wanderers, Norwich City 2; Huddersfield Town, Bristol City, Brentford, Bury, Bradford City, Everton, Fulham, Sheffield United, Newcastle United, Coventry City, Blackpool, Blackburn Rovers, Sunderland, Crystal Palace, Luton Town, Queen's Park Rangers, Chelsea, Oxford United, Millwall 1.

Football League champions

Season ending	Champions	Matches	Pts	Home W	D	L	F	A	Pts	Away W	D	L	F	A	Pts	Goal av.	No. of players	Ever present	Winning margin (pts)
1889	Preston North End	22	40	10	1	0	39	7	21	8	3	0	35	8	19	3.36	18	2	11
1890	Preston North End	22	33	8	1	2	41	12	17	7	2	2	30	18	16	3.23	19	3	2
1891	Everton	22	29	9	0	2	39	12	18	5	1	5	24	17	11	2.86	21	3	2
1892	Sunderland	26	42	13	0	0	55	11	26	8	0	5	38	25	16	3.57	15	2	5
1893	Sunderland	30	48	13	2	0	58	17	28	9	2	4	42	19	20	3.33	15	3	11
1894	Aston Villa	30	44	12	2	1	49	13	26	7	4	4	35	29	18	2.80	24	1	6
1895	Sunderland	30	47	13	2	0	51	14	28	8	3	4	29	23	19	2.66	16	2	5
1896	Aston Villa	30	45	14	1	0	47	17	29	6	4	5	31	28	16	2.60	17	2	4
1897	Aston Villa	30	47	10	3	2	36	16	23	11	2	2	37	22	24	2.43	17	4	11
1898	Sheffield United	30	42	9	4	2	27	14	22	8	4	3	29	17	20	1.86	23	1	5
1899	Aston Villa	34	45	15	2	0	58	13	32	4	5	8	18	27	13	2.23	24	1	2
1900	Aston Villa	34	50	12	4	1	45	18	28	10	2	5	32	17	22	2.26	21	2	2
1901	Liverpool	34	45	12	2	3	36	13	26	7	5	5	23	22	19	1.73	18	3	2
1902	Sunderland	34	44	12	3	2	32	14	27	7	3	7	18	21	17	1.47	19	1	3
1903	Sheffield Wednesday	34	42	12	3	2	31	7	27	7	1	9	23	29	15	1.58	23	3	1
1904	Sheffield Wednesday	34	47	14	3	0	34	10	31	6	4	7	14	18	16	1.41	22	2	3
1905	Newcastle United	34	48	14	1	2	41	12	29	9	1	7	31	21	19	2.11	21	0	1
1906	Liverpool	38	51	14	3	2	49	15	31	9	2	8	30	31	20	2.07	21	1	4
1907	Newcastle United	38	51	18	1	0	51	12	37	4	6	9	23	34	14	1.94	27	0	3
1908	Manchester United	38	52	15	1	3	43	19	31	8	5	6	38	29	21	2.13	25	0	9
1909	Newcastle United	38	53	14	1	4	32	20	29	10	4	5	33	21	24	1.71	25	1	7
1910	Aston Villa	38	53	17	2	0	62	19	36	6	5	8	22	23	17	2.21	18	0	5
1911	Manchester United	38	52	14	4	1	47	18	32	8	4	7	25	22	20	1.89	26	0	1
1912	Blackburn Rovers	38	49	13	6	0	35	10	32	7	3	9	25	33	17	1.57	21	0	3
1913	Sunderland	38	54	14	2	3	47	17	30	11	2	6	39	26	24	2.26	22	1	4
1914	Blackburn Rovers	38	51	14	5	0	51	15	33	6	7	6	27	27	19	2.05	21	1	7
1915	Everton	38	46	8	5	6	44	29	21	11	3	5	32	18	25	2.00	24	0	1
No national competition 1916, 1917, 1918 or 1919 when regional leagues in operation																			
1920	West Bromwich Albion	42	60	17	1	3	65	21	35	11	3	7	39	26	25	2.47	18	1	9
1921	Burnley	42	59	17	3	1	56	16	37	6	10	5	23	20	22	1.88	23	1	5
1922	Liverpool	42	57	15	4	2	43	15	34	7	9	5	20	21	23	1.50	22	2	6
1923	Liverpool	42	60	17	3	1	50	13	37	9	5	7	20	18	23	1.66	19	3	6
1924	Huddersfield Town	42	57	15	5	1	35	9	35	8	6	7	25	24	22	1.42	22	1	gl av.
1925	Huddersfield Town	42	58	10	8	3	31	10	28	11	8	2	38	18	30	1.64	22	0	2
1926	Huddersfield Town	42	57	14	6	1	50	17	34	9	5	7	42	43	23	2.19	24	0	5
1927	Newcastle United	42	56	19	1	1	64	20	39	6	5	10	32	38	17	2.28	21	3	5
1928	Everton	42	53	11	8	2	60	28	30	9	5	7	42	38	23	2.42	24	2	2
1929	Sheffield Wednesday	42	52	18	3	0	55	16	39	3	7	11	31	46	13	2.04	22	4	1
1930	Sheffield Wednesday	42	60	15	4	2	56	20	34	11	4	6	49	37	26	2.50	22	1	10
1931	Arsenal	42	66	14	5	2	67	27	33	14	5	2	60	32	33	3.02	22	1	7
1932	Everton	42	56	18	0	3	84	30	36	8	4	9	32	34	20	2.76	20	0	2
1933	Arsenal	42	58	14	3	4	70	27	31	11	5	5	48	34	27	2.80	23	1	4
1934	Arsenal	42	59	15	4	2	45	19	34	10	5	6	30	28	25	1.78	23	1	3
1935	Arsenal	42	58	15	4	2	74	17	34	8	8	5	41	29	24	2.73	25	0	4
1936	Sunderland	42	56	17	2	2	71	33	36	8	4	9	38	41	20	2.59	23	2	8

Division 3

Portsmouth, Oxford United 2; Plymouth Argyle, Southampton, Bury, Northampton Town, Coventry City, Carlisle United, Hull City, Queen's Park Rangers, Watford, Leyton Orient, Preston North End, Aston Villa, Bolton Wanderers, Oldham Athletic, Blackburn Rovers, Hereford United, Mansfield Town, Wrexham, Shrewsbury Town, Grimsby Town. Rotherham United, Burnley. Bradford City, Bournemouth, Reading, Sunderland 1.

Division 4

Doncaster Rovers, Peterborough United, Chesterfield 2; Port Vale, Walsall, Millwall, Brentford, Gillingham, Brighton & Hove Albion, Stockport County, Luton Town, Notts County, Grimsby Town, Southport, Mansfield Town, Lincoln City, Cambridge United, Watford, Reading, Huddersfield Town, Southend United, Sheffield United, Wimbledon, York City, Swindon Town, Northampton Town, Wolverhampton Wanderers 1.

Division 3 Southern

Bristol City 3; Charlton Athletic, Ipswich Town, Millwall, Notts County, Plymouth Argyle, Swansea Town 2; Brentford, Bristol Rovers, Cardiff City, Crystal Palace, Coventry City, Fulham, Leyton Orient, Luton Town, Newport County, Nottingham Forest, Norwich City, Portsmouth, Queen's Park Rangers, Reading, Southampton, Brighton and Hove Albion 1.

Division 3 Northern

Barnsley, Doncaster Rovers, Lincoln City 3; Chesterfield, Grimsby Town, Hull City, Port Vale, Stockport County 2; Bradford Park Avenue, Bradford City, Darlington, Derby County, Nelson, Oldham Athletic, Rotherham United, Stoke City, Tranmere Rovers, Wolverhampton Wanderers, Scunthorpe United 1.

Season ending	Champions	Matches	Pts	Home W	D	L	F	A	Pts	Away W	D	L	F	A	Pts	Goal av.	No. of players	Ever present	Winning margin (pts)
1937	Manchester City	42	57	15	5	1	56	22	35	7	8	6	51	39	22	2.54	22	4	3
1938	Arsenal	42	52	15	4	2	52	16	34	6	6	9	25	28	18	1.83	29	0	1
1939	Everton	42	59	17	3	1	60	18	37	10	2	9	28	34	22	2.09	22	1	4

No national competition 1940, 1941, 1942, 1943, 1944, 1945 or 1946 when regional leagues were in operation

Season ending	Champions	Matches	Pts	Home W	D	L	F	A	Pts	Away W	D	L	F	A	Pts	Goal av.	No. of players	Ever present	Winning margin (pts)
1947	Liverpool	42	57	13	3	5	42	24	29	12	4	5	42	28	28	2.00	26	0	1
1948	Arsenal	42	52	15	3	3	56	15	33	8	10	3	25	17	26	1.92	19	2	7
1949	Portsmouth	42	58	18	3	0	52	12	39	7	5	9	32	30	19	2.00	18	2	5
1950	Portsmouth	42	56	12	7	2	44	15	31	10	2	9	30	23	22	1.76	25	2	gl av.
1951	Tottenham Hotspur	42	60	17	2	2	54	21	36	8	8	5	28	23	24	1.95	19	2	4
1952	Manchester United	42	57	15	3	3	55	21	33	8	8	5	40	31	24	2.26	24	1	4
1953	Arsenal	42	54	15	3	3	60	30	33	6	9	6	37	34	21	2.30	21	0	gl av.
1954	Wolverhampton Wanderers	42	57	16	1	4	61	25	33	9	6	6	35	31	24	2.28	22	1	4
1955	Chelsea	42	52	11	5	5	43	29	27	9	7	5	38	28	25	1.92	20	2	4
1956	Manchester United	42	60	18	3	0	51	20	39	7	7	7	32	31	21	1.97	24	1	11
1957	Manchester United	42	64	14	4	3	55	25	32	14	4	3	48	29	22	2.45	24	0	8
1958	Wolverhampton Wanderers	42	64	17	3	1	60	21	37	11	5	5	43	26	27	2.45	21	0	5
1959	Wolverhampton Wanderers	42	61	15	3	3	68	19	33	13	2	6	42	30	28	2.61	22	0	6
1960	Burnley	42	55	15	2	4	52	28	32	9	5	7	33	33	23	2.02	18	3	1
1961	Tottenham Hotspur	42	66	15	3	3	65	28	33	16	1	4	50	27	33	2.73	17	4	8
1962	Ipswich Town	42	56	17	2	2	58	28	36	7	6	8	35	39	20	2.21	16	3	3
1963	Everton	42	61	14	7	0	48	17	35	11	4	6	36	25	26	2.00	20	2	6
1964	Liverpool	42	57	16	0	5	60	18	32	10	5	6	32	27	25	2.19	17	3	4
1965	Manchester United	42	61	16	4	1	52	13	36	10	5	6	37	26	25	2.11	18	4	gl av.
1966	Liverpool	42	61	17	2	2	52	15	36	9	7	5	27	19	25	1.88	14	5	6
1967	Manchester United	42	60	17	4	0	51	13	38	7	8	6	33	32	22	2.00	20	2	4
1968	Manchester City	42	58	17	2	2	52	16	36	9	4	8	34	27	22	2.04	21	1	2
1969	Leeds United	42	67	18	3	0	41	9	39	9	10	2	25	17	28	1.57	17	4	6
1970	Everton	42	66	17	3	1	46	19	37	12	5	4	26	15	29	1.71	17	4	9
1971	Arsenal	42	65	18	3	0	41	6	39	11	4	6	30	23	26	1.69	16	3	1
1972	Derby County	42	58	16	4	1	43	10	36	8	6	7	26	23	22	1.64	16	2	1
1973	Liverpool	42	60	17	3	1	45	19	37	8	7	6	27	23	23	1.71	16	3	3
1974	Leeds United	42	62	12	8	1	38	18	32	12	6	3	28	13	30	1.57	20	2	5
1975	Derby County	42	53	14	4	3	41	18	32	7	7	7	26	31	21	1.59	16	2	2
1976	Liverpool	42	60	14	5	2	41	21	33	9	9	3	25	10	27	1.57	19	2	1
1977	Liverpool	42	57	18	3	0	47	11	39	5	8	8	15	22	18	1.47	17	3	1
1978	Nottingham Forest	42	64	15	6	0	37	8	36	10	8	3	32	16	28	1.64	16	1	7
1979	Liverpool	42	68	19	2	0	51	4	40	11	6	4	34	12	28	2.02	15	4	8
1980	Liverpool	42	60	15	6	0	46	8	36	10	8	3	35	22	24	1.92	17	3	2
1981	Aston Villa	42	60	16	3	2	40	13	35	10	5	6	32	27	25	1.71	14	7	4
1982	Liverpool	42	87	14	3	4	39	14	45	12	6	3	41	18	42	1.90	16	3	4
1983	Liverpool	42	82	16	4	1	55	16	52	8	6	7	32	21	30	2.07	16	4	11
1984	Liverpool	42	80	14	5	2	50	12	47	8	9	4	23	20	33	1.73	15	5	3
1985	Everton	42	90	16	3	2	58	17	51	12	3	6	30	26	42	2.09	25	1	13
1986	Liverpool	42	88	16	4	1	58	14	52	10	6	5	31	23	36	2.11	18	1	3
1987	Everton	42	86	16	4	1	49	11	52	10	4	7	27	20	34	1.80	23	1	9
1988	Liverpool	40	90	15	5	0	49	9	50	11	7	2	38	15	40	2.17	22	2	9

Teams with the longest unbeaten runs in Football League matches from the start of a season

Season	Team	Division	Unbeaten in first
1888–89	Preston North End	1	all 22
1889–90	Accrington Stanley	1	3
1889–90	Aston Villa	1	3
1890–91	Everton	1	7
1891–92	Aston Villa	1	4
1891–92	Bolton Wanderers	1	4
1892–93	Sunderland	1	8
1893–94	Liverpool	2	all 28*
1894–95	Everton	1	8
1895–96	Liverpool	2	5
1895–96	Newton Heath	2	5
1896–97	Sheffield United	1	8
1897–98	Sheffield United	1	14
1898–99	Sheffield United	1	11
1899–1900	Sheffield United	1	22
1900–01	Small Heath	2	14
1901–02	Lincoln City	2	7
1902–03	Blackpool	2	6
1903–04	Preston North End	2	13
1904–05	Liverpool	2	13
1905–06	Sheffield Wednesday	1	7
1905–06	Manchester United	2	7
1906–07	Bolton Wanderers	1	7
1906–07	Hull City	2	7
1907–08	Everton	1	6
1908–09	Birmingham City	2	8
1909–10	Sheffield United	1	9
1910–11	Sunderland	1	14
1911–12	Clapton Orient	2	7
1912–13	Hull City	2	8
1913–14	Blackburn Rovers	1	10
1914–15	Manchester City	1	11
1919–20	Tottenham Hotspur	2	12
1920–21	South Shields	2	7
1921–22	Portsmouth	3S	10
1922–23	Portsmouth	3S	8
1923–24	Cardiff City	1	11
1924–25	Huddersfield Town	1	10
1925–26	Chelsea	2	14
1926–27	Stoke City	3N	9
1927–28	Charlton Athletic	3S	12
1928–29	Luton Town	3S	10
1928–29	Wrexham	3N	10
1929–30	Plymouth Argyle	3S	18
1930–31	Notts County	3S	18
1931–32	Southend United	3S	15
1932–33	Brentford	3S	14
1933–34	Aldershot	3S	8
1934–35	Tranmere Rovers	3N	8
1935–36	Huddersfield Town	1	9
1935–36	Chesterfield	3N	9
1935–36	Tranmere Rovers	3N	9
1936–37	Chester	3N	9
1936–37	Hull City	3N	9
1937–38	Coventry City	2	15
1938–39	Southport	3N	9
1946–47	Barnsley	2	10
1947–48	Arsenal	1	17
1948–49	Derby County	1	16
1949–50	Liverpool	1	19
1950–51	Newcastle United	1	11
1951–52	Oldham Athletic	3N	9
1952–53	Oldham Athletic	3N	13
1953–54	Norwich City	3S	12
1954–55	Bristol City	3S	13
1955–56	Blackpool	1	8
1956–57	Manchester United	1	12
1957–58	Scunthorpe United	3N	8
1958–59	Fulham	2	12
1959–60	Millwall	4	19
1960–61	Tottenham Hotspur	1	16
1961–62	Bournemouth	3	14
1962–63	Huddersfield Town	2	13
1963–64	Gillingham	4	13
1964–65	Bradford Park Avenue	4	12
1965–66	Bristol City	2	7
1966–67	Chelsea	1	10
1967–68	Torquay United	3	10
1968–69	Darlington	4	14
1969–70	Port Vale	4	18
1970–71	Notts County	4	9
1971–72	Norwich City	2	13
1972–73	Burnley	2	16
1973–74	Leeds United	1	29
1974–75	Manchester United	2	9
1975–76	Bury	3	10
1976–77	Leicester City	1	6
1976–77	Manchester City	1	6
1976–77	Wolverhampton Wanderers	2	6
1976–77	Stockport County	4	6
1977–78	Manchester City	1	8
1977–78	Brighton & Hove Albion	2	8
1977–78	Tottenham Hotspur	2	8
1977–78	Southend United	4	8
1978–79	Everton	1	19
1979–80	Walsall	4	13
1980–91	Ipswich Town	1	14
1981–82	Oldham Athletic	2	9
1982–83	Wimbledon	4	11
1983–84	Sheffield Wednesday	2	15
1984–85	Portsmouth	2	10
1985–86	Reading	3	14
1986–87	Exeter City	4	13
1987–88	Liverpool	1	29

* Liverpool also won one test match and then began the next season with two games undefeated.

Home and away oddments

No home defeat or away win since Football League increased to 20 clubs per division in 1905–06

No home defeat

Div	Team	Season
1	Newcastle United	1906–07
2	Oldham Athletic	1907–08
1	Aston Villa	1909–10
1	Blackburn Rovers	1909–10
2	Bolton Wanderers	1910–11
2	Chelsea	1910–11
1	Blackburn Rovers	1911–12
2	Burnley	1911–12
2	Clapton Orient	1913–14
2	Tottenham Hotspur	1919–20

Div	Team	Season
1	Bolton Wanderers	1920–21
1	Manchester City	1920–21
3S	Plymouth Argyle	1921–22
3S	Southampton	1921–22
3N	Grimsby Town	1921–22
3S	Plymouth Argyle	1922–23
3N	Darlington	1923–24
3N	Rochdale	1923–24
3N	Wolverhampton Wanderers	1923–24
3S	Swansea Town	1924–25
3S	Reading	1925–26
3N	Grimsby Town	1925–26
3S	Luton Town	1926–27
3S	Plymouth Argyle	1926–27
3N	Bradford	1926–27
3S	Millwall	1927–28
3N	Stockport County	1927–28
1	Leicester City	1928–29
1	Sheffield Wednesday	1928–29
3N	Stockport County	1928–29
3S	Brentford	1929–30
3S	Plymouth Argyle	1929–30
3S	Crystal Palace	1931–32
2	Tottenham Hotspur	1932–33
3S	Northampton Town	1932–33
3N	Doncaster Rovers	1932–33
3N	Hull City	1932–33
1	Blackburn Rovers	1933–34
3S	Reading	1933–34
3N	Barnsley	1933–34
3N	Stockport County	1933–34
1	Sheffield Wednesday	1934–35
2	Brentford	1934–35
3S	Reading	1934–35
2	Charlton Athletic	1935–36
3N	Gateshead	1935–36
3S	Cardiff City	1946–47
3N	Rotherham United	1946–47
1	Portsmouth	1948–49
3S	Swansea Town	1948–49
3N	Mansfield Town	1950–51
3N	Port Vale	1953–54
1	Manchester United	1955–56
3S	Colchester United	1956–57
3S	Torquay United	1956–57
3	Walsall	1960–61
2	Liverpool	1961–62
1	Everton	1962–63
3	Bournemouth	1962–63
2	Leeds United	1963–64
3	Mansfield Town	1963–64
4	Gillingham	1963–64
1	Tottenham Hotspur	1964–65
2	Northampton Town	1964–65
4	Brighton & Hove Albion	1964–65
4	Millwall	1964–65
2	Manchester City	1965–66
3	Millwall	1965–66
1	Manchester United	1966–67
4	Wrexham	1966–67
4	Barnsley	1967–68
4	Crewe Alexandra	1967–68
1	Leeds United	1968–69
3	Luton Town	1968–69
4	Wrexham	1969–70
1	Arsenal	1970–71
1	Liverpool	1970–71
3	Preston North End	1970–71
4	Notts County	1970–71
1	Leeds United	1971–72
2	Birmingham City	1971–72
2	Millwall	1971–72
2	Norwich City	1971–72
4	Peterborough United	1973–74
4	Mansfield Town	1974–75
1	Queen's Park Rangers	1975–76
2	Sunderland	1975–76
4	Lincoln City	1975–76
4	Northampton Town	1975–76
1	Liverpool	1976–77
2	Chelsea	1976–77
3	Mansfield Town	1976–77
4	Bradford City	1976–77
1	Nottingham Forest	1977–78
4	Aldershot	1977–78
1	Liverpool	1978–79
1	Nottingham Forest	1978–79
3	Shrewsbury Town	1978–79
1	Liverpool	1979–80
2	Sunderland	1979–80
1	Arsenal	1980–81
3	Rotherham United	1980–81
4	Southend United	1980–81
4	Sheffield United	1981–82
1	Manchester United	1982–83
3	Huddersfield Town	1982–83
4	Reading	1983–84
3	Millwall	1984–85
1	Liverpool	1987–88

No away win

Div	Team	Season
1	Middlesbrough	1905–06
2	Blackpool	1907–08
2	Chesterfield	1907–08
2	Barnsley	1908–09
2	Blackpool	1908–09
2	Gainsborough Trinity	1910–11
1	Bury	1911–12
2	Stockport County	1912–13
2	Nottingham Forest	1913–14
1	Chelsea	1914–15
3S	Northampton Town	1921–22
2	Wolverhampton Wanderers	1922–23
3S	Newport County	1922–23
3N	Hartlepools United	1922–23
3S	Merthyr Town	1923–24
3S	Merthyr Town	1924–25
2	Stockport County	1925–26
1	Sheffield Wednesday	1926–27
3N	Barrow	1927–28
3S	Merthyr Town	1928–29
3S	Bristol Rovers	1929–30
2	Barnsley	1930–31
3S	Norwich City	1930–31
3N	Nelson	1930–31
3S	Mansfield Town	1931–32
3N	New Brighton	1931–32
3N	Rochdale	1931–32
3S	Cardiff City	1932–33
3N	Rotherham United	1932–33
2	Southampton	1933–34
2	Swansea Town	1933–34
2	Oldham Athletic	1934–35
1	Huddersfield Town	1936–37
3N	Hartlepools United	1937–38
2	Tranmere Rovers	1938–39
1	Leeds United	1946–47
1	Bolton Wanderers	1949–50
3N	Halifax Town	1950–51
3N	Bradford City	1952–53
3N	Bradford	1955–56
3N	Crewe Alexandra	1955–56
1	Sheffield Wednesday	1957–58
3	Rochdale	1958–59
4	Southport	1958–59
1	Everton	1959–60
4	Gateshead	1959–60
1	Ipswich Town	1963–64
1	Stoke City	1968–69
1	Queen's Park Rangers	1968–69
4	Bradford	1968–69
2	Charlton Athletic	1969–70
4	Bradford	1969–70
2	Watford	1971–72
4	Chester	1971–72
2	Cardiff City	1972–73
4	Mansfield Town	1973–74
2	Oldham Athletic	1974–75
4	Scunthorpe United	1974–75
1	Aston Villa	1975–76
2	Plymouth Argyle	1975–76
3	Sheffield Wednesday	1975–76
1	Derby County	1976–77
4	Halifax Town	1976–77
4	Southport	1976–77
3	Hereford United	1977–78
4	Rochdale	1977–78

1	Norwich City	1978-79
1	Bolton Wanderers	1979-80
2	Charlton Athletic	1979-80
1	Crystal Palace	1980-81
1	Swansea City	1982-83
4	Rochdale	1982-83
2	Swansea City	1983-84
2	Cambridge United	1983-84
3	Scunthorpe United	1983-84
4	Chester City	1983-84
1	Stoke City	1984-85
1	Manchester City	1986-87
4	Exeter City	1986-87

Highest number of goals scored by each Football League club in one season

(Descending Order)

Goals	Team	Division	Season
134	Peterborough United	4	1960-61
128	Aston Villa	1	1930-31
128	Bradford City	3N	1928-29
127	Arsenal	1	1930-31
127	Millwall	3S	1927-28
123	Doncaster Rovers	3N	1946-47
122	Middlesbrough	2	1926-27
121	Everton	2	1930-31
121	Lincoln City	3N	1951-52
119	Chester	4	1964-65
118	Barnsley	3N	1933-34
115	Stockport County	3N	1933-34
115	Tottenham Hotspur	1	1960-61
115	Wolverhampton Wanderers	2	1931-32
114	Rotherham United	3N	1946-47
114	Blackburn Rovers	2	1954-55
113	Carlisle United	4	1963-64
112	Brighton & Hove Albion	3S	1955-56
112	Reading	3S	1951-52
112	Southampton	3S	1957-58
111	Derby County	3N	1956-57
111	Fulham	3S	1931-32
111	Queen's Park Rangers	3	1961-62
111	Tranmere Rovers	3N	1930-31
110	Crystal Palace	4	1960-61
110	Nottingham Forest	3S	1950-51
110	Port Vale	4	1958-59
109	Hull City	3	1965-66
109	Leicester City	2	1956-57
109	Northampton Town	3	1962-63
		and 3S	and 1952-53
109	Sunderland	1	1935-36
108	Bury	3	1960-61
108	Coventry City	3S	1931-32
108	Darlington	3N	1929-30
108	Manchester City	2	1926-27
108	Mansfield Town	4	1962-63
107	Charlton Athletic	2	1957-58
107	Notts County	4	1959-60
107	Plymouth Argyle	3S	1925-26
		and	1951-52
106	Ipswich Town	3S	1955-56
106	Liverpool	2	1895-96
106	Orient	3S	1955-56
106	Sheffield Wednesday	2	1958-59
106	Wrexham	3N	1932-33
105	Rochdale	3N	1926-27
105	West Bromwich Albion	2	1929-30
104	Bristol City	3S	1926-27
104	Colchester United	4	1961-62
103	Birmingham City	2	1893-94
103	Grimsby Town	2	1933-34
103	Luton Town	3S	1936-37
103	Manchester United	1	1956-57
		and	1958-59
102	Burnley	1	1960-61
102	Chesterfield	3N	1930-31
102	Sheffield United	1	1925-26
102	Walsall	4	1959-60
101	Huddersfield Town	4	1979-80
101	Shrewsbury Town	4	1958-59
101	West Ham United	2	1957-58
100	Preston North End	2	1927-28
		and 1	and 1957-58
100	Swindon Town	3S	1926-27
99	Norwich City	3S	1952-53
98	Blackpool	2	1929-30
98	Brentford	4	1962-63
98	Chelsea	1	1960-61
98	Leeds United	2	1927-28
98	Newcastle United	1	1951-52
97	Wimbledon	3	1983-84
96	Bolton Wanderers	2	1934-35
96	York City	4	1983-84
95	Crewe Alexandra	3N	1931-32
95	Oldham Athletic	4	1962-63
93	Cardiff City	3S	1946-47
92	Bristol Rovers	3S	1952-53
92	Southend United	3S	1950-51
92	Stoke City	3N	1926-27
92	Watford	4	1959-60
91	Oxford United	3	1983-84
91	Portsmouth	4	1979-80
90	Gillingham	3N	1956-57
90	Hartlepools United	3N	1956-57
90	Swansea City	2	1956-57
89	Torquay United	3S	1956-57
88	Bournemouth	3S	1956-57
88	Exeter City	3S	1932-33
88	Scunthorpe United	3N	1957-58
87	Cambridge United	4	1976-77
86	Hereford United	3	1975-76
85	Newport County	4	1964-65
83	Aldershot	4	1963-64
83	Halifax Town	3N	1957-58
80	Wigan Athletic	4	1981-82
56	Scarborough	4	1987-88

Scottish League clubs

Goals	Team	Division	Season
142	Raith Rovers	2	1937-38
135	Morton	2	1963-64
132	Heart of Midlothian	1	1957-58
132	Falkirk	2	1935-36
122	Clyde	2	1956-57
120	Cowdenbeath	2	1938-39
120	Dunfermline Athletic	2	1957-58
119	Motherwell	1	1931-32
118	Rangers	1	1931-32
		and	1933-34
117	Ayr United	2	1927-28
115	Celtic	1	1935-36
114	East Fife	2	1929-30
114	St Mirren	2	1935-36
112	Dundee	2	1946-47
111	East Stirling	2	1931-32
108	Dundee United	2	1935-36

107	Airdrieonians	2	1965–66	92	Hamilton Academicals	1	1932–33
106	Hibernian	1	1959–60	92	Kilmarnock	1	1962–63
105	Stirling Albion	2	1959–60	91	Partick Thistle	1	1928–29
102	St Johnstone	2	1931–32	90	Forfar Athletic	2	1931–32
101	Albion Rovers	2	1929–30	87	Arbroath	2	1967–68
101	Dumbarton	2	1956–57	83	Berwick Rangers	2	1961–62
100	Queen's Park	1	1928–29	83	Stranraer	2	1961–62
99	Stenhousemuir	2	1960–61	80	Brechin City	2	1957–58
96	Aberdeen	1	1935–36	78	Clydebank	1	1978–79
94	Queen of the South	2	1959–60	78	Montrose	2	1970–71
92	Alloa	2	1961–62	69	Meadowbank Thistle	2	1986–87

Record wins

Football League clubs (in descending order of scoring)

Team	Score	Opponents	Competition	Date
Preston North End	26–0	Hyde	FA Cup 1st rd	15.10.1887
Scarborough	16–1	Leeds Amateurs	FA Amateur Cup	9.11.07
Notts County	15–0	Thornhill United	FA Cup 1st rd	24.10.1885
Bristol Rovers	15–1	Weymouth	FA Cup Pr rd	17.11.1900
Nottingham Forest	14–0	Clapton	FA Cup 1st rd	17.1.1891
Southampton	14–0	Newbury	FA Cup 1st rd	10.9.1894
Wolverhampton Wanderers	14–0	Crosswell's Brewery	FA Cup 2nd rd	13.11.1886
Wimbledon	15–2	Polytechnic	FA Cup Pr rd	21.9.29
Aston Villa	13–0	Wednesday Old Alliance	FA Cup 1st rd	30.10.1886
Bolton Wanderers	13–0	Sheffield United	FA Cup 2nd rd	1.2.1890
Chelsea	13–0	Jeunesse Hautcharage	Cup Winners' Cup 1st rd	29.9.71
Newcastle United	13–0	Newport County	Division 2	5.10.46
Stockport County	13–0	Halifax Town	Division 3N	6.1.34
Arsenal	12–0	Loughborough Town	Division 2	12.3.1900
Birmingham City	12–0	Walsall Town Swifts	Division 2	17.12.1892
Birmingham City	12–0	Doncaster Rovers	Division 2	11.4.03
Chester	12–0	York City	Division 3N	1.2.36
Derby County	12–0	Finn Harps	UEFA Cup 3rd rd	15.9.76
Luton Town	12–0	Bristol Rovers	Division 3S	13.4.36
Sheffield Wednesday	12–0	Halliwell	FA Cup 1st rd	10.9.1894
West Bromwich Albion	12–0	Darwen	Division 1	4.4.1892
Tottenham Hotspur	13–2	Crewe Alexandra	FA Cup 4th rd replay	3.2.60
Bury	12–1	Stockton	FA Cup 1st rd replay	2.2.1897
Blackburn Rovers	11–0	Rossendale United	FA Cup 1st rd	25.10.84
Bournemouth	11–0	Margate	FA Cup 1st rd	20.11.71
Bristol City	11–0	Chichester	FA Cup 1st rd	5.11.60
Hereford United	11–0	Thynnes	FA Cup qual rd	13.9.47
Liverpool	11–0	Stromsgodset Drammen	Cup Winners' Cup 1st rd	17.9.74
Oldham Athletic	11–0	Southport	Division 4	26.12.62
Bradford City	11–1	Rotherham United	Division 3N	25.8.28
Hull City	11–1	Carlisle United	Division 3N	14.1.39
Lincoln City	11–1	Crewe Alexandra	Division 3N	29.9.51
Northampton Town	11–1	Southend United	Southern League	30.12.09
Sunderland	11–1	Fairfield	FA Cup 1st rd	2.2.1895
Blackpool	10–0	Lanerossi Vicenza	Anglo-Italian Cup	10.6.72
Chesterfield	10–0	Glossop North End	Division 2	17.1.03
Doncaster Rovers	10–0	Darlington	Division 4	25.1.64
Gillingham	10–0	Chesterfield	Division 3	5.9.87
Ipswich Town	10–0	Floriana	European Cup 1st rd	25.9.62
Leeds United	10–0	Lyn Oslo	European Cup 1st rd	17.9.69
Leicester City	10–0	Portsmouth	Division 1	20.10.28
Manchester United	10–0	Anderlecht	European Cup Pr rd	26.9.56
Newport County	10–0	Merthyr Town	Division 3S	10.4.30
Walsall	10–0	Darwen	Division 2	4.3.1899
West Ham United	10–0	Bury	Milk Cup 2nd rd 2nd leg	25.10.83
Tranmere Rovers	13–4	Oldham Athletic	Division 3N	26.12.35
Everton	11–2	Derby County	FA Cup 1st rd	18.1.1890
Sheffield United	11–2	Cardiff City	Division 1	1.1.26
Brighton & Hove Albion	10–1	Wisbech	FA Cup 1st rd	13.11.65
Fulham	10–1	Ipswich Town	Division 1	26.12.63
Hartlepool United	10–1	Barrow	Division 4	4.4.59
Huddersfield Town	10–1	Blackpool	Division 1	13.12.30
Manchester City	10–1	Huddersfield Town	Division 2	7.11.87
Southend United	10–1	Golders Green	FA Cup 1st rd	24.11.34
Southend United	10–1	Brentwood	FA Cup 2nd rd	7.12.68
Swindon Town	10–1	Farnham United Breweries	FA Cup 1st rd	28.11.25
Watford	10–1	Lowestoft Town	FA Cup 1st rd	27.11.26
Wrexham	10–1	Hartlepool United	Division 4	3.3.62

Barnsley	9-0	Loughborough Town	Division 2	29.1.1899
Barnsley	9-0	Accrington Stanley	Division 3N	3.2.34
Brentford	9-0	Wrexham	Division 3	15.10.63
Burnley	9-0	Darwen	Division 1	9.1.1892
Burnley	9-0	Crystal Palace	FA Cup 2nd rd replay	27.1.09
Burnley	9-0	New Brighton	FA Cup 4th rd	26.1.57
Burnley	9-0	Penrith	FA Cup 1st rd	17.11.84
Coventry City	9-0	Bristol City	Division 3S	28.4.34
Crystal Palace	9-0	Barrow	Division 4	10.10.59
Scunthorpe United	9-0	Boston United	FA Cup 1st rd	21.11.53
Torquay United	9-0	Swindon Town	Division 3S	8.3.52
Norwich City	10-2	Coventry City	Division 3S	15.3.30
Reading	10-2	Crystal Palace	Division 3S	4.9.46
Colchester United	9-1	Bradford City	Division 4	30.12.61
Milwall	9-1	Torquay United	Division 3S	29.8.27
Millwall	9-1	Coventry City	Division 3S	19.11.27
Portsmouth	9-1	Notts County	Division 2	9.4.27
Port Vale	9-1	Chesterfield	Division 2	24.9.32
York City	9-1	Southport	Division 3N	2.2.57
Carlisle United	8-0	Hartlepool United	Division 3N	1.9.28
Carlisle United	8-0	Scunthorpe United	Division 3N	25.12.52
Crewe Alexandra	8-0	Rotherham United	Division 3N	1.10.32
Rotherham United	8-0	Oldham Athletic	Division 3N	26.5.47
Swansea City	8-0	Hartlepool United	Division 4	1.4.78
Middlesbrough	10-3	Sheffield United	Division 1	18.11.33
Stoke City	10-3	West Bromwich Albion	Division 1	4.2.37
Cardiff City	9-2	Thames	Division 3S	6.2.32
Darlington	9-2	Lincoln City	Division 3N	7.1.28
Grimsby Town	9-2	Darwen	Division 2	15.4.1899
Mansfield Town	9-2	Rotherham United	Division 3N	27.12.32
Mansfield Town	9-2	Hounslow Town	FA Cup 1st rd replay	5.11.62
Orient	9-2	Aldershot	Division 3S	10.2.34
Orient	9-2	Chester	League Cup 3rd rd	17.10.62
Queen's Park Rangers	9-2	Tranmere Rovers	Division 3	3.12.60
Aldershot	8-1	Gateshead	Division 4	13.9.58
Charlton Athletic	8-1	Middlesbrough	Division 1	12.9.53
Exeter City	8-1	Coventry City	Division 3S	4.12.26
Exeter City	8-1	Aldershot	Division 3S	4.5.35
Peterborough United	8-1	Oldham Athletic	Division 4	26.11.69
Plymouth Argyle	8-1	Millwall	Division 2	16.1.32
Rochdale	8-1	Chesterfield	Division 3N	18.12.26
Halifax Town	7-0	Bishop Auckland	FA Cup 2nd rd replay	10.1.67
Oxford United	7-0	Barrow	Division 4	19.12.64
Shrewsbury Town	7-0	Swindon Town	Division 3S	6.5.55
Cambridge United	6-0	Darlington	Division 4	18.9.71
Wigan Athletic	7-2	Scunthorpe United	Division 4	12.3.82

Scottish League clubs (in descending order)

Team	Score	Opponents	Competition	Date
Arbroath	36-0	Bon Accord	Scottish Cup 1st rd	12.9.1885
Stirling Albion	20-0	Selkirk	Scottish Cup 1st rd	9.12.84
Partick Thistle	16-0	Royal Albert	Scottish Cup 1st rd	17.1.31
Queen's Park	16-0	St Peter's	Scottish Cup 1st rd	12.9.1885
Heart of Midlothian	15-0	King's Park	Scottish Cup 2nd rd	13.3.37
St Mirren	15-0	Glasgow University	Scottish Cup 1st rd	10.1.60
Airdrieonians	15-1	Dundee Wanderers	Division 2	1.11.1894
Hibernian	15-1	Peebles Rovers	Scottish Cup 2nd rd	11.2.61
Dundee United	14-0	Nithsdale Wanderers	Scottish Cup 1st rd	17.1.31
Forfar Athletic	14-1	Lindertis	Scottish Cup 1st rd	1.9.1888
Aberdeen	13-0	Peterhead	Scottish Cup 3rd rd	10.2.23
Dumbarton	13-1	Kirkintilloch Central	Scottish Cup 1st rd	1.9.1888
Albion Rovers	12-0	Airdriehill	Scottish Cup 1st rd	3.9.1887
Cowdenbeath	12-0	Johnstone	Scottish Cup 1st rd	21.1.28
Montrose	12-0	Vale of Leithen	Scottish Cup 2nd rd	4.1.75
Rangers	14-2	Whitehill	Scottish Cup 2nd rd	22.9.83
Rangers	14-2	Blairgowrie	Scottish Cup 1st rd	20.1.34
Brechin City	12-1	Thornhill	Scottish Cup 1st rd	28.1.26
Falkirk	12-1	Laurieston	Scottish Cup 2nd rd	1.9.1888
Motherwell	12-1	Dundee United	Division 2	23.1.54
East Fife	13-2	Edinburgh City	Division 2	11.12.37
Celtic	11-0	Dundee	Division 1	26.10.1895
Morton	11-0	Carfin Shamrock	Scottish Cup 1st rd	13.11.1886
Ayr United	11-1	Dumbarton	League Cup	13.8.52
Clyde	11-1	Cowdenbeath	Division 2	6.10.51
Queen of the South	11-1	Stranraer	Scottish Cup 1st rd	16.1.32
Dundee	10-0	Alloa	Division 2	8.3.47
Dundee	10-0	Dunfermline Athletic	Division 2	22.3.47
Dunfermline Athletic	11-2	Stenhousemuir	Division 2	27.9.30
Kilmarnock	13-2	Saltcoats Victoria	Scottish Cup 2nd rd	12.9.1896
East Stirlingshire	10-1	Stenhousemuir	Scottish Cup 1st rd	1.9.1888

Raith Rovers	10–1	Coldstream	Scottish Cup 2nd rd	13.3.54
Hamilton Academicals	10–2	Cowdenbeath	Division 1	15.10.32
Alloa	9–2	Forfar Athletic	Division 2	18.3.33
Berwick Rangers	8–1	Forfar Athletic	Division 2	25.12.65
Berwick Rangers	8–1	Vale of Leithen	Scottish Cup 1st rd	30.9.67
Clydebank	8–1	Arbroath	Division 1	3.1.77
St Johnstone	8–1	Partick Thistle	League Cup	16.8.69
Stenhousemuir	9–2	Dundee United	Division 2	17.4.37
Stranraer	7–0	Brechin City	Division 2	6.2.65
Meadowbank Thistle	6–1	Stenhousemuir	Division 2	6.2.82

Heaviest defeats

Football League clubs (in descending order)

Team	Score	Opponents	Competition	Date
Reading	0–18	Preston North End	FA Cup 1st rd	27.1.1894
Scarborough	1–16	South Bank	Northern League	15.11.19
Halifax Town	0–13	Stockport County	Division 3N	6.1.34
Newport County	0–13	Newcastle United	Division 2	5.10.46
Sheffield United	0–13	Bolton Wanderers	FA Cup 2nd rd	1.2.1890
Bristol Rovers	0–12	Luton Town	Division 3S	13.4.36
Doncaster Rovers	0–12	Small Heath	Division 2	11.4.03
Leicester City	0–12	Nottingham Forest	Division 1	21.4.09
Walsall	0–12	Small Heath	Division 2	17.12.1892
Walsall	0–12	Darwen	Division 2	26.12.1896
York City	0–12	Chester	Division 3N	1.2.36
Crewe Alexandra	2–13	Tottenham Hotspur	FA Cup 4th rd replay	3.2.60
Carlisle United	1–11	Hull City	Division 3N	14.1.39
Charlton Athletic	1–11	Aston Villa	Division 2	14.11.59
Rotherham United	1–11	Bradford City	Division 3N	25.8.28
Burnley	0–10	Aston Villa	Division 1	29.8.25
Burnley	0–10	Sheffield United	Division 1	19.1.29
Bury	0–10	Blackburn Rovers	FA Cup Pr rd	1.10.1887
Bury	0–10	West Ham United	Milk Cup 2nd rd 2nd leg	25.10.83
Chesterfield	0–10	Gillingham	Division 3	5.9.87
Darlington	0–10	Doncaster Rovers	Division 4	25.1.64
Fulham	0–10	Liverpool	Littlewoods Cup 2nd rd 1st leg	23.9.86
Northampton Town	0–10	Bournemouth	Division 3S	2.9.39
Portsmouth	0–10	Leicester City	Division 1	20.10.28
Port Vale	0–10	Sheffield United	Division 2	10.12.1892
Port Vale	0–10	Notts County	Division 2	26.2.1895
Sheffield Wednesday	0–10	Aston Villa	Division 1	5.10.12
Stoke City	0–10	Preston North End	Division 1	14.9.1889
Watford	0–10	Wolverhampton Wanderers	FA Cup 1st rd replay	13.1.12
Oldham Athletic	4–13	Tranmere Rovers	Division 3N	26.12.35
Derby County	2–11	Everton	FA Cup 1st rd	18.1.1890
Chester City	2–11	Oldham Athletic	Division 3N	19.1.52
Cardiff City	2–11	Sheffield United	Division 1	1.1.26
Blackpool	1–10	Small Heath	Division 2	2.3.01
Blackpool	1–10	Huddersfield Town	Division 1	13.12.30
Hartlepools United	1–10	Wrexham	Division 4	3.3.62
Huddersfield Town	1–10	Manchester City	Division 2	7.11.87
Ipswich Town	1–10	Fulham	Division 1	26.12.63
Swindon Town	1–10	Manchester City	FA Cup 4th rd replay	25.1.30
Wolverhampton Wanderers	1–10	Newton Heath	Division 1	15.10.1892
Aldershot	0–9	Bristol City	Division 3S	28.12.46
Barnsley	0–9	Notts County	Division 2	19.11.27
Bournemouth	0–9	Lincoln City	Division 3	18.12.82
Brighton & Hove Albion	0–9	Middlesbrough	Division 2	23.8.58
Bristol City	0–9	Coventry City	Division 3S	28.4.34
Exeter City	0–9	Notts County	Division 3S	16.10.48
Exeter City	0–9	Northampton Town	Division 3S	12.4.58
Middlesbrough	0–9	Blackburn Rovers	Division 2	6.11.54
Newcastle United	0–9	Burton Wanderers	Division 2	15.4.1895
Plymouth Argyle	0–9	Stoke City	Division 2	17.12.60
Wrexham	0–9	Brentford	Division 3	15.10.63
Lincoln City	3–11	Manchester City	Division 2	23.3.1895
Coventry City	2–10	Norwich City	Division 3S	15.3.30
Norwich City	2–10	Swindon Town	Southern League	5.9.08
Torquay United	2–10	Fulham	Division 3S	7.9.31
Torquay United	2–10	Luton Town	Division 3S	2.9.33
Birmingham City	1–9	Sheffield Wednesday	Division 1	13.12.30
Birmingham City	1–9	Blackburn Rovers	Division 1	5.1.1895
Bradford City	1–9	Colchester United	Division 4	30.12.61
Grimsby Town	1–9	Arsenal	Division 1	28.1.31
Liverpool	1–9	Birmingham City	Division 2	11.12.54
Luton Town	1–9	Small Heath	Division 2	12.11.1898
Manchester City	1–9	Everton	Division 1	3.9.06

Team	Score	Opponent	Competition	Date
Millwall	1–9	Aston Villa	FA Cup 4th rd	28.1.46
Nottingham Forest	1–9	Blackburn Rovers	Division 2	10.4.37
Notts County	1–9	Blackburn Rovers	Division 1	16.11.1889
Notts County	1–9	Aston Villa	Division 1	29.9.1888
Notts County	1–9	Portsmouth	Division 2	9.4.27
Rochdale	1–9	Tranmere Rovers	Division 3N	25.12.31
Southend United	1–9	Brighton & Hove Albion	Division 3	27.11.65
Tranmere Rovers	1–9	Tottenham Hotspur	FA Cup 3rd rd replay	14.1.53
Arsenal	0–8	Loughborough Town	Division 2	12.12.1896
Blackburn Rovers	0–8	Arsenal	Division 1	25.2.33
Hull City	0–8	Wolverhampton Wanderers	Division 2	4.11.11
Orient	0–8	Aston Villa	FA Cup 4th rd	30.1.29
Scunthorpe United	0–8	Carlisle United	Division 3N	25.12.52
Southampton	0–8	Tottenham Hotspur	Division 2	28.3.36
Southampton	0–8	Everton	Division 1	20.11.71
Sunderland	0–8	West Ham United	Division 1	19.10.68
Sunderland	0–8	Watford	Division 1	25.9.82
Wimbledon	0–8	Everton	League Cup 2nd rd	29.8.78
West Bromwich Albion	3–10	Stoke City	Division 1	4.2.57
Gillingham	2–9	Nottingham Forest	Division 3S	18.11.50
Aston Villa	1–8	Blackburn Rovers	FA Cup 3rd rd	16.2.1889
Chelsea	1–8	Wolverhampton Wanderers	Division 1	26.9.53
Leeds United	1–8	Stoke City	Division 1	27.8.34
Mansfield Town	1–8	Walsall	Division 3N	19.1.33
Peterborough United	1–8	Northampton Town	FA Cup 2nd rd 2nd replay	18.12.46
Queen's Park Rangers	1–8	Mansfield Town	Division 3	15.3.65
Queen's Park Rangers	1–8	Manchester United	Division 1	19.3.69
Shrewsbury Town	1–8	Norwich City	Division 3S	13.9.52
Shrewsbury Town	1–8	Coventry City	Division 3	22.10.63
Stockport County	1–8	Chesterfield	Division 2	19.4.02
Swansea City	1–8	Fulham	Division 2	22.1.38
Crystal Palace	4–11	Manchester City	FA Cup 5th rd	20.2.26
Bolton Wanderers	0–7	Manchester City	Division 1	21.3.36
Brentford	0–7	Swansea Town	Division 3S	8.11.24
Brentford	0–7	Walsall	Division 3S	19.1.57
Colchester United	0–7	Leyton Orient	Division 3S	5.1.52
Colchester United	0–7	Reading	Division 3S	18.9.57
Manchester United	0–7	Blackburn Rovers	Division 1	10.4.26
Manchester United	0–7	Aston Villa	Division 1	27.12.30
Manchester United	0–7	Wolverhampton Wanderers	Division 2	26.12.31
Preston North End	0–7	Blackpool	Division 1	1.5.48
Tottenham Hotspur	0–7	Liverpool	Division 1	2.9.78
Everton	4–10	Tottenham Hotspur	Division 1	11.10.58
West Ham United	2–8	Blackburn Rovers	Division 1	26.12.63
Cambridge United	0–6	Aldershot	Division 3	13.4.74
Cambridge United	0–6	Darlington	Division 4	28.9.74
Cambridge United	0–6	Chelsea	Division 2	15.1.83
Oxford United	0–6	Liverpool	Division 1	22.3.86
Hereford United	2–7	Arsenal	FA Cup 3rd rd replay	22.1.85
Wigan Athletic	0–5	Bristol Rovers	Division 3	26.2.83
Wigan Athletic	0–5	Chelsea	FA Cup 3rd rd replay	26.1.85

Scottish League clubs (in descending order)

Team	Score	Opponent	Competition	Date
Montrose	0–13	Aberdeen Reserves	Division C	17.3.51
Dundee United	1–12	Motherwell	Division 2	23.1.54
East Stirlingshire	1–12	Dundee United	Division 2	13.4.36
Clyde	0–11	Dumbarton	Scottish Cup 4th rd	22.11.79
Clyde	0–11	Rangers	Scottish Cup 4th rd	13.11.80
Dundee	0–11	Celtic	Division 1	26.10.1895
Forfar Athletic	2–12	King's Park	Division 2	2.1.30
Airdrieonians	1–11	Hibernian	Division 1	24.10.59
Cowdenbeath	1–11	Clyde	Division 2	6.10.51
Dumbarton	1–11	Albion Rovers	Division 2	30.1.26
Dumbarton	1–11	Ayr United	League Cup qual rd	13.8.52
Falkirk	1–11	Airdrieonians	Division 1	28.4.51
Hamilton Academicals	1–11	Hibernian	Division 1	6.11.65
Stranraer	1–11	Queen of the South	Scottish Cup 1st rd	16.1.32
Dunfermline Athletic	0–10	Dundee	Division 2	22.3.47
Hibernian	0–10	Rangers	Division 1	24.12.1898
Partick Thistle	0–10	Queen's Park	Scottish Cup 5th rd	3.12.81
Brechin City	1–10	Dunfermline Athletic	Division 2	14.12.29
Morton	1–10	Port Glasgow Athletic	Division 2	5.5.1894
St Johnstone	1–10	Third Lanark	Scottish Cup 1st rd	24.1.03
Alloa	2–11	Hibernian	League Cup qual rd	26.9.65
Stenhousemuir	2–11	Dunfermline Athletic	Division 2	27.9.30
Raith Rovers	2–11	Morton	Division 2	18.3.36
Ayr United	0–9	Rangers	Division 1	16.11.29
Ayr United	0–9	Heart of Midlothian	Division 1	28.2.31
East Fife	0–9	Heart of Midlothian	Division 1	5.10.57
Stirling Albion	0–9	Dundee United	Division 1	30.12.67
Albion Rovers	1–9	Motherwell	Division 1	2.1.37

Team 1	Score	Team 2	Competition	Date
Clydebank	1–9	Gala Fairydean	Scottish Cup qual rd	15.9.65
Aberdeen	0–8	Celtic	Division 1	30.1.65
Arbroath	0–8	Kilmarnock	Division 2	3.1.49
Berwick Rangers	0–8	Morton	Division 2	21.12.57
Celtic	0–8	Motherwell	Division 1	30.4.37
Kilmarnock	0–8	Hibernian	Division 1	22.8.37
Kilmarnock	0–8	Rangers	Division 1	27.2.37
Meadowbank Thistle	0–8	Hamilton Academical	Division 2	14.12.74
Motherwell	0–8	Aberdeen	Division 1	26.3.79
Queen of the South	2–10	Dundee	Division 1	1.12.62
Queen's Park	3–10	Heart of Midlothian	Division 1	24.8.12
St Mirren	2–9	Dundee	Division 1	24.8.12
Heart of Midlothian	0–7	Hibernian	Division 1	1.1.73
Rangers	1–7	Celtic	League Cup Final	19.10.57

Goal bonanzas

There have been only two drawn matches in Football League history in which each side scored as many as six goals – 6–6 draws between Leicester City and Arsenal in 1930 and Charlton Athletic and Middlesbrough in 1960. Below are the details of the matches in which each team scored five times or more:

Match and score				Division	Date
Blackburn Rovers	5	Accrington Stanley	5	F.Lge	9.9.1888
Derby County	8	Blackburn Rovers	5	1	6.9.1890
Crewe Alexandra	5	Walsall Town S.	6	2	5.11.1892
Burton Swifts	8	Walsall Town S.	5	2	24.2.1894
Manchester United	5	Lincoln City	5	2	16.11.1895
Derby County	5	Everton	5	1	15.10.1898
Sheffield Wed.	5	Everton	5	1	12.11.04
Sunderland	5	Liverpool	5	1	19.1.07
Liverpool	6	Newcastle United	5	1	4.12.09
Middlesbrough	7	Tottenham Hotspur	5	1	13.2.15
Tottenham Hotspur	5	Huddersfield Town	5	1	19.9.25
Wrexham	5	Accrington Stanley	6	3N	24.10.25
Crystal Palace	5	Plymouth Argyle	5	3S	28.11.25
Bury	6	Manchester City	5	1	25.12.25
Aberdare Athletic	5	Plymouth Argyle	6	3S	2.1.27
Newcastle United	7	Aston Villa	5	1	10.3.27
Northampton Town	6	Luton Town	5	3S	26.12.27
Swansea Town	5	Blackpool	5	2	27.8.28
Blackburn Rovers	7	Birmingham City	5	1	28.9.29
Sheffield United	5	Blackburn Rovers	7	1	3.3.30
Leicester City	6	Arsenal	6	1	21.4.30
Millwall	5	Preston North End	7	2	4.10.30
Sunderland	6	Liverpool	5	1	6.12.30
West Ham United	5	Aston Villa	5	1	3.1.31
Coventry City	5	Fulham	5	3S	2.1.32
Walsall	5	Accrington Stanley	5	3N	2.4.32
W.B.A.	5	Grimsby Town	6	1	30.4.32
Grimsby Town	5	Port Vale	5	2	15.10.32
Blackburn Rovers	6	Blackpool	5	1	2.1.33
Grimsby Town	5	Charlton Athletic	5	2	7.1.33
Luton Town	5	Brentford	5	3S	1.2.33
Stockport County	8	Chester	5	3N	6.5.33
W.B.A.	6	Sunderland	5	1	24.3.34
Bristol Rovers	5	Exeter City	5	3S	10.11.34
York City	7	Mansfield Town	5	3N	16.11.35
Crewe Alexandra	5	Chesterfield	6	3N	1.2.36
Middlesbrough	5	Sunderland	5	1	17.10.36
Darlington	5	Hartlepools United	5	3N	21.11.36
Bolton Wanderers	5	Chelsea	5	1	30.10.37
Walsall	5	Millwall	6	3S	13.11.48
Derby County	6	Sunderland	5	1	16.12.50
Leicester City	5	Sheffield United	5	2	3.11.51
Chelsea	5	Manchester United	6	1	16.10.54
Charlton Athletic	7	Huddersfield Town	6	2	21.12.57
Chelsea	6	Newcastle United	5	1	10.9.58
Charlton Athletic	6	Middlesbrough	6	2	22.10.60
Newcastle United	5	West Ham United	5	1	10.12.60
Blackburn Rovers	5	Arsenal	5	1	3.11.62
Birmingham City	5	Blackburn Rovers	5	1	24.4.65
Tottenham Hotspur	5	Aston Villa	5	1	19.3.66
Birmingham City	5	Derby County	5	2	9.4.66
Chelsea	5	West Ham United	5	1	17.12.66
Bristol Rovers	5	Charlton Athletic	5	2	18.11.78
Southampton	5	Coventry City	5	1	4.5.82
Doncaster Rovers	7	Reading	5	3	25.9.82
Q.P.R.	5	Newcastle United	5	1	22.9.84

Champions in reserve

Instances since the 1914–18 war of clubs winning the First Division championship and their reserves also being champions:

Season	Club	Reserve winners
1919–20	West Bromwich Albion	Birmingham League
1924–25	Huddersfield Town	Central League
1925–26	Huddersfield Town	Central League
1928–29	Sheffield Wednesday	Central League
1930–31	Arsenal	London Combination
1933–34	Arsenal	London Combination
1934–35	Arsenal	London Combination
1937–38	Arsenal	London Combination
1947–48	Arsenal	Football Combination
1954–55	Chelsea	Football Combination
1955–56	Manchester United	Central League
1957–58	Wolverhampton Wanderers*	Central League
1971–72	Derby County	Central League
1972–73	Liverpool	Central League
1975–76	Liverpool	Central League
1976–77	Liverpool	Central League
1978–79	Liverpool	Central League
1979–80	Liverpool	Central League
1981–82	Liverpool	Central League
1983–84	Liverpool	Central League

* Wolverhampton Wanderers third team won the Birmingham League (First Division) championship, the fourth team the Worcester Combination title and their youth team the FA Youth Cup in the same season.

Over forties

Post-war players who have made Football League appearances at the age of 40 or over.

Neil McBain (New Brighton)	1946–47
Stanley Matthews (Stoke City)	1964–65
Alec Ferguson (Swindon Town)	1947–48
Ted Sagar (Everton)	1952–53
Alf Wood (Coventry City)	1958–59
Sam Bartram (Charlton Athletic)	1955–56
John Oakes (Plymouth Argyle)	1947–48
Bobby Collins (Oldham Athletic)	1972–73
Jack Brownsword (Scunthorpe United)	1964–65
Alan Oakes (Port Vale)	1983–84
Roy Sproson (Port Vale)	1971–72
Terry Cooper (Bristol City)	1984–85
Jimmy Dickinson (Portsmouth)	1964–65
John Jackson (Hereford United)	1982–83
Billy Bonds (West Ham United)	1986–87
Tommy Hutchison (Swansea City)	1987–88
Billy Cairns (Grimsby Town)	1952–53

Sir Stanley Matthews on his retirement from first-class football at 50.

The great derby showdowns

The League's greatest rivalry – **Everton v Liverpool**

Everton were founded in 1878 as St Domingo Church Sunday School team, becoming Everton the following year. Liverpool came into being in 1892 following a split which led to the Everton club moving from Anfield to Goodison Park.

Of the 138 matches played between the sides in the League Everton have won 48, Liverpool 49 and 41 have been drawn.

League results at Goodison Park (Everton's score first)

Season	Score	Season	Score
1894–95	3–0	1936–37	2–0
1896–97	2–1	1937–38	1–3
1897–98	3–0	1938–39	2–1
1898–99	1–2	1946–47	1–0
1899–1900	3–1	1947–48	0–3
1900–01	1–1	1948–49	1–1
1901–02	4–0	1949–50	0–0
1902–03	3–1	1950–51	1–3
1903–04	5–2	1962–63	2–2
1905–06	4–2	1963–64	3–1
1906–07	0–0	1964–65	2–1
1907–08	2–4	1965–66	0–0
1908–09	5–0	1966–67	3–1
1909–10	2–3	1967–68	1–0
1910–11	0–1	1968–69	0–0
1911–12	2–1	1969–70	0–3
1912–13	0–2	1970–71	0–0
1913–14	1–2	1971–72	1–0
1914–15	1–3	1972–73	0–2
1919–20	0–0	1973–74	0–1
1920–21	0–3	1974–75	0–0
1921–22	1–1	1975–76	0–0
1922–23	0–1	1976–77	0–0
1923–24	1–0	1977–78	0–1
1924–25	0–1	1978–79	1–0
1925–26	3–3	1979–80	1–2
1926–27	1–0	1980–81	2–2
1927–28	1–1	1981–82	1–3
1928–29	1–0	1982–83	0–5
1929–30	3–3	1983–84	1–1
1931–32	2–1	1984–85	1–0
1932–33	3–1	1985–86	2–3
1933–34	0–0	1986–87	0–0
1934–35	1–0	1987–88	1–0
1935–36	0–0		

League results at Anfield (Liverpool's score first)

Season	Score	Season	Score
1894–95	2–2	1905–06	1–1
1896–97	0–0	1906–07	1–2
1897–98	3–1	1907–08	0–0
1898–99	2–0	1908–09	0–1
1899–1900	1–2	1909–10	0–1
1900–01	1–2	1910–11	0–2
1901–02	2–2	1911–12	1–3
1902–03	0–0	1912–13	0–2
1903–04	2–2	1913–14	1–2

116

Season	Score	Season	Score
1914–15	0–5	1963–64	2–1
1919–20	3–1	1964–65	0–4
1920–21	1–0	1965–66	5–0
1921–22	1–1	1966–67	0–0
1922–23	5–1	1967–68	1–0
1923–24	1–2	1968–69	1–1
1924–25	3–1	1969–70	0–2
1925–26	5–1	1970–71	3–2
1926–27	1–0	1971–72	4–0
1927–28	3–3	1972–73	1–0
1928–29	1–2	1973–74	0–0
1929–30	0–3	1974–75	0–0
1931–32	1–3	1975–76	1–0
1932–33	7–4	1976–77	3–1
1933–34	3–2	1977–78	0–0
1934–35	2–1	1978–79	1–1
1935–36	6–0	1979–80	2–2
1936–37	3–2	1980–81	1–0
1937–38	1–2	1981–82	3–1
1938–39	0–3	1982–83	0–0
1946–47	0–0	1983–84	3–0
1947–48	4–0	1984–85	0–1
1948–49	0–0	1985–86	0–2
1949–50	3–1	1986–87	3–1
1950–51	0–2	1987–88	2–0
1962–63	0–0		

Season	Score	Season	Score
1913–14	0–1	1960–61	5–1
1914–15	0–0	1961–62	3–2
1919–20	1–0	1962–63	2–3
1920–21	1–1	1966–67	1–0
1921–22	3–1	1967–68	1–3
1925–26	1–6	1968–69	0–1
1928–29	1–2	1969–70	1–2
1929–30	1–3	1970–71	1–4
1930–31	1–3	1971–72	1–3
1936–37	3–2	1972–73	0–0
1947–48	1–1*	1973–74	0–1
1948–49	0–0*	1975–76	2–0
1949–50	2–1	1976–77	3–1
1951–52	1–1	1977–78	2–2
1952–53	1–1	1978–79	1–0
1953–54	1–1	1979–80	1–0
1954–55	0–5	1980–81	2–2
1955–56	2–1	1981–82	1–1
1956–57	2–0	1982–83	2–2
1957–58	4–1	1985–86	2–2
1958–59	4–1	1986–87	2–0
1959–60	0–0	* United played at Maine Road	

The two Manchesters – **Manchester City v Manchester United**

City were founded in 1887 as Ardwick FC and became Manchester City in 1894. United were formed a few years earlier in 1878 as Newton Heath and became Manchester United in 1902.

Of the110 League matches played between the sides City won 31, United 40 and 39 were drawn.

Rivalry in the North-East – **Newcastle United v Sunderland**

Sunderland were founded in 1879 as Sunderland and District Teachers AFC and became known under their present title in 1881. Newcastle were founded in 1882 as Newcastle East End and changed to Newcastle United in 1892.

Of the 108 League matches played between the two sides, Sunderland have won 38, Newcastle 39 and 31 have been drawn.

League results at Maine Road (City's score first)

Season	Score	Season	Score
1894–95	2–5	1954–55	3–2
1895–96	2–1	1955–56	1–0
1896–97	0–0	1956–57	2–4
1897–98	0–1	1957–58	2–2
1898–99	4–0	1958–59	1–1
1902–03	0–2	1959–60	3–0
1906–07	3–0	1960–61	1–3
1907–08	0–0	1961–62	0–2
1908–09	1–2	1962–63	1–1
1910–11	1–1	1966–67	1–1
1911–12	0–0	1967–68	1–2
1912–13	0–2	1968–69	0–0
1913–14	0–2	1969–70	4–0
1914–15	1–1	1970–71	3–4
1919–20	3–3	1971–72	3–3
1920–21	3–0	1972–73	3–0
1921–22	4–1	1973–74	0–0
1925–26	1–1	1975–76	2–2
1928–29	2–2	1976–77	1–3
1929–30	0–1	1977–78	3–1
1930–31	4–1	1978–79	0–3
1936–37	1–0	1979–80	2–0
1947–48	0–0	1980–81	1–0
1948–49	0–0	1981–82	0–0
1949–50	1–2	1982–83	1–2
1951–52	1–2	1985–86	0–3
1952–53	2–1	1986–87	1–1
1953–54	2–0		

League results at Roker Park (Sunderland's score first)

Season	Score	Season	Score
1898–99	2–3	1929–30	1–0
1899–1900	1–2	1930–31	5–0
1900–01	1–1	1931–32	1–4
1901–02	0–0	1932–33	0–2
1902–03	0–0	1933–34	2–0
1903–04	1–1	1948–49	1–1
1904–05	3–1	1949–50	2–2
1905–06	3–2	1950–51	2–1
1906–07	2–0	1951–52	1–4
1907–08	2–4	1952–53	0–2
1908–09	3–1	1953–54	1–1
1909–10	0–2	1954–55	4–2
1910–11	2–1	1955–56	1–6
1911–12	1–2	1956–57	1–2
1912–13	2–0	1957–58	2–0
1913–14	1–2	1961–62	3–0
1914–15	2–4	1962–63	0–0
1919–20	2–0	1963–64	2–1
1920–21	0–2	1965–66	2–0
1921–22	0–0	1966–67	3–0
1922–23	2–0	1967–68	3–3
1923–24	3–2	1968–69	1–1
1924–25	1–1	1969–70	1–1
1925–26	2–2	1976–77	2–2
1926–27	2–0	1978–79	1–1
1927–28	1–1	1979–80	1–0
1928–29	5–2	1984–85	0–0

League results at Old Trafford (United's score first)

Season	Score	Season	Score
1894–95	4–1	1906–07	1–1
1895–96	1–1	1907–08	3–1
1896–97	2–1	1908–09	3–1
1897–98	1–1	1910–11	2–1
1898–99	3–0	1911–12	0–0
1902–03	1–1	1912–13	0–1

League results at St James's Park (Newcastle's score first)

Season	Score	Season	Score
1898–99	0–1	1904–05	1–3
1899–1900	2–4	1905–06	1–1
1900–01	0–2	1906–07	4–2
1901–02	0–1	1907–08	1–3
1902–03	1–0	1908–09	1–9
1903–04	1–3	1909–10	1–0

Season	Score	Season	Score	Season	Score	Season	Score
1910–11	1–1	1949–50	2–2	1950–51	1–0	1969–70	1–0
1911–12	3–1	1950–51	2–2	1951–52	1–2	1970–71	0–1
1912–13	1–1	1951–52	2–2	1952–53	1–3	1971–72	1–1
1913–14	2–1	1952–53	2–2	1953–54	1–4	1972–73	1–2
1914–15	2–5	1953–54	2–1	1954–55	0–1	1973–74	2–0
1919–20	2–3	1954–55	1–2	1955–56	3–1	1974–75	2–0
1920–21	6–1	1955–56	3–1	1956–57	1–3	1975–76	0–0
1921–22	2–2	1956–57	6–2	1957–58	3–1	1976–77	2–2
1922–23	2–1	1957–58	2–2	1958–59	1–4	1978–79	0–5
1923–24	0–2	1961–62	2–2	1959–60	3–0	1979–80	1–2
1924–25	2–0	1962–63	1–1	1960–61	4–2	1980–81	2–0
1925–26	0–0	1963–64	1–0	1961–62	4–3	1981–82	2–2
1926–27	1–0	1965–66	2–0	1962–63	4–4	1982–83	5–0
1927–28	3–1	1966–67	0–3	1963–64	3–1	1983–84	2–4
1928–29	4–3	1967–68	2–1	1964–65	3–1	1984–85	0–2
1929–30	3–0	1968–69	1–1	1965–66	2–2	1985–86	1–0
1930–31	2–0	1969–70	3–0	1966–67	3–1	1986–87	1–2
1931–32	1–2	1976–77	2–0	1967–68	1–0	1987–88	1–2
1932–33	0–1	1978–79	1–4	1968–69	1–2		
1933–34	2–1	1979–80	3–1				
1948–49	2–1	1984–85	3–1				

North London encounters – **Arsenal v Tottenham Hotspur**

Arsenal were founded in 1886 as Royal Arsenal, becoming Woolwich Arsenal in 1891 and Arsenal from 1914. Tottenham Hotspur were founded four years earlier in 1882 and were known as the Hotspur Football Club before becoming Tottenham Hotspur in 1885.

Of the 102 League matches played between the two sides, Tottenham have won 39, Arsenal 42, and 21 have been drawn

League results at Highbury (Arsenal's score first)

Season	Score	Season	Score
1909–10	1–0	1962–63	2–3
1910–11	2–0	1963–64	4–4
1911–12	3–1	1964–65	3–1
1912–13	0–3	1965–66	1–1
1920–21	3–2	1966–67	0–2
1921–22	1–0	1967–68	4–0
1922–23	0–2	1968–69	1–0
1923–24	1–1	1969–70	2–3
1924–25	1–0	1970–71	2–0
1925–26	0–1	1971–72	0–2
1926–27	2–4	1972–73	1–1
1927–28	1–1	1973–74	0–1
1933–34	1–3	1974–75	1–0
1934–35	5–1	1975–76	0–2
1950–51	2–2	1976–77	1–0
1951–52	1–1	1978–79	1–0
1952–53	4–0	1979–80	1–0
1953–54	0–3	1980–81	2–0
1954–55	2–0	1981–82	1–3
1955–56	0–1	1982–83	2–0
1956–57	3–1	1983–84	3–2
1957–58	4–4	1984–85	1–2
1958–59	3–1	1985–86	0–0
1959–60	1–1	1986–87	0–0
1960–61	2–3	1987–88	2–1
1961–62	2–1		

League results at White Hart Lane (Tottenham's score first)

Season	Score	Season	Score
1909–10	1–1	1923–24	3–0
1910–11	3–1	1924–25	2–0
1911–12	5–0	1925–26	1–1
1912–13	1–1	1926–27	0–4
1920–21	2–1	1927–28	2–0
1921–22	2–0	1933–34	1–1
1922–23	1–2	1934–35	0–6

Duel of the Nottinghams – **Notts County v Nottingham Forest**

Notts County were founded in 1862 and are the oldest club in the Football League. Nottingham Forest came into being in 1865, but did not enter the League until 1882, four years after Notts County had become a founder member.

Of the 82 League matches played between the two sides, Forest have won 33, County 27, and 22 have been drawn.

League results at Meadow Lane (Notts County's score first)

Season	Score	Season	Score
1892–93	3–0	1928–29	1–1
1897–98	1–3	1929–30	0–0
1898–99	2–2	1931–32	2–6
1899–1900	1–2	1932–33	2–4
1900–01	1–0	1933–34	1–0
1901–02	3–0	1934–35	3–5
1902–03	1–1	1949–50	2–0
1903–04	1–3	1951–52	2–2
1904–05	1–2	1952–53	3–2
1905–06	1–1	1953–54	1–1
1907–08	2–0	1954–55	4–1
1908–09	3–0	1955–56	1–3
1909–10	4–1	1956–57	1–2
1910–11	1–1	1973–74	0–1
1913–14	2–2	1974–75	2–2
1920–21	2–0	1975–76	0–0
1921–22	1–1	1976–77	1–1
1923–24	2–1	1981–82	1–2
1924–25	0–0	1982–83	3–2
1926–27	1–2	1983–84	0–0
1927–28	1–2		

League results at the City Ground (Forest's score first)

Season	Score	Season	Score
1892–93	3–1	1920–21	1–0
1897–98	1–1	1921–22	0–0
1898–99	0–0	1923–24	1–0
1899–1900	0–3	1924–25	0–0
1900–01	5–0	1926–27	2–0
1901–02	1–0	1927–28	2–1
1902–03	0–0	1928–29	1–2
1903–04	0–1	1929–30	1–1
1904–05	2–1	1931–32	2–1
1905–06	1–2	1932–33	3–0
1907–08	2–0	1933–34	2–0
1908–09	1–0	1934–35	2–3
1909–10	2–1	1949–50	1–2
1910–11	0–2	1951–52	3–2
1913–14	1–0	1952–53	1–0

Season	Score	Season	Score
1953-54	5-0	1975-76	0-1
1954-55	0-1	1976-77	1-2
1955-56	0-2	1981-82	0-2
1956-57	2-4	1982-83	2-1
1973-74	0-0	1983-84	3-1
1974-75	0-2		

Sheffield steel – **Sheffield United v Sheffield Wednesday**

United were founded in 1889, Wednesday in 1867. Of the 92 matches played between the clubs United have won 35, Wednesday 30, and 27 have been drawn.

League results at Bramall Lane (United's score first)

Season	Score	Season	Score
1893-94	1-1	1927-28	1-1
1894-95	1-0	1928-29	1-1
1895-96	1-1	1929-30	2-2
1896-97	2-0	1930-31	1-1
1897-98	1-1	1931-32	1-1
1898-99	2-1	1932-33	2-3
1900-01	1-0	1933-34	5-1
1901-02	3-0	1937-38	2-1
1902-03	2-3	1938-39	0-0
1903-04	1-1	1949-50	2-0
1904-05	4-2	1951-52	7-3
1905-06	0-2	1953-54	2-0
1906-07	2-1	1954-55	1-0
1907-08	1-3	1958-59	1-0
1908-09	2-1	1961-62	1-0
1909-10	3-3	1962-63	2-2
1910-11	0-1	1963-64	1-1
1911-12	1-1	1964-65	2-3
1912-13	0-2	1965-66	1-0
1913-14	0-1	1966-67	1-0
1914-15	0-1	1967-68	0-1
1919-20	3-0	1970-71	3-2
1926-27	2-0	1979-80	1-1

League results at Hillsborough (Wednesday's score first)

Season	Score	Season	Score
1893-94	1-2	1927-28	3-3
1894-95	2-3	1928-29	5-2
1895-96	1-0	1929-30	1-1
1896-97	1-1	1930-31	1-3
1897-98	0-1	1931-32	2-1
1898-99	1-1	1932-33	3-3
1900-01	1-0	1933-34	0-1
1901-02	1-0	1937-38	0-1
1902-03	0-1	1938-39	1-0
1903-04	3-0	1949-50	2-1
1904-05	1-3	1951-52	1-3
1905-06	1-0	1953-54	3-2
1906-07	2-2	1954-55	1-2
1907-08	2-0	1958-59	2-0
1908-09	1-0	1961-62	1-2
1909-10	1-3	1962-63	3-1
1910-11	2-0	1963-64	3-0
1911-12	1-1	1964-65	0-2
1912-13	1-0	1965-66	2-2
1913-14	2-1	1966-67	2-2
1914-15	1-1	1967-68	1-1
1919-20	2-1	1970-71	0-0
1926-27	2-3	1979-80	4-0

West Country clashes – **Bristol City v Bristol Rovers**

Bristol City were founded in 1894 as Bristol South End and became known under their present title in 1897. Bristol Rovers were founded in 1883 as Black Arabs, changed to Eastville Rovers in 1884, Bristol Eastville Rovers in 1897

and became known as Bristol Rovers in 1898. The 68 League meetings between the two clubs have resulted in Bristol City winning 26 matches, Rovers 17, with the other 25 drawn. Bristol Rovers moved to Bath City's ground in 1986.

League results at Ashton Gate (City's score first)

Season	Score	Season	Score
1922-23	0-1	1952-53	0-0
1924-25	2-0	1955-56	1-1
1925-26	0-0	1956-57	5-3
1926-27	3-1	1957-58	3-2
1932-33	3-1	1958-59	1-1
1933-34	0-3	1959-60	2-1
1934-35	1-1	1962-63	4-1
1935-36	0-2	1963-64	3-0
1936-37	4-1	1964-65	2-1
1937-38	0-0	1974-75	1-1
1938-39	2-1	1975-76	1-1
1946-47	4-0	1980-81	0-0
1947-48	5-2	1981-82	1-2
1948-49	1-1	1984-85	3-0
1949-50	1-2	1985-86	2-0
1950-51	1-0	1986-87	0-1
1951-52	1-1	1987-88	3-3

League results at Eastville and Twerton Park* (Rovers' score first)

Season	Score	Season	Score
1922-23	1-2	1952-53	0-0
1924-25	0-0	1955-56	0-3
1925-26	0-1	1956-57	0-0
1926-27	0-5	1957-58	3-3
1932-33	1-1	1958-59	1-2
1933-34	5-1	1959-60	2-1
1934-35	2-2	1962-63	1-2
1935-36	1-1	1963-64	4-0
1936-37	3-1	1964-65	1-1
1937-38	1-0	1974-75	1-4
1938-39	1-1	1975-76	0-0
1946-47	0-3	1980-81	0-0
1947-48	0-2	1981-82	1-0
1948-49	3-1	1984-85	1-0
1949-50	2-3	1985-86	1-1
1950-51	2-1	1986-87*	0-0
1951-52	2-0	1987-88*	1-0

Midland rivals – **Aston Villa v Birmingham City**

Aston Villa were founded in 1874. Birmingham were originally known as Small Heath Alliance from their formation in 1875 until 1888 when they dropped 'Alliance'. In 1905 they became Birmingham and added City in 1945. Of the 96 League meetings between them, Villa have won 39, Birmingham 32, with 25 drawn.

League results at Villa Park (Aston Villa's score first)

Season	Score	Season	Score
1894-95*	2-1	1931-32	3-2
1895-96*	7-3	1932-33	1-0
1901-02	1-0	1933-34	1-1
1903-04	1-1	1934-35	2-2
1904-05	2-1	1935-36	2-1
1905-06	1-3	1938-39	5-1
1906-07	4-1	1948-49	0-3
1907-08	2-3	1949-50	1-1
1921-22	1-1	1955-56	0-0
1922-23	3-0	1956-57	3-1
1923-24	0-0	1957-58	0-2
1924-25	1-0	1958-59	1-1
1925-26	3-3	1960-61	6-2
1926-27	4-2	1961-62	1-3
1927-28	1-1	1962-63	4-0
1928-29	1-2		
1929-30	2-1		
1930-31	1-1	* at Perry Barr	

Season	Score	Season	Score
1963-64	0-3	1978-79	1-0
1964-65	3-0	1980-81	3-0
1967-68	2-4	1981-82	0-0
1968-69	1-0	1982-83	1-0
1969-70	0-0	1983-84	1-0
1975-76	2-1	1985-86	0-3
1976-77	1-2	1987-88	0-2
1977-78	0-1		

League results at St Andrew's (Birmingham City's score first)

Season	Score	Season	Score
1894-95*	2-2	1948-49	0-1
1895-96*	1-4	1949-50	2-2
1901-02*	0-2	1955-56	2-2
1903-04*	2-2	1956-57	1-2
1904-05*	0-3	1957-58	3-1
1905-06*	2-0	1958-59	4-1
1906-07	3-2	1960-61	1-1
1907-08	2-3	1961-62	0-2
1921-22	1-0	1962-63	3-2
1922-23	1-0	1963-64	3-3
1923-24	3-0	1964-65	0-1
1924-25	1-0	1967-68	2-1
1925-26	2-1	1968-69	4-0
1926-27	1-2	1969-70	0-2
1927-28	1-1	1975-76	3-2
1928-29	2-4	1976-77	2-1
1929-30	1-1	1977-78	1-0
1930-31	0-4	1978-79	0-1
1931-32	1-1	1980-81	1-2
1932-33	3-2	1981-82	0-1
1933-34	0-0	1982-83	3-0
1934-35	2-1	1983-84	2-1
1935-36	2-2	1985-86	0-0
1938-39	3-0	1987-88	1-2

* at Small Heath

Glasgow divided – **Rangers v Celtic**

Rangers were founded in 1873, Celtic in 1888. Of the 208 Scottish League matches played between the clubs, Rangers have won 78, Celtic 67 and 63 have been drawn.

League results at Ibrox Park (Rangers' score first)

Season	Score	Season	Score
1890-91	1-2	1923-24	0-0
1891-92	1-1	1924-25	4-1
1892-93	2-2	1925-26	1-0
1893-94	5-0	1926-27	2-1
1894-95	1-1	1927-28	1-0
1895-96	2-4	1928-29	3-0
1896-97	2-0	1929-30	1-0
1897-98	0-4	1930-31	1-0
1898-99	4-1	1931-32	0-0
1899-1900	3-3	1932-33	0-0
1900-01	2-1	1933-34	2-2
1901-02	2-2	1934-35	2-1
1902-03	3-3	1935-36	1-2
1903-04	0-0	1936-37	1-0
1904-05	1-4	1937-38	3-1
1905-06	3-2	1938-39	2-1
1906-07	2-1	1946-47	1-1
1907-08	0-1	1947-48	2-0
1908-09	1-3	1948-49	4-0
1909-10	0-0	1949-50	4-0
1910-11	1-1	1950-51	1-0
1911-12	3-1	1951-52	1-1
1912-13	0-1	1952-53	1-0
1913-14	0-2	1953-54	1-1
1914-15	2-1	1954-55	4-1
1915-16	3-0	1955-56	0-0
1916-17	0-0	1956-57	2-0
1917-18	1-2	1957-58	2-3
1918-19	1-1	1958-59	2-1
1919-20	3-0	1959-60	3-1
1920-21	0-2	1960-61	2-1
1921-22	1-1	1961-62	2-2
1922-23	2-0	1962-63	4-0

Season	Score	Season	Score
1963-64	2-1	1979-80	2-2
1964-65	1-0		1-1
1965-66	2-1	1980-81	3-0
1966-67	2-2		0-1
1967-68	1-0	1981-82	0-2
1968-69	1-0		1-0
1969-70	0-1	1982-83	1-2
1970-71	1-1		2-4
1971-72	2-3	1983-84	1-2
1972-73	2-1		1-0
1973-74	0-1	1984-85	0-0
1974-75	3-0		1-2
1975-76	2-1	1985-86	3-0
	1-0		4-4
1976-77	0-1	1986-87	1-0
	2-2		2-0
1977-78	3-2	1987-88	2-2
	3-1		1-2
1978-79	1-1		
	1-0		

League results at Parkhead (Celtic's score first)

Season	Score	Season	Score
1890-91	2-2	1949-50	1-1
1891-92	3-0	1950-51	3-2
1892-93	3-0	1951-52	1-4
1893-94	3-2	1952-53	2-1
1894-95	5-3	1953-54	1-0
1895-96	6-2	1954-55	2-0
1896-97	1-1	1955-56	0-1
1897-98	0-0	1956-57	0-2
1898-99	0-4	1957-58	0-1
1899-1900	3-2	1958-59	2-2
1900-01	2-1	1959-60	0-1
1901-02	2-4	1960-61	1-5
1902-03	1-1	1961-62	1-1
1903-04	2-2	1962-63	0-1
1904-05	2-2	1963-64	0-1
1905-06	1-0	1964-65	3-1
1906-07	2-1	1965-66	5-1
1907-08	2-1	1966-67	2-0
1908-09	2-3	1967-68	2-2
1909-10	1-1	1968-69	2-4
1910-11	0-1	1969-70	0-0
1911-12	3-0	1970-71	2-0
1912-13	3-2	1971-72	2-1
1913-14	4-0	1972-73	3-1
1914-15	2-1	1973-74	1-0
1915-16	2-2	1974-75	1-2
1916-17	0-0	1975-76	1-1
1917-18	0-0		0-0
1918-19	0-3	1976-77	2-2
1919-20	1-1		1-0
1920-21	1-2	1977-78	1-1
1921-22	0-0		2-0
1922-23	1-3	1978-79	3-1
1923-24	2-2		4-2
1924-25	0-1	1979-80	1-0
1925-26	2-2		1-0
1926-27	0-1	1980-81	1-2
1927-28	1-0		3-1
1928-29	1-2	1981-82	3-3
1929-30	1-2		2-1
1930-31	2-0	1982-83	3-2
1931-32	1-2		0-0
1932-33	1-1	1983-84	2-1
1933-34	2-2		3-0
1934-35	1-1	1984-85	1-1
1935-36	3-4		1-1
1936-37	1-1	1985-86	1-1
1937-38	3-0		2-0
1938-39	6-2	1986-87	1-1
1946-47	2-3		3-1
1947-48	0-4	1987-88	1-0
1948-49	0-1		2-0

Dundee v Dundee United

Dundee were founded in 1893 while Dundee United were formed in 1909 as Dundee

Hibernians; they became known as Dundee United in 1923.

The 78 League meetings between the two clubs have resulted in Dundee United winning 38 times to Dundee's 25 with 15 drawn matches.

Season	Score	Season	Score
1921-22	0-2	1960-61	1-2
1922-23	2-2	1961-62	4-2
1923-24	1-1	1962-63	3-3
1924-25	2-0	1963-64	4-2
1925-26	1-4	1964-65	0-1
1926-27	2-2	1965-66	0-4
1927-28	2-2	1966-67	0-0
1928-29	1-1	1967-68	1-4
1929-30	1-1	1968-69	0-0
1930-31	4-1	1969-70	0-2
1933-34	0-0	1970-71	0-0
1934-35	5-2	1971-72	0-2
1935-36	8-3	1972-73	0-7
1936-37	3-2	1973-74	4-1
1937-38	3-2	1974-75	0-0
1938-39	0-1	1975-76	1-1
1946-47	2-3		0-1
1947-48	2-1	1976-77	0-1
1948-49	3-2		2-2
1949-50	5-2	1978-79	1-1
1950-51	2-1		1-2
1951-52	1-1	1983-84	3-2
1952-53	1-2		1-1
1953-54	4-0	1984-85	0-0
1954-55	5-1		2-2
1955-56	0-1	1985-86	2-1
1956-57	0-2		3-1
1957-58	3-1	1986-87	1-1
1958-59	1-3		2-1
1959-60	2-2	1987-88	1-0
			0-0

League results at Dens Park (Dundee's score first)

Season	Score	Season	Score
1925-26	0-0	1974-75	2-0
1926-27	5-0	1975-76	0-0
1929-30	1-0		2-1
1931-32	1-1	1979-80	1-0
1938-39	2-0		1-1
1946-47	2-0	1981-82	1-3
1960-61	3-0		0-2
1961-62	4-1	1982-83	0-2
1962-63	1-2		1-2
1963-64	1-1	1983-84	1-4
1964-65	2-4		2-5
1965-66	0-5	1984-85	0-2
1966-67	2-3		1-0
1967-68	2-2	1985-86	0-3
1968-69	1-2		0-1
1969-70	1-2	1986-87	0-2
1970-71	2-3		1-1
1971-72	6-4	1987-88	1-1
1972-73	3-0		0-2
1973-74	0-1		

League results at Tannadice Park (Dundee United's score first)

Season	Score	Season	Score
1925-26	0-1	1974-75	3-0
1926-27	1-0	1975-76	1-2
1929-30	0-1		1-0
1931-32	0-3	1979-80	3-0
1938-39	3-0		2-0
1946-47	1-2	1981-82	5-2
1960-61	3-1		1-1
1961-62	1-2	1982-83	1-0
1962-63	1-1		5-3
1963-64	2-1	1983-84	0-1
1964-65	1-4		1-1
1965-66	2-1	1984-85	3-4
1966-67	1-4		4-0
1967-68	0-0	1985-86	2-0
1968-69	3-1		0-0
1969-70	4-1	1986-87	0-3
1970-71	3-2		1-1
1971-72	1-1	1987-88	1-3
1972-73	2-1		1-0
1973-74	1-2		

Capital clashes – Heart of Midlothian v Hibernian

Heart of Midlothian were founded in 1874 and Hibernian in 1875. The two clubs have played each other 174 times in the League; Hearts have won 75 matches, Hibs 50 and 49 have been drawn.

League results at Tynecastle (Hearts' score first)

Season	Score	Season	Score
1895-96	4-3	1908-09	1-1
1896-97	1-0	1909-10	1-0
1897-98	3-2	1910-11	2-0
1898-99	4-0	1911-12	3-0
1899-1900	1-3	1912-13	1-0
1900-01	0-3	1913-14	3-1
1901-02	2-1	1914-15	3-1
1902-03	1-1	1915-16	1-3
1903-04	2-0	1916-17	2-1
1904-05	1-0	1917-18	1-0
1905-06	1-0	1918-19	3-1
1906-07	4-1	1919-20	1-3
1907-08	1-2	1920-21	5-1

League results at Easter Road (Hibs' score first)

Season	Score	Season	Score
1895-96	3-2	1948-49	3-1
1896-97	2-0	1949-50	1-2
1897-98	1-1	1950-51	0-1
1898-99	5-1	1951-52	2-3
1899-1900	1-0	1952-53	3-1
1900-01	0-0	1953-54	1-2
1901-02	1-2	1954-55	2-3
1902-03	0-0	1955-56	2-2
1903-04	4-2	1956-57	2-3
1904-05	3-0	1957-58	0-2
1905-06	0-3	1958-59	0-4
1906-07	0-0	1959-60	1-5
1907-08	2-3	1960-61	1-4
1908-09	0-1	1961-62	1-4
1909-10	1-4	1962-63	0-4
1910-11	1-0	1963-64	1-1
1911-12	0-4	1964-65	3-5
1912-13	0-3	1965-66	2-3
1913-14	1-2	1966-67	3-1
1914-15	2-2	1967-68	1-0
1915-16	1-2	1968-69	1-3
1916-17	0-2	1969-70	0-0
1917-18	1-3	1970-71	0-0
1918-19	1-3	1971-72	0-0
1919-20	2-4	1972-73	2-0
1920-21	3-0	1973-74	3-1
1921-22	2-1	1974-75	2-1
1922-23	2-1	1975-76	3-0
1923-24	1-1		1-0
1924-25	2-1	1976-77	3-1
1925-26	0-0		1-1
1926-27	2-2	1978-79	1-1
1927-28	2-1		1-2
1928-20	1-0	1983-84	1-1
1929-30	1-1		0-0
1930-31	2-2	1984-85	1-2
1933-34	1-4		1-2
1934-35	1-0	1985-86	0-0
1935-36	1-1		1-2
1936-37	3-3	1986-87	1-3
1937-38	2-2		2-2
1938-39	4-0	1987-88	2-1
1946-47	0-1		0-0
1947-48	3-1		

Teams who have scored eight or more goals in post-war Football League matches

Season	Match				Other 10-goal games not shown on left			
1946-47	Newcastle United	13	Newport County	0	Liverpool	7	Chelsea	4
	Reading	10	Crystal Palace	2	Wolverhampton W	6	Chelsea	4
	Bristol City	9	Aldershot	0				
	Doncaster Rovers	9	Carlisle United	2				
	Doncaster Rovers	8	Barrow	0				
	Accrington Stanley	8	Lincoln City	4				
	Northampton Town	0	Walsall	8				
	Rotherham United	8	Oldham Athletic	0				
1947-48	Arsenal	8	Grimsby Town	0	Preston North End	7	Derby County	4
	Wolverhampton W	8	Grimsby Town	1	Port Vale	6	Aldershot	4
1948-49	Notts County	11	Newport County	1	Walsall	5	Millwall	6
	Notts County	9	Exeter City	0				
	Notts County	9	Ipswich Town	2				
	Brentford	8	Bury	2				
	Carlisle United	1	Rotherham United	8				
1949-50					Newport County	6	Bristol City	4
1950-51	Gillingham	9	Exeter City	4	Derby County	6	Sunderland	5
	Nottingham Forest	9	Gillingham	2	Middlesbrough	7	Charlton Athletic	3
	Brighton & Hove Albion	9	Newport County	1				
	Lincoln City	9	Accrington Stanley	1				
	Middlesbrough	8	Huddersfield Town	0				
	Southend United	8	Swindon	2				
1951-52	Oldham Athletic	11	Chester	2	Sheffield United	7	Sheffield Wednesday	3
	Lincoln City	11	Crewe Alexandra	1	Leicester City	5	Sheffield United	5
	Torquay United	9	Swindon Town	0				
	Bury	8	Southampton	2				
	Grimsby Town	8	Halifax Town	1				
	Norwich City	8	Walsall	0				
1952-53	Blackpool	8	Charlton Athletic	4	Wolverhampton W	7	Manchester City	3
	Huddersfield Town	8	Everton	2	Fulham	4	Leicester City	6
	Carlisle United	8	Scunthorpe United	0	Nottingham Forest	6	Swansea City	4
	Shrewsbury Town	1	Norwich City	8	Bolton Wanderers	4	Arsenal	6
1953-54	Leicester City	9	Lincoln City	2	Newcastle United	3	West Bromwich Albion	7
	Lincoln City	8	Blackburn Rovers	0	Bradford City	6	Accrington Stanley	4
	Everton	8	Plymouth Argyle	4	Shrewsbury	6	Watford	4
	Charlton Athletic	8	Middlesbrough	1				
	Wolverhampton W	8	Chelsea	1				
	Hull	8	Oldham Athletic	0				
	Wrexham	8	Workington	0				
1954-55	Birmingham City	9	Liverpool	1	Chelsea	5	Manchester United	6
	Blackburn Rovers	9	Middlesbrough	0	Luton Town	7	Blackburn Rovers	3
	Blackburn Rovers	8	Bristol Rovers	3	West Bromwich Albion	6	Leicester City	4
					Chesterfield	3	Stockport County	7
					Southampton	6	Brentford	4
					Wolverhampton W	6	Huddersfield Town	4
1955-56	Cardiff City	1	Wolverhampton W	9	Blackpool	7	Sunderland	3
	Leyton Orient	8	Aldershot	3	Blackburn Rovers	4	Bristol City	6
	Leyton Orient	8	Crystal Palace	0				
	Luton Town	8	Sunderland	2				
	Chesterfield	8	Crewe Alexandra	0				
	Stockport County	8	Carlisle United	1				
1956-57	York City	9	Southport	1	Wolverhampton W	7	Charlton Athletic	3
	Sunderland	8	Charlton Athletic	1	Arsenal	7	Manchester City	3
	Stoke City	8	Lincoln City	0	Fulham	7	Swansea City	3
					Mansfield Town	7	Darlington	3
					Shrewsbury Town	7	Swindon Town	3
					Crewe Alexandra	6	Mansfield Town	4
					Wrexham	6	Carlisle United	4

Season	Match				Other 10-goal games not shown on left			
1957–58	West Bromwich Albion	9	Manchester City	2	Charlton Athletic	7	Huddersfield Town	6
	Chester	9	York City	2	Chelsea	7	Portsmouth	4
	Northampton Town	9	Exeter City	0	Burnley	7	Leicester City	3
	Hull	9	Oldham Athletic	0	Southampton	7	Norwich City	3
	Leicester City	8	Manchester City	4	Mansfield Town	6	Bury	4
	Bury	8	Tranmere Rovers	2	Swansea City	6	Bristol Rovers	4
	Preston North End	8	Birmingham City	0				
	West Ham United	8	Rotherham United	0				
1958–59	Tottenham Hotspur	10	Everton	4	Bristol Rovers	7	Grimsby Town	3
	Hartlepools United	10	Barrow	1	Chelsea	6	Newcastle United	5
	Middlesbrough	9	Brighton & Hove Albion	0	Barnsley	4	Bristol City	7
	Tranmere Rovers	9	Accrington Stanley	0	Brighton & Hove Albion	4	Middlesbrough	6
	Plymouth Argyle	8	Mansfield Town	3	Doncaster Rovers	4	Plymouth Argyle	6
	Colchester United	8	Stockport County	2				
	Aldershot	8	Gateshead	1				
	Port Vale	8	Gateshead	0				
1959–60	Aston Villa	11	Charlton Athletic	1	Newcastle United	7	Manchester United	3
	Wolverhampton W	9	Fulham	0	Manchester City	4	Wolverhampton W	6
	Crystal Palace	9	Barrow	0	Plymouth Argyle	6	Charlton Athletic	4
	Crystal Palace	8	Watford	1				
	Newcastle United	8	Everton	2				
	Burnley	8	Nottingham Forest	0				
	Northampton Town	8	Oldham Athletic	1				
	Walsall	8	Southport	0				
1960–61	Stoke City	9	Plymouth Argyle	0	Charlton Athletic	6	Middlesbrough	6
	Queen's Park Rangers	9	Tranmere Rovers	2	Charlton Athletic	7	Portsmouth	4
	Crystal Palace	9	Accrington Stanley	2	Charlton Athletic	6	Plymouth	4
					Plymouth Argyle	6	Charlton Athletic	4
					Newcastle United	5	West Ham United	5
1961–62	Wrexham	10	Hartlepools United	1	Barnsley	7	Bristol City	3
	Colchester United	9	Bradford City	1	Southampton	6	Scunthorpe United	4
	Aston Villa	8	Leicester City	3				
	Everton	8	Cardiff City	3				
	Notts County	8	Newport County	1				
1962–63	Oldham Athletic	11	Southport	0	Blackburn Rovers	5	Arsenal	5
	Tottenham Hotspur	9	Nottingham Forest	2				
	Wolverhampton W	8	Manchester City	1				
1963–64	Fulham	10	Ipswich Town	1	Southampton	6	Derby County	4
	Stoke City	9	Ipswich Town	1				
	West Ham United	2	Blackburn Rovers	8				
	Doncaster Rovers	10	Darlington	0				
	Brentford	9	Wrexham	0				
	Torquay United	8	Newport County	3				
	Aldershot	8	Barrow	2				
	Manchester City	8	Scunthorpe United	1				
	Coventry City	8	Shrewsbury Town	1				
1964–65	Mansfield Town	8	Queen's Park Rangers	1	Birmingham City	5	Blackburn	5
	Scunthorpe United	8	Luton Town	1	Tottenham Hotspur	7	Wolverhampton W	4
					Oldham Athletic	7	Bristol City	3
1965–66	Southampton	9	Wolverhampton W	3	Tottenham Hotspur	5	Aston Villa	5
	Preston North End	9	Cardiff City	0	Birmingham City	5	Derby County	5
	Brighton & Hove Albion	9	Southend United	1	Rotherham United	6	Cardiff City	4
					Brighton & Hove Albion	6	Mansfield Town	4
1966–67	Lincoln City	8	Luton Town	1	Chelsea	5	West Ham United	5
					Doncaster Rovers	4	Mansfield Town	6
1967–68	West Bromwich Albion	8	Burnley	1				
1968–69	Manchester United	8	Queen's Park Rangers	1				
	West Ham United	8	Sunderland	0				
1969–70	Bradford City	8	Bournemouth	1	Bolton Wanderers	6	Queen's Park Rangers	4
	Preston North End	8	Oldham Athletic	1				
	Halifax Town	0	Fulham	8				
	Reading	8	Southport	0				
1970–71					Shrewsbury Town	7	Port Vale	3
					Brentford	6	York City	4
1971–72	Everton	8	Southmpton	0				
1972–73	Chester	8	Peterborough United	2				

Season	Match				Other 10-goal games not shown on left			
1973–74	Brighton & Hove Albion	2	Bristol Rovers	8				
	Crewe Alexandra	1	Rotherham United	8				
1974–75					Shrewsbury Town	7	Doncaster Rovers	4
					Bournemouth	3	Plymouth Argyle	7
1976–77	Derby County	8	Tottenham Hotspur	2				
1977–78	Tottenham Hotspur	9	Bristol Rovers	0	Crewe Alexandra	4	Brentford	6
	Swansea City	8	Hartlepool United	0				
1978–79					Bristol Rovers	5	Charlton Athletic	5
1979–80	Swindon Town	8	Bury	0	Orient	3	Chelsea	7
1980–81	Lincoln City	8	Northampton Town	0				
1981–82					Southampton	5	Coventry City	5
					Sheffield United	7	Northampton Town	3
1982–83	Watford	8	Sunderland	0	Doncaster Rovers	7	Reading	5
					Aldershot	6	Rochdale	4
1983–84	Southampton	8	Coventry City	2				
	Bolton Wanderers	8	Walsall	1				
1984–85					Queen's Park Rangers	5	Newcastle United	5
					Plymouth Argyle	6	Preston North End	4
1985–86	West Ham United	8	Newcastle United	1				
1987–88	Manchester City	10	Huddersfield Town	1	Luton Town	7	Oxford United	4
	Gillingham	10	Chesterfield	0				

Football League goalscorers

Division 1 from 1888–89, other divisions since 1919–20 because of the difficulty in checking accuracy of earlier scorers.

1888–1915

Season	Leading scorer	Team	Goals
1888–89	John Goodall	Preston North End	21
1889–90	Jimmy Ross	Preston North End	24
1890–91	Jack Southworth	Blackburn Rovers	26
1891–92	John Campbell	Sunderland	32
1892–93	John Campbell	Sunderland	31
1893–94	Jack Southworth	Everton	27
1894–95	John Campbell	Sunderland	22
1895–96	Steve Bloomer	Derby County	22
1896–97	Steve Bloomer	Derby County	24
1897–98	Fred Wheldon	Aston Villa	21
1898–99	Steve Bloomer	Derby County	24
1899–1900	Bill Garratt	Aston Villa	27
1900–01	Steve Bloomer	Derby County	24
1901–02	James Settle	Everton	18
1901–02	Fred Priest	Sheffield United	18
1902–03	Alec Raybould	Liverpool	31
1903–04	Steve Bloomer	Derby County	20
1904–05	Arthur Brown	Sheffield United	23
1905–06	Bullet Jones	Birmingham City	26
1905–06	Albert Shepherd	Bolton Wanderers	26
1906–07	Alec Young	Everton	28
1907–08	Enoch West	Nottingham Forest	27
1908–09	Bert Freeman	Everton	36
1909–10	John Parkinson	Liverpool	30
1910–11	Albert Shepherd	Newcastle United	25
1911–12	Harold Hampton	Aston Villa	25
1911–12	Dave McLean	Sheffield Wednesday	25
1911–12	George Holley	Sunderland	35
1912–13	David McLean	Sheffield Wednesday	30
1913–14	George Elliot	Middlesbrough	31
1914–15	Bobby Parker	Everton	36

Division 1 1919–39

Season	Leading scorer	Team	Goals
1919–20	Fred Morris	West Bromwich Albion	37
1920–21	Joe Smith	Bolton Wanderers	38
1921–22	Andy Wilson	Middlesbrough	31
1922–23	Charlie Buchan	Sunderland	30
1923–24	Wilf Chadwick	Everton	28
1924–25	Fred Roberts	Manchester City	31
1925–26	Ted Harper	Blackburn Rovers	43
1926–27	Jimmy Trotter	Sheffield Wednesday	37
1927–28	Dixie Dean	Everton	60
1928–29	Dave Halliday	Sunderland	43
1929–30	Vic Watson	West Ham United	42
1930–31	Pongo Waring	Aston Villa	49
1931–32	Dixie Dean	Everton	45
1932–33	Jack Bowers	Derby County	35
1933–34	Jack Bowers	Derby County	34
1934–35	Ted Drake	Arsenal	42
1935–36	Ginger Richardson	West Bromwich Albion	39
1936–37	Freddie Steele	Stoke City	33
1937–38	Tommy Lawton	Everton	28
1938–39	Tommy Lawton	Everton	34

Division 1 1946–88

Season	Leading scorer	Team	Goals
1946–47	Dennis Westcott	Wolverhampton Wanderers	38
1947–48	Ronnie Rooke	Arsenal	33
1948–49	Willie Moir	Bolton Wanderers	25
1949–50	Dickie Davis	Sunderland	25
1950–51	Stan Mortensen	Blackpool	30
1951–52	George Robledo	Newcastle United	33

Season	Leading scorer	Team	Goals
1952-53	Charlie Wayman	Preston North End	24
1953-54	Jimmy Glazzard	Huddersfield Town	29
1953-54	Johnny Nicholls	West Bromwich Albion	28
1954-55	Ronnie Allen	West Bromwich Albion	27
1955-56	Nat Lofthouse	Bolton Wanderers	33
1956-57	John Charles	Leeds United	38
1957-58	Bobby Smith	Tottenham Hotspur	36
1958-59	Jimmy Greaves	Chelsea	32
1959-60	Dennis Viollet	Manchester United	32
1960-61	Jimmy Greaves	Chelsea	41
1961-62	Ray Crawford	Ipswich Town	33
1961-62	Derek Kevan	West Bromwich Albion	33
1962-63	Jimmy Greaves	Tottenham Hotspur	37
1963-64	Jimmy Greaves	Tottenham Hotspur	35
1964-65	Jimmy Greaves	Tottenham Hotspur	29
1964-65	Andy McEvoy	Blackburn Rovers	29
1965-66	Roger Hunt	Liverpool	30
1966-67	Ron Davies	Southampton	37
1967-68	George Best	Manchester United	28
1967-68	Ron Davies	Southampton	28
1968-69	Jimmy Greaves	Tottenham Hotspur	27
1969-70	Jeff Astle	West Bromwich Albion	25
1970-71	Tony Brown	West Bromwich Albion	28
1971-72	Francis Lee	Manchester City	33
1972-73	Bryan Robson	West Ham United	28
1973-74	Mick Channon	Southampton	21
1974-75	Malcolm Macdonald	Newcastle United	21
1975-76	Ted MacDougall	Norwich City	23
1976-77	Malcolm Macdonald	Arsenal	25
1976-77	Andy Gray	Aston Villa	25
1977-78	Bob Latchford	Everton	30
1978-79	Frank Worthington	Bolton Wanderers	24
1979-80	Phil Boyer	Southampton	23
1980-81	Steve Archibald	Tottenham Hotspur	20
1980-81	Peter Withe	Aston Villa	20
1981-82	Kevin Keegan	Southampton	26
1982-83	Luther Blissett	Watford	27
1983-84	Ian Rush	Liverpool	32
1984-85	Kerry Dixon	Chelsea	24
1984-85	Gary Lineker	Leicester City	24
1985-86	Gary Lineker	Everton	30
1986-87	Clive Allen	Tottenham Hotspur	33
1987-88	John Aldridge	Liverpool	26

Division 2 1919-39

Season	Leading scorer	Team	Goals
1919-20	Sam Taylor	Huddersfield Town	35
1920-21	Syd Puddefoot	West Ham United	29
1921-22	Jimmy Broad	Stoke City	25
1922-23	Harry Bedford	Blackpool	32
1923-24	Harry Bedford	Blackpool	34
1924-25	Arthur Chandler	Leicester City	33
1925-26	Bob Turnbull	Chelsea	39
1926-27	George Camsell	Middlesbrough	59
1927-28	Jimmy Cookson	West Bromwich Albion	38
1928-29	Jimmy Hampson	Blackpool	40
1929-30	Jimmy Hampson	Blackpool	45
1930-31	Dixie Dean	Everton	39
1931-32	Cyril Pearce	Swansea Town	35
1932-33	Ted Harper	Preston North End	37
1933-34	Pat Glover	Grimsby Town	42
1934-35	Jack Milsom	Bolton Wanderers	31
1935-36	Jack Dodds	Sheffield United	34
1935-36	Bob Finan	Blackpool	34
1936-37	Jack Bowers	Leicester City	33
1937-38	George Henson	Bradford Park Avenue	27
1938-39	Hugh Billington	Luton Town	28

Division 2 1946-88

Season	Leading scorer	Team	Goals
1946-47	Charlie Waymen	Newcastle United	30
1947-48	Eddie Quigley	Sheffield Wednesday	22

Steve Bloomer who regularly featured as Derby County's leading scorer.

Kevin Keegan who was Liverpool's capture from Scunthorpe United, but Southampton's top scorer in 1981-82.

Season	Leading scorer	Team	Goals
1948-49	Charlie Wayman	Southampton	32
1949-50	Tommy Briggs	Grimsby Town	35
1950-51	Cecil McCormack	Barnsley	33
1951-52	Derek Dooley	Sheffield Wednesday	46
1952-53	Arthur Rowley	Leicester City	39
1953-54	John Charles	Leeds United	42
1954-55	Tommy Briggs	Blackburn Rovers	33
1955-56	Bill Gardiner	Leicester City	34
1956-57	Arthur Rowley	Leicester City	44
1957-58	Tom Johnston	Leyton Orient (35) and Blackburn Rovers (8)	43
1958-59	Brian Clough	Middlesbrough	42
1959-60	Brian Clough	Middlesbrough	39
1960-61	Ray Crawford	Ipswich Town	39
1961-62	Roger Hunt	Liverpool	41
1961-62	Barrie Thomas	Scunthorpe United (31) and Newcastle United (10)	41
1962-63	Bobby Tambling	Chelsea	35
1963-64	Ron Saunders	Portsmouth	33
1964-65	George O'Brien	Southampton	32
1965-66	Martin Chivers	Southampton	30
1966-67	Bobby Gould	Coventry City	24
1967-68	John Hickton	Middlesbrough	24
1968-69	John Toshack	Cardiff City	22
1969-70	John Hickton	Middlesbrough	24
1970-71	John Hickton	Middlesbrough	25
1971-72	Bob Latchford	Birmingham City	23
1972-73	Don Givens	Queen's Park Rangers	23
1973-74	Duncan McKenzie	Nottingham Forest	26
1974-75	Brian Little	Aston Villa	20
1975-76	Derek Hales	Charlton Athletic	28
1976-77	Mickey Walsh	Blackpool	26
1977-78	Bob Hatton	Blackpool	22
1978-79	Bryan Robson	West Ham United	24
1979-80	Clive Allen	Queen's Park Rangers	28
1980-81	David Cross	West Ham United	22
1981-82	Ronnie Moore	Rotherham United	22
1982-83	Gary Lineker	Leicester City	26
1983-84	Kerry Dixon	Chelsea	28
1984-85	John Aldridge	Oxford United	30
1985-86	Kevin Drinkell	Norwich City	22
1986-87	Mike Quinn	Portsmouth	22
1987-88	Mark Bright	Crystal Palace	25

Division 3 (South) 1920-39

Season	Leading scorer	Team	Goals
1920-21	John Connor	Crystal Palace	28
1920-21	Ernie Simms	Luton Town	28
1920-21	George Whitworth	Northampton Town	28
1921-22	Frank Richardson	Plymouth Argyle	31
1922-23	Fred Pagnam	Watford	30
1923-24	Billy Haines	Portsmouth	28
1924-25	Jack Fowler	Swansea Town	28
1925-26	Jack Cock	Plymouth Argyle	32
1926-27	Harry Morris	Swindon Town	47
1927-28	Harry Morris	Swindon Town	38
1928-29	Andrew Rennie	Luton Town	43
1929-30	George Goddard	Queen's Park Rangers	37
1930-31	Peter Simpson	Crystal Palace	46
1931-32	Clarrie Bourton	Coventry City	49
1932-33	Clarrie Bourton	Coventry City	40
1933-34	Albert Dawes	Northampton Town (11) and Crystal Palace (16)	27
1934-35	Ralph Allen	Charlton Athletic	32
1935-36	Albert Dawes	Crystal Palace	38
1936-37	Joe Payne	Luton Town	55
1937-38	Harry Crawshaw	Mansfield Town	25
1938-39	Ben Morton	Swindon Town	28

Division 3 (South) 1946-58

Season	Leading scorer	Team	Goals
1946-47	Don Clark	Bristol City	36
1947-48	Len Townsend	Bristol City	31
1948-49	Don McGibbon	Bournemouth	30
1949-50	Tommy Lawton	Notts County	31
1950-51	Wally Ardron	Nottingham Forest	35
1951-52	Ronnie Blackman	Reading	39
1952-53	Geoff Bradford	Bristol Rovers	33
1953-54	Jack English	Northampton Town	28
1954-55	Ernie Morgan	Gillingham	31
1955-56	Sammy Collins	Torquay United	40
1956-57	Ted Phillips	Ipswich Town	41
1957-58	Sam McCrory	Southend United	31
1957-58	Derek Reeves	Southampton	31

Division 3 (North) 1921-39

Season	Leading scorer	Team	Goals
1921-22	Jim Carmichael	Grimsby Town	37
1922-23	George Beel	Chesterfield	23
1922-23	Jim Carmichael	Grimsby Town	23
1923-24	David Brown	Darlington	27
1924-25	David Brown	Darlington	39
1925-26	Jimmy Cookson	Chesterfield	44
1926-27	Albert Whitehurst	Rochdale	44
1927-28	Joe Smith	Stockport County	38
1928-29	Jimmy McConnell	Carlisle United	43
1929-30	Frank Newton	Stockport County	36
1930-31	Jimmy McConnell	Carlisle United	37
1931-32	Alan Hall	Lincoln City	42
1932-33	Bill McNaughton	Hull City	39
1933-34	Alf Lythgoe	Stockport County	46
1934-35	Gilbert Alsop	Walsall	40
1935-36	Bunny Bell	Tranmere Rovers	33
1936-37	Ted Harston	Mansfield Town	55
1937-38	John Roberts	Port Vale	28
1938-39	Sam Hunt	Carlisle United	32

Division 3 (North) 1946–58

Season	Leading scorer	Team	Goals
1946–47	Clarrie Jordan	Doncaster Rovers	42
1947–48	Jimmy Hutchinson	Lincoln City	32
1948–49	Wally Ardron	Rotherham United	29
1949–50	Peter Doherty	Doncaster Rovers	26
1949–50	Reg Phillips	Crewe Alexandra	26
1950–51	Jack Shaw	Rotherham United	37
1951–52	Andy Graver	Lincoln City	36
1952–53	Jimmy Whitehouse	Carlisle United	29
1953–54	Jack Connor	Stockport County	31
1954–55	Jack Connor	Stockport County	30
1954–55	Arthur Bottom	York City	30
1954–55	Don Travis	Oldham Athletic	30
1955–56	Bob Crosbie	Grimsby Town	36
1956–57	Ray Straw	Derby County	37
1957–58	Alf Ackerman	Carlisle United	35

Division 3 1958–88

Season	Leading scorer	Team	Goals
1958–59	Jim Towers	Brentford	32
1959–60	Derek Reeves	Southampton	39
1960–61	Tony Richards	Walsall	36
1961–62	Cliff Holton	Northampton Town (36) and Walsall (1)	37
1962–63	George Hudson	Coventry City	30
1963–64	Alf Biggs	Bristol Rovers	30
1964–65	Ken Wagstaff	Mansfield Town (8) and Hull City (23)	31
1965–66	Les Allen	Queen's Park Rangers	30
1966–67	Rodney Marsh	Queen's Park Rangers	30
1967–68	Don Rogers	Swindon Town	25
1967–68	Bobby Owen	Bury	25
1968–69	Brian Lewis	Luton Town	22
1968–69	Don Rogers	Swindon Town	22
1969–70	George Jones	Bury	26
1970–71	Gerry Ingram	Preston North End	22
1970–71	Dudley Roberts	Mansfield Town	22
1971–72	Ted MacDougall	Bournemouth	35
1971–72	Alf Wood	Shrewsbury Town	35
1972–73	Bruce Bannister	Bristol Rovers	25
1972–73	Arthur Horsfield	Charlton Athletic	25
1973–74	Billy Jennings	Watford	26
1974–75	Dixie McNeil	Hereford United	31
1975–76	Dixie McNeil	Hereford United	35
1976–77	Peter Ward	Brighton & Hove Albion	32
1977–78	Alex Bruce	Preston North End	27
1978–79	Ross Jenkins	Watford	29
1979–80	Terry Curran	Sheffield Wednesday	22
1980–81	Tony Kellow	Exeter City	25
1981–82	Gordon Davies	Fulham	24
1982–83	Kerry Dixon	Reading	26
1983–84	Keith Edwards	Sheffield United	33
1984–85	Tommy Tynan	Plymouth Argyle	31
1985–86	Trevor Senior	Reading	27
1986–87	Andy Jones	Port Vale	29
1987–88	Steve Lovell	Gillingham	25

Division 4 1958–88

Season	Leading scorer	Team	Goals
1958–59	Arthur Rowley	Shrewsbury Town	37
1959–60	Cliff Holton	Watford	42
1960–61	Terry Bly	Peterborough United	52
1961–62	Bobby Hunt	Colchester United	41
1962–63	Ken Wagstaff	Mansfield Town	34
1962–63	Colin Booth	Doncaster Rovers	34
1963–64	Hugh McIlmoyle	Carlisle United	39
1964–65	Alick Jeffrey	Doncaster Rovers	36
1965–66	Kevin Hector	Bradford Park Avenue	44
1966–67	Ernie Phythian	Hartlepools United	23
1967–68	Roy Chapman	Port Vale	25
1967–68	Les Massie	Halifax Town	25
1968–69	Gary Talbot	Chester	22
1969–70	Albert Kinsey	Wrexham	27
1970–71	Ted MacDougall	Bournemouth	42
1971–72	Peter Price	Peterborough United	28
1972–73	Fred Binney	Exeter City	28
1973–74	Brian Yeo	Gillingham	31
1974–75	Ray Clarke	Mansfield Town	28
1975–76	Ronnie Moore	Tranmere Rovers	34
1976–77	Brian Joicey	Barnsley	25
1977–78	Steve Phillips	Brentford	32
1977–78	Alan Curtis	Swansea City	32
1978–79	John Dungworth	Aldershot	26
1979–80	Colin Garwood	Portsmouth (17) and Aldershot (10)	27
1980–81	Alan Cork	Wimbledon	23
1981–82	Keith Edwards	Sheffield United (35) and Hull City (1)	36
1982–83	Steve Cammack	Scunthorpe United	25
1983–84	Trevor Senior	Reading	36
1984–85	John Clayton	Tranmere Rovers	31
1985–86	Richard Cadette	Southend United	25
1985–86	Steve Taylor	Rochdale	25
1986–87	Richard Hill	Northampton Town	29
1987–88	Steve Bull	Wolverhampton Wanderers	34

Leading goalscorer for each Football League Championship-winning team

Season	Player and team	Goals
1888–89	J. Goodall, Preston North End	21
1889–90	J. Ross, Preston North End	24
1890–91	F. Geary, Everton	20
1891–92	J. M. Campbell, Sunderland	32
1892–93	J. M. Campbell, Sunderland	31
1893–94	J. H. G. Devey, Aston Villa	21
1894–95	J. M. Campbell, Sunderland	25
1895–96	J. Campbell, Aston Villa	20
1896–97	G. F. Wheldon, Aston Villa	17
1897–98	W. Bennett, Sheffield United	12
1898–99	J. H. G. Devey, Aston Villa	22
1899–1900	W. Garratty, Aston Villa	27
1900–01	S. A. Raybould, Liverpool	16
1901–02	W. Hogg, Sunderland	10
1902–03	H. Davis, Sheffield Wednesday	13
1903–04	H. Chapman, Sheffield Wednesday	16
1904–05	W. Appleyard, Newcastle United	14
1905–06	J. Hewitt, Liverpool	23
1906–07	W. Appleyard, Newcastle United	17
1907–08	A. Turnbull, Manchester United	25
1908–09	A. Shepherd, Newcastle United	12
1909–10	H. Hampton, Aston Villa	26
1910–11	E. West, Manchester United	19
1911–12	W. Aitkenhead, Blackburn Rovers	16
1912–13	C. M. Buchan, Sunderland	27
1913–14	D. Shea, Blackburn Rovers	27
1914–15	R. N. Parker, Everton	36
1919–20	F. Morris, West Bromwich Albion	37

Graeme Sharp of Everton made his goalscoring mark in the Goodison Park's most recent championship success.

1920–21	J. Anderson, Burnley	25
1921–22	H. Chambers, Liverpool	19
1922–23	H. Chambers, Liverpool	22
1923–24	C. Wilson, Huddersfield Town	18
1924–25	C. Wilson, Huddersfield Town	24
1925–26	G. Brown, Huddersfield Town	35
1926–27	H. Gallacher, Newcastle United	36
1927–28	W. R. Dean, Everton	60
1928–29	J. D. W. Allen, Sheffield Wednesday	33
1929–30	J. D. W. Allen, Sheffield Wednesday	33
1930–31	J. Lambert, Arsenal	38
1931–32	W. R. Dean, Everton	45
1932–33	C. S. Bastin, Arsenal	33
1933–34	C. S. Bastin and E. R. Bowden, Arsenal	13
1934–35	E. J. Drake, Arsenal	42
1935–36	H. S. Carter, Sunderland	31
1936–37	P. D. Doherty, Manchester City	30
1937–38	E. J. Drake, Arsenal	17
1938–39	T. Lawton, Everton	34
1946–47	J. Balmer, Liverpool	24
1947–48	R. L. Rooke, Arsenal	33
1948–49	P. P. Harris, Portsmouth	17
1949–50	I. Clarke, Portsmouth	17
1950–51	W. E. Walters, Tottenham Hotspur	15
1951–52	J. F. Rowley, Manchester United	30
1952–53	D. Lishman, Arsenal	22
1953–54	J. Hancocks, Wolverhampton Wanderers	25
1954–55	R. T. F. Bentley, Chelsea	21
1955–56	T. Taylor, Manchester United	25
1956–57	W. Whelan, Manchester United	26
1957–58	J. Murray, Wolverhampton Wanderers	29
1958–59	J. Murray, Wolverhampton Wanderers	21
1959–60	J. Connelly, Burnley	20
1960–61	R. A. Smith, Tottenham Hotspur	28
1961–62	R. Crawford, Ipswich Town	33
1962–63	T. R. Vernon, Everton	24
1963–64	R. Hunt, Liverpool	31
1964–65	D. Law, Manchester United	28
1965–66	R. Hunt, Liverpool	30
1966–67	D. Law, Manchester United	23
1967–68	N. J. Young, Manchester City	19
1968–69	M. D. Jones, Leeds United	14
1969–70	J. Royle, Everton	23
1970–71	R. Kennedy, Arsenal	19
1971–72	A. Hinton, Derby County	15
1972–73	J. B. Toshack and J. K. Keegan, Liverpool	13
1973–74	M. D. Jones, Leeds United	14
1974–75	B. D. Rioch, Derby County	15
1975–76	J. B. Toshack, Liverpool	16
1976–77	J. K. Keegan, Liverpool	12
1977–78	P. Withe and J. M. Robertson, Nottingham Forest	12
1978–79	K. M. Dalglish, Liverpool	21
1979–80	D. E. Johnson, Liverpool	21
1980–81	P. Withe, Aston Villa	20
1981–82	I. J. Rush, Liverpool	17
1982–83	I. J. Rush, Liverpool	24
1983–84	I. J. Rush, Liverpool	32
1984–85	G. Sharp, Everton	21
1985–86	I. J. Rush, Liverpool	22
1986–87	T. Steven, Everton	14
1987–88	J. Aldridge, Liverpool	26

Highest aggregate goalscorers for each Football League club, in descending order

Goals	Player	Club	Years
349	Dixie Dean	Everton	1925–37
326	George Camsell	Middlesbrough	1925–39
314	John Atyeo	Bristol City	1951–66
298	Vic Watson	West Ham United	1920–35
292	Steve Bloomer	Derby County	1892–1906 1910–14
259	Arthur Chandler	Leicester City	1923–35
255	Nat Lofthouse	Bolton Wanderers	1946–61
249	Joe Bradford	Birmingham City	1920–35
247	Jimmy Hampson	Blackpool	1927–38
245	Geoff Bradford	Bristol Rovers	1949–64
245	Roger Hunt	Liverpool	1959–69
243	Gordon Turner	Luton Town	1949–64
220	Jimmy Greaves	Tottenham Hotspur	1961–70
218	Tony Brown	West Bromwich Albion	1963–79
216	Harry Morris	Swindon Town	1926–33
213	Harry Hampton	Aston Villa	1904–20
213	Billy Walker	Aston Villa	1919–34
209	Charlie Buchan	Sunderland	1911–25
205	Harry Johnson	Sheffield United	1919–30
204	Sammy Collins	Torquay United	1948–58
203	Ray Crawford	Ipswich Town	1958–63 1966–69
202	Ron Eyre	Bournemouth	1924–33
199	Andy Wilson	Sheffield Wednesday	1900–20
199	Grenville Morris	Nottingham Forest	1898–1913
199	Bobby Charlton	Manchester United	1956–73
195	Chris Chilton	Hull City	1960–71
194	Peter Harris	Portsmouth	1946–60
187	Tom Finney	Preston North End	1946–60
185	Mike Channon	Southampton	1966–77 1979–82
184	Tony Richards	Walsall	1954–63
184	Colin Taylor	Walsall	1958–63 1964–68 1969–73
182	Pat Glover	Grimsby Town	1930–39
180	Sammy Black	Plymouth Argyle	1924–38
180	Tom Keetley	Doncaster Rovers	1923–29
178	George Beel	Burnley	1923–32
177	Jackie Milburn	Newcastle United	1946–57
175	Tom Bamford	Wrexham	1928–34
172	George Goddard	Queen's Park Rangers	1926–34
171	Jack Howarth	Aldershot	1965–71 1972–77
171	Clarrie Bourton	Coventry City	1931–37
168	Peter Lorimer	Leeds United	1965–78 1984–86
166	Ivor Allchurch	Swansea City	1949–58 1965–68
164	Bobby Tambling	Chelsea	1958–70
164	Bill Hartill	Wolverhampton Wanderers	1928–35
161	Ernie Moss	Chesterfield	1969–76 1979–81 1984–86
158	Tommy Johnson	Manchester City	1919–30
158	Ronnie Blackman	Reading	1947–54
154	Peter Simpson	Crystal Palace	1930–36
154	Bedford Jezzard	Fulham	1948–56
154	Wilf Kirkham	Port Vale	1923–29 1931–33
153	Stuart Leary	Charlton Athletic	1953–62
153	Jim Towers	Brentford	1954–61
152	Arthur Rowley	Shrewsbury Town	1958–65
150	Cliff Bastin	Arsenal	1930–47
144	Andy Graver	Lincoln City	1950–55 1958–61
144	Tom Barnett	Watford	1928–39
142	George Brown	Huddersfield Town	1921–29
142	Jimmy Glazzard	Huddersfield Town	1946–56
142	Freddie Steele	Stoke City	1934–39
140	Tommy Briggs	Blackburn Rovers	1952–58
135	Brian Yeo	Gillingham	1963–75
135	Jack English	Northampton Town	1947–60
132	Jack Connor	Stockport County	1951–56
131	Martyn King	Colchester United	1959–65
131	Alan Cork	Wimbledon	1977–88
130	Gladstone Guest	Rotherham United	1946–56
129	Tony Kellow	Exeter City	1976–78 1980–83 1985–88
129	Ernest Dixon	Halifax Town	1922–30
127	Len Davies	Cardiff City	1921–29
126	Jimmy McConnell	Carlisle United	1928–32
126	Bert Swindells	Crewe Alexandra	1928–37
125	Les Bradd	Notts County	1967–78
125	Norman Wilkinson	York City	1954–66
124	Norman Bullock	Bury	1920–35

Nat Lofthouse (left) who set up Bolton Wanderers scoring record in the years after the Second World War and **Jackie Milburn** (right) the Newcastle United top scorer in the same era.

Cliff Holton who was Watford's ace marksman in 1959–60. **Charlie Buchan**, Sunderland's leading scorer in 1912–13 and a later star with Arsenal as well.

122	Ernest Hine	Barnsley	1921–26
			1934–38
122	Johnny Gavin	Norwich City	1946–54
			1955–58
122	Roy Hollis	Southend United	1953–60
122	Jim Hall	Peterborough United	1967–75
121	Tom Johnston	Orient	1956–58
			1959–61
121	Bobby Campbell	Bradford City	1981–84
			1984–86
119	Reg Jenkins	Rochdale	1964–73
113	Tommy Cook	Brighton & Hove Albion	1922–29
110	Eric Gemmell	Oldham Athletic	1947–54
110	Steve Cammack	Scunthorpe United	1979–81
			1981–86
104	Harry Johnson	Mansfield Town	1931–36
104	Bunny Bell	Tranmere Rovers	1931–36
99	Reg Parker	Newport County	1948–54
98	Ken Johnson	Hartlepool United	1949–64
90	Alan Walsh	Darlington	1978–84
85	Dixie McNeil	Hereford United	1974–77
83	Gary Talbot	Chester	1963–67
			1968–70

79	Derek Possee	Millwall	1967–73
74	Alan Biley	Cambridge United	1975–80
73	Graham Atkinson	Oxford United	1962–73
62	Peter Houghton	Wigan Athletic	1978–84
8	Stewart Mell	Scarborough	1987–88

Record aggregate goalscorers in League and Cup games in post-war matches

| 54 | Terry Bly, Peterborough United (52 League, 2 FA Cup) | 1960–61 |
| 52 | Steve Bull, Wolverhampton Wanderers (34 League, 12 Sherpa Van, 3 FA Cup, 3 Littlewoods Cup) | 1987–88 |

Cliff Bastin (below, left) who was Arsenal's goalscoring winger in the 1930s and **Ernie Moss** (below) who had three successful scoring spells with Chesterfield.

Players who, since the 1914–18 War, have scored as many as half of a team's **131**
Football League goals in a completed season

Player	Team	Division	Season	Goals	Out of
George Elliott	Middlesbrough	1	1919–20	31	61
Bob Blood	Port Vale	2	1919–20	24	42
Dave McLean	Bradford Park Avenue	1	1920–21	22	43
John McIntyre	Sheffield Wednesday	2	1920–21	27	48
Sid Puddefoot	West Ham United	2	1920–21	29	51
Jack Doran	Brighton & Hove Albion	3S	1920–21	22	42
Jack Doran	Brighton & Hove Albion	3S	1921–22	23	45
Jim Carmichael	Grimsby Town	3N	1921–22	37	72
Harry Bedford	Blackpool	2	1922–23	32	60
Fred Pagnam	Watford	3S	1922–23	30	57
Joe Bradford	Birmingham	1	1923–24	24	41
Tommy Roberts	Preston North End	1	1923–24	26	52
Hugh Davey	Bournemouth	3S	1923–24	20	40
Bertie Mills	Hull City	2	1924–25	25	50
Wilf Kirkham	Port Vale	2	1924–25	26	48
David Brown	Darlington	3N	1924–25	39	78
Tom Jennings	Leeds United	1	1926–27	35	69
Dixie Dean	Everton	1	1927–28	60	102
Tom Keetley	Doncaster Rovers	3N	1928–29	40	76
Jim McConnell	Carlisle United	3N	1928–29	43	86
Jimmy Dunne	Sheffield United	1	1930–31	41	78
Leopold Stevens	New Brighton	3N	1931–32	20	38
Ted Harper	Preston North End	2	1932–33	37	74
Jack Bowers	Derby County	1	1933–34	35	68
Albert Valentine	Halifax Town	3N	1935–36	29	57
Joe Payne	Luton Town	3S	1936–37	55	103
Ted Harston	Mansfield Town	3N	1936–37	55	91
John Charles	Leeds United	1	1956–57	38	72
Gordon Turner	Luton Town	1	1956–57	30	58
Colin Booth	Doncaster Rovers	4	1962–63	34	64
Ron Davies	Southampton	1	1966–67	37	74
Ted MacDougall	Bournemouth	4	1970–71	42	81

Note: Jack Doran, Irish international centre-forward, is the only player to have achieved this feat twice, and he did it in successive seasons.

Players scoring five goals or more in a Football League post-war match

Division 1

Player	For	Goals	Against	Home or Away	Date
J. McIntosh	Blackpool	5	Preston North End	away	1.5.48
E. R. Firmani	Charlton Athletic	5	Aston Villa	home	5.2.55
A. Stokes	Tottenham Hotspur	5	Birmingham City	home	18.9.57
R. Smith	Tottenham Hotspur	5	Aston Villa	home	29.3.58
J. Greaves	Chelsea	5	Wolverhampton Wanderers	home	30.8.58
P. Harris	Portsmouth	5	Aston Villa	home	3.9.58
J. Robson	Burnley	5	Nottingham Forest	home	21.11.59
J. Greaves	Chelsea	5	Preston North End	away	19.12.59
D. T. Kevan	West Bromwich Albion	5	Everton	home	19.3.60
J. Greaves	Chelsea	5	West Bromwich Albion	home	3.12.60
B. Dear	West Ham United	5	West Bromwich Albion	home	16.3.65
A. Lochhead	Burnley	5	Chelsea	home	24.4.65
R. Tambling	Chelsea	5	Aston Villa	away	17.9.66
G. Hurst	West Ham United	6	Sunderland	home	19.10.68
R. Davies	Derby County	5	Luton Town	home	29.3.75
A. Brazil	Ipswich Town	5	Southampton	home	16.2.82
I. Rush	Liverpool	5	Luton Town	home	29.10.83
T. Woodcock	Arsenal	5	Aston Villa	away	29.10.83

Division 2

Player	For	Goals	Against	Home or Away	Date
L. F. Shackleton	Newcastle United	6	Newport County	home	5.10.46
E. Quigley	Bury	5	Millwall	home	15.2.47
G. Smith	Manchester City	5	Newport County	home	14.6.47
J. Dailey	Sheffield Wednesday	5	Barnsley	home	6.9.47
C. Wayman	Southampton	5	Leicester City	home	23.10.48
P. McKennan	Brentford	5	Bury	home	19.2.49
C. McCormack	Barnsley	5	Luton Town	home	9.9.50
D. Dooley	Sheffield Wednesday	5	Notts County	home	3.11.51
T. J. Eglington	Everton	5	Doncaster Rovers	home	27.9.52
D. Hines	Leicester City	5	Lincoln City	home	21.11.53
J. Evans	Liverpool	5	Bristol Rovers	home	15.9.54
T. H. Briggs	Blackburn Rovers	7	Bristol Rovers	home	5.2.55
B. Jezzard	Fulham	5	Hull City	home	8.10.55

N. Coleman	Stoke City	7	Lincoln City	home	23.2.57
J. Summers	Charlton Athletic	5	Huddersfield	home	21.12.57
J. Hill	Fulham	5	Doncaster Rovers	away	15.3.58
B. Clough	Middlesbrough	5	Brighton & Hove Albion	home	23.8.58
G. Hitchens	Aston Villa	5	Charlton Athletic	home	14.11.59
J. Summers	Charlton Athletic	5	Portsmouth	home	1.10.60
W. Carter	Plymouth Argyle	5	Charlton Athletic	home	27.12.60
D. Sharkey	Sunderland	5	Norwich City	home	20.3.63
R. Pointer	Bury	5	Rotherham United	home	2.10.65
S. Garner	Blackburn Rovers	5	Derby County	home	10.9.83

Division 3 (Southern section)

Player	For	Goals	Against	Home or Away	Date
J. Devlin	Walsall	5	Torquay United	home	1.9.49
C. Mortimore	Aldershot	5	Leyton Orient	away	25.2.50
R. H. Blackman	Reading	5	Brighton & Hove Albion	home	11.11.50
R. W. Hollis	Norwich City	5	Walsall	home	29.12.51
R. H. Blackman	Reading	5	Southend United	home	14.4.52
A. Thorne	Brighton & Hove Albion	5	Watford	home	30.4.58

Division 3 (Northern section)

Player	For	Goals	Against	Home or Away	Date
A. Patrick	York City	5	Rotherham United	home	20.11.48
E. Passmore	Gateshead	5	Hartlepool United	away	5.9.49
A. Graver	Lincoln City	6	Crewe Alexandra	home	29.9.51
E. Gemmell	Oldham Athletic	7	Chester	home	19.1.52
J. T. Connor	Stockport County	5	Workington	home	8.11.52
J. E. Whitehouse	Carlisle United	5	Scunthorpe United	home	25.12.52
G. T. S. Stewart	Accrington Stanley	5	Gateshead	home	27.11.54
J. T. Connor	Stockport County	5	Carlisle United	home	7.4.56
J. Dailey	Rochdale	5	Hartlepools United	home	2.11.57
B. Jepson	Chester	5	York City	home	8.2.58

Division 3

Player	For	Goals	Against	Home or Away	Date
B. Thomas	Scunthorpe United	5	Luton Town	home	24.4.65
K. East	Swindon Town	5	Mansfield Town	home	20.11.65
S. Earle	Fulham	5	Halifax Town	away	16.9.69
A. Wood	Shrewsbury	5	Blackburn Rovers	home	2.10.71
T. Caldwell	Bolton Wanderers	5	Walsall	home	10.9.83
A. Jones	Port Vale	5	Newport County	home	4.5.87

Division 4

Player	For	Goals	Against	Home or Away	Date
R. Folland	Hartlepools United	5	Oldham Athletic	home	1.4.61
R. Lister	Oldham Athletic	6	Southport	home	26.12.62
R. Stubbs	Torquay United	5	Newport County	home	19.10.63
K. Hector	Bradford	5	Barnsley	home	20.11.65
D. Banton	Aldershot	5	Halifax Town	home	7.5.83

Football League post-war hat-tricks from three penalty-kicks

Player	For	Against	Date
George Milburn	Chesterfield	Sheffield Wednesday	June 1947
Charlie Mitten	Manchester United	Aston Villa	March 1950
Joe Willets	Hartlepools United	Darlington	March 1951
Ken Barnes	Manchester City	Everton	December 1957
Trevor Anderson	Swindon Town	Walsall	April 1976
Alan Slough	Peterborough	Chester	April 1978
Andy Blair	Sheffield Wednesday	Luton Town	November 1984

Players scoring hat-tricks in the Football League against their former clubs during the last 20 years

Player	For	Against	Date
Ivor Allchurch	Cardiff City	Swansea Town	April 1965
Barry Hutchinson	Darlington	Chesterfield	April 1966
Derek Dougan	Leicester City	Aston Villa	September 1966
Harry Burrows	Stoke City	Aston Villa	December 1966
Ray Smith	Wrexham	Southend United	October 1967
Terry Harkin	Shrewsbury Town	Southport	May 1969
John Fairbrother	Mansfield Town	Peterborough United	October 1972
Peter Noble	Burnley	Newcastle United	November 1974
Derek Hales	Charlton Athletic	Luton Town	September 1976
Malcolm Macdonald	Arsenal	Newcastle United	December 1976

*Edward Woods	Newport County	Scunthorpe United	October 1977
Phil Boyer	Southampton	Derby County	September 1979
David Kemp	Plymouth Argyle	Carlisle United	September 1980
Leighton James	Swansea City	Derby County	October 1980
Paul Goddard	West Ham United	Queen's Park Rangers	April 1981
Trevor Christie	Notts County	Leicester City	August 1983
Wayne Biggins	Burnley	Lincoln City	February 1984

* Woods had been on loan to Scunthorpe

Post-war instances of two Football League hat-tricks scored by a player against the same opponents in the same season

Player	For	Against	Division	Season
†L. F. Shackleton	Newcastle United	Newport County	2	1946–47
H. Billington	Luton Town	Brentford	2	1947–48
G. B. Sutherland	Leyton Orient	Ipswich Town	3S	1949–50
W. Ardron	Nottingham Forest	Gillingham	3S	1950–51
*J. Shaw	Rotherham United	New Brighton	3N	1950–51
E. Gemmell	Oldham Athletic	Chester	3N	1951–52
*G. A. Rowley	Leicester City	Fulham	2	1952–53
E. Carr	Bradford City	Carlisle United	3N	1952–53
W. J. Charles	Leeds United	Rotherham United	2	1953–54
†T. Briggs	Blackburn Rovers	Bristol Rovers	2	1954–55
W. Grant	Ipswich Town	Millwall	3S	1955–56
R. Dwight	Fulham	Swansea Town	2	1956–57
†N. Coleman	Stoke City	Lincoln City	2	1956–57
B. Clough	Middlesbrough	Brighton & Hove Albion	2	1958–59
B. Clough	Middlesbrough	Scunthorpe United	2	1958–59
J. Rogers	Coventry City	Aldershot	4	1958–59
B. Frear	Chesterfield	Southend United	3	1958–59
J. Greaves	Chelsea	Preston North End	1	1959–60
D. Viollet	Manchester United	Burnley	1	1960–61
T. Bly	Peterborough United	Exeter City	4	1960–61
P. Dobing	Manchester City	West Ham United	1	1961–62
K. Havenhand	Derby County	Bristol Rovers	2	1961–62
R. Saunders	Portsmouth	Leyton Orient	2	1963–64
C. Napier	Workington	Swansea Town	3	1965–66
†G. Hurst	West Ham United	Sunderland	1	1968–69

* Against his former club
† Two hat-tricks in one game

Post-war Football League matches in which players on both sides scored hat-tricks

(Home team given first)

Division	Player	For	Against	Date	Result
1	Fenton Steele	Middlesbrough Stoke City	Stoke City Middlesbrough	7.9.46	5–4
3N	Mercer Cheetham	Accrington Stanley Lincoln City	Lincoln City Accrington Stanley	31.5.47	8–4
3S	Allen Jones McNicol	Port Vale Port Vale Aldershot	Aldershot Aldershot Port Vale	6.9.47	6–4
2	Carter Milburn	Bury Newcastle United	Newcastle United Bury	18.10.47	3–5
2	Jezzard Allchurch, I.	Fulham Swansea Town	Swansea Town Fulham	19.4.54	4–3
1	O'Connell, S. Viollet	Chelsea Manchester United	Manchester United Chelsea	16.10.54	5–6
2	Chappell Atyeo	Barnsley Bristol City	Bristol City Barnsley	27.8.58	4–7
1	Smith Harris, J.	Tottenham Hotspur Everton	Everton Tottenham Hotspur	11.10.58	10–4
1	Thompson Greaves	Preston North End Chelsea	Chelsea Preston North End	19.12.59	4–5
2	Edwards Clough	Charlton Athletic Middlesbrough	Middlesbrough Charlton Athletic	22.10.60	6–6

(Home team given first)

Division	Player	For	Against	Date	Result
3	Bly Beesley	Coventry City Southend United	Southend United Coventry City	1.9.62	3-4
1	Keyworth Law	Leicester City Manchester United	Manchester United Leicester City	16.4.63	4-3
1	Kevan Lee	West Bromwich Albion Bolton Wanderers	Bolton Wanderers West Bromwich Albion	22.9.62	5-4
1	Jones Baker	Tottenham Hotspur Ipswich Town	Ipswich Town Tottenham Hotspur	4.4.64	6-3
3	McKinven Hamilton	Southend United Bristol Rovers	Bristol Rovers Southend United	24.10.64	6-3
3	Large Mabbutt	Northampton Town Bristol Rovers	Bristol Rovers Northampton Town	28.10.67	4-5
1	Francis MacDonald	Birmingham City Arsenal	Arsenal Birmingham City	18.1.77	3-3
4	Ingram Daniels	Bradford City Stockport County	Stockport County Bradford City	11.9.76	3-3
4	Cooke Houchen	Peterborough United Hartlepool United	Hartlepool United Peterborough United	27.2.82	4-4
3	Snodin, G. Dixon	Doncaster Reading	Reading Doncaster	25.9.82	7-5
3	White Neville	Gillingham Exeter City	Exeter City Gillingham	8.1.83	4-4

Players scoring three or more Division 1 hat-tricks in one post-war season

Six hat-tricks

Jimmy Greaves	Chelsea	1960-61

Four hat-tricks

Doug Lishman	Arsenal	1951-52
Jack Rowley	Manchester United	1951-52
Eddie Firmani	Charlton Athletic	1954-55
Alex Govan	Birmingham City	1956-57
Gordon Turner	Luton Town	1956-57
Bobby Smith	Tottenham Hotspur	1957-58
Jimmy Greaves	Tottenham Hotspur	1962-63
Andy McEvoy	Blackburn Rovers	1963-64
Fred Pickering	Blackburn Rovers and Everton	1963-64
Jimmy Greaves	Tottenham Hotspur	1963-64

Three hat-tricks

Jack Balmer	Liverpool	1946-47
Freddie Steele	Stoke City	1946-47
Jack Rowley	Manchester United	1947-48
Willie Moir	Bolton Wanderers	1948-49
Doug Reid	Portsmouth	1949-50
Jack Lee	Derby County	1950-51
Alex McCrae	Middlesbrough	1950-51
Nat Lofthouse	Bolton Wanderers	1952-53
Ronnie Allen	West Bromwich Albion	1953-54
Jimmy Glazzard	Huddersfield Town	1953-54
Nat Lofthouse	Bolton Wanderers	1955-56
Roy Swinbourne	Wolverhampton Wanderers	1955-56
Gordon Turner	Luton Town	1957-58
Jimmy Greaves	Chelsea	1959-60
Billy McAdams	Manchester City	1959-60
Jimmy Robson	Burnley	1960-61
Peter Dobing	Manchester City	1961-62
Derek Kevan	West Bromwich Albion	1962-63
Denis Law	Manchester United	1963-64
Willie Irvine	Burnley	1965-66
Ron Davies	Southampton	1966-67

Jeff Astle	West Bromwich Albion	1967-68
Jimmy Greaves	Tottenham Hotspur	1968-69
Kevin Hector	Derby County	1973-74
Mick Ferguson	Coventry City	1977-78
Dennis Tueart	Manchester City	1977-78
Phil Boyer	Southampton	1979-80
Ian Rush	Liverpool	1982-83
Paul Walsh	Luton Town	1982-83
Ian Rush	Liverpool	1983-84

Three hat-tricks for one Football League team in a game

Enoch West, Arthur Spouncer and Billy Hooper, Nottingham Forest v Leicester Fosse, Division 1, 21.4.09
Ron Barnes, Roy Ambler and Wyn Davies, Wrexham v Hartlepools United, Division 4, 3.3.62
Tony Adcock, Paul Stewart and David White, Manchester City v Huddersfield Town, Division 2, 7.11.87

Youngest players scoring Division 1 hat-tricks in a game

Alan Shearer, 17 years 240 days, Southampton v Arsenal, 9.4.88
Jimmy Greaves, 17 years 10 months, Chelsea v Portsmouth, 25.12.57

Total Football League attendances since 1946–47

Season	Matches	Total	Division 1	Division 2	Division 3S	Division 3N
1946–47	1 848	35 604 606	15 005 316	11 071 572	5 664 004	3 863 714
1947–48	1 848	40 259 130	16 732 341	12 286 350	6 653 610	4 586 829
1948–49	1 848	41 271 414	17 914 667	11 353 237	6 998 429	5 005 081
1949–50	1 848	40 517 865	17 278 625	11 694 158	7 104 155	4 440 927
1950–51	2 028	39 584 967	16 679 454	10 780 580	7 367 884	4 757 109
1951–52	2 028	39 015 866	16 110 322	11 066 189	6 958 927	4 880 428
1952–53	2 028	37 149 966	16 050 278	9 686 654	6 704 299	4 708 735
1953–54	2 028	36 174 590	16 154 915	9 510 053	6 311 508	4 198 114
1954–55	2 028	34 133 103	15 087 221	8 988 794	5 966 017	4 051 071
1955–56	2 028	33 150 809	14 108 961	9 080 002	5 692 479	4 269 367
1956–57	2 028	33 744 405	13 803 037	8 718 162	5 622 189	4 691 017
1957–58	2 028	33 562 208	14 468 652	8 663 712	6 097 183	4 332 661

Season	Matches	Total	Division 1	Division 2	Division 3	Division 4
1958–59	2 028	33 610 985	14 727 691	8 641 997	5 946 600	4 276 697
1959–60	2 028	32 538 611	14 391 227	8 399 627	5 739 707	4 008 050
1960–61	2 028	28 619 754	12 926 948	7 033 936	4 784 256	3 874 614
1961–62	2 015	27 979 902	12 061 194	7 453 089	5 199 106	3 266 513
1962–63	2 028	28 885 852	12 490 239	7 792 770	5 341 362	3 261 481
1963–64	2 028	28 535 022	12 486 626	7 594 158	5 419 157	3 035 081
1964–65	2 028	27 641 168	12 708 752	6 984 104	4 436 245	3 512 067
1965–66	2 028	27 206 980	12 480 644	6 914 757	4 779 150	3 032 429
1966–67	2 028	28 902 596	14 242 957	7 253 819	4 421 172	2 984 648
1967–68	2 028	30 107 298	15 289 410	7 450 410	4 013 087	3 354 391
1968–69	2 028	29 382 172	14 584 851	7 382 390	4 339 656	3 075 275
1969–70	2 028	29 600 972	14 868 754	7 581 728	4 223 761	2 926 729
1970–71	2 028	28 194 146	13 954 337	7 098 265	4 377 213	2 764 331
1971–72	2 028	28 700 729	14 484 603	6 769 308	4 697 392	2 749 426
1972–73	2 028	25 448 642	13 998 154	5 631 730	3 737 252	2 081 506
1973–74	2 027	24 982 203	13 070 991	6 326 108	3 421 624	2 163 480
1974–75	2 028	25 577 977	12 613 178	6 955 970	4 086 145	1 992 684
1975–76	2 028	24 896 053	13 089 861	5 798 405	3 948 449	2 059 338
1976–77	2 028	26 182 800	13 647 585	6 250 597	4 152 218	2 132 400
1977–78	2 028	25 392 872	13 255 677	6 474 763	3 332 042	2 330 390
1978–79	2 028	24 540 627	12 704 549	6 153 223	3 374 558	2 308 297
1979–80	2 028	24 623 975	12 163 002	6 112 025	3 999 328	2 349 620
1980–81	2 028	21 907 569	11 392 894	5 175 442	3 637 854	1 701 379
1981–82	2 028	20 006 961	10 420 793	4 750 463	2 836 915	1 998 790
1982–83	2 028	18 766 158	9 295 613	4 974 937	2 943 568	1 552 040
1983–84	2 028	18 342 116	8 701 230	5 359 757	2 726 062	1 555 067
1984–85	2 028	17 849 835	9 761 404	4 030 823	2 667 008	1 390 600
1985–86	2 028	16 488 577	9 037 854	3 551 968	2 490 481	1 408 274
1986–87	2 028	17 379 218	9 144 676	4 168 131	2 350 970	1 715 441

Highest attendances

At each Football League club's current ground, listed in descending order

Team	Attendance	Opponents	Match	Date
Manchester City	84 569	Stoke City	FA Cup 6th rd	3.3.34
Chelsea	82 905	Arsenal	Division 1	12.10.35
Everton	78 299	Liverpool	Division 1	18.9.48
Aston Villa	76 588	Derby County	FA Cup 6th rd	2.3.46
Sunderland	75 118	Derby County	FA Cup 6th rd replay	8.3.33
Tottenham Hotspur	75 038	Sunderland	FA Cup 6th rd	5.3.38
Charlton Athletic	75 031	Aston Villa	FA Cup 5th rd	12.2.38
Arsenal	73 295	Sunderland	Division 1	9.3.35
Sheffield Wednesday	72 841	Manchester City	FA Cup 5th rd	17.2.34
Manchester United	70 504	Aston Villa	Division 1	27.12.20
Bolton Wanderers	69 912	Manchester City	FA Cup 5th rd	18.2.33
Newcastle United	68 386	Chelsea	Division 1	3.9.30
Sheffield United	68 287	Leeds United	FA Cup 5th rd	15.2.36
Huddersfield Town	67 037	Arsenal	FA Cup 6th rd	27.2.32
Birmingham City	66 844	Everton	FA Cup 5th rd	11.2.39
West Bromwich Albion	64 815	Arsenal	FA Cup 6th rd	6.3.37
Liverpool	61 905	Wolverhampton Wanderers	FA Cup 4th rd	2.2.52
Blackburn Rovers	61 783	Bolton Wanderers	FA Cup 6th rd	2.3.29
Wolverhampton Wanderers	61 315	Liverpool	FA Cup 5th rd	11.2.39
Leeds United	57 892	Sunderland	FA Cup 5th rd replay	15.3.67
Cardiff City	57 800	Arsenal	Division 1	22.4.53
Hull City	55 019	Manchester United	FA Cup 6th rd	26.2.49
Burnley	54 775	Huddersfield Town	FA Cup 3rd rd	23.2.24
Middlesbrough	53 596	Newcastle United	Division 1	27.12.49

Team	Attendance	Opponents	Match	Date
Crystal Palace	51 801	Burnley	Division 2	11.5.79
Coventry City	51 457	Wolverhampton Wanderers	Division 2	29.4.67
Portsmouth	51 385	Derby County	FA Cup 6th rd	26.2.49
Stoke City	51 380	Arsenal	Division 1	29.3.37
Port Vale	50 000	Aston Villa	FA Cup 5th rd	20.2.60
Nottingham Forest	49 945	Manchester United	Division 1	28.10.67
Fulham	49 335	Millwall	Division 2	8.10.38
Millwall	48 672	Derby County	FA Cup 5th rd	20.2.37
Oldham Athletic	47 671	Sheffield Wednesday	FA Cup 4th rd	25.1.30
Notts County	47 310	York City	FA Cup 6th rd	12.3.55
Leicester City	47 298	Tottenham Hotspur	FA Cup 5th rd	18.2.58
Norwich City	43 984	Leicester City	FA Cup 6th rd	30.3.63
Plymouth Argyle	43 596	Aston Villa	Division 2	10.10.36
Bristol City	43 335	Preston North End	FA Cup 5th rd	16.2.35
Preston North End	42 684	Arsenal	Division 1	23.4.68
West Ham United	42 322	Tottenham Hotspur	Division 1	17.10.70
Derby County	41 826	Tottenham Hotspur	Division 1	20.9.69
Barnsley	40 255	Stoke City	FA Cup 5th rd	15.2.36
Brentford	39 626	Preston North End	FA Cup 6th rd	5.3.38
Bradford City	39 146	Burnley	FA Cup 4th rd	11.3.11
Blackpool	39 118	Manchester United	Division 1	19.4.52
Bristol Rovers*	38 472	Preston North End	FA Cup 4th rd	30.1.60
Ipswich Town	38 010	Leeds United	FA Cup 6th rd	8.3.75
Doncaster Rovers	37 149	Hull City	Division 3N	2.10.48
Halifax Town	36 885	Tottenham Hotspur	FA Cup 5th rd	14.2.53
Brighton & Hove Albion	36 747	Fulham	Division 2	27.12.58
Queen's Park Rangers	35 353	Leeds United	Division 1	28.4.74
Bury	35 000	Bolton Wanderers	FA Cup 3rd rd	9.1.60
Wrexham	34 445	Manchester United	FA Cup 4th rd	26.1.57
Orient	34 345	West Ham United	FA Cup 4th rd	25.1.64
Watford	34 099	Manchester United	FA Cup 4th rd	3.2.69
Reading	33 042	Brentford	FA Cup 5th rd	19.2.27
Swansea City	32 796	Arsenal	FA Cup 4th rd	17.2.68
Swindon Town	32 000	Arsenal	FA Cup 3rd rd	15.1.72
Grimsby Town	31 657	Wolverhampton Wanderers	FA Cup 5th rd	20.2.37
Southampton	31 044	Manchester United	Division 1	8.10.69
Southend United	31 036	Liverpool	FA Cup 3rd rd	10.1.79
Chesterfield	30 968	Newcastle United	Division 2	7.4.39
Peterborough United	30 096	Swansea Town	FA Cup 5th rd	20.2.65
Luton Town	30 069	Blackpool	FA Cup 6th rd replay	4.3.59
Bournemouth	28 799	Manchester United	FA Cup 6th rd	2.3.57
York City	28 123	Huddersfield Town	FA Cup 6th rd	5.3.38
Stockport County	27 833	Liverpool	FA Cup 5th rd	11.2.50
Carlisle United	27 500	Birmingham City	FA Cup 3rd rd	5.1.57
Carlisle United	27 500	Middlesbrough	FA Cup 5th rd	7.2.70
Wigan Athletic	27 500	Hereford United	FA Cup 2nd rd	12.12.53
Walsall	25 453	Newcastle United	Division 2	29.8.61
Rotherham United	25 000	Sheffield United	Division 2	13.12.52
Rotherham United	25 000	Sheffield Wednesday	Division 2	26.1.52
Northampton Town	24 523	Fulham	Division 1	23.4.66
Mansfield Town	24 467	Nottingham Forest	FA Cup 3rd rd	10.1.53
Tranmere Rovers	24 424	Stoke City	FA Cup 4th rd	5.2.72
Newport County	24 268	Cardiff City	Division 3S	16.10.37
Rochdale	24 231	Notts County	FA Cup 2nd rd	10.12.49
Scunthorpe United	23 935	Portsmouth	FA Cup 4th rd	30.1.54
Lincoln City	23 196	Derby County	League Cup 4th rd	15.11.67
Gillingham	23 002	Queen's Park Rangers	FA Cup 3rd rd	10.1.48
Oxford United	22 730	Preston North End	FA Cup 6th rd	29.2.64
Torquay United	21 908	Huddersfield Town	FA Cup 4th rd	29.1.55
Darlington	21 023	Bolton Wanderers	League Cup 3rd rd	14.11.60
Exeter City	20 984	Sunderland	FA Cup 6th rd replay	4.3.31
Chester City	20 500	Chelsea	FA Cup 3rd rd replay	16.1.52
Crewe Alexandra	20 000	Tottenham Hotspur	FA Cup 4th rd	30.1.60
Aldershot	19 138	Carlisle United	FA Cup 4th rd replay	28.1.70
Colchester United	19 072	Reading	FA Cup 1st rd	27.11.48
Shrewsbury Town	18 917	Walsall	Division 2	26.4.61
Hereford United	18 114	Sheffield Wednesday	FA Cup 3rd rd	4.1.58
Wimbledon	18 000	HMS Victory	Amateur Cup 3rd rd	23.2.35
Hartlepools United	17 426	Manchester United	FA Cup 3rd rd	5.1.57
Cambridge United	14 000	Chelsea	Friendly	1.5.70
Scarborough	11 130	Luton Town	FA Cup 3rd rd	8.1.38

*Eastville attendance record; club now at Twerton Park, Bath.

At each Scottish League club's current ground, in descending order

Team	Attendance	Opponents	Match	Date
Rangers	118 567	Celtic	Division 1	2.1.39
Queen's Park	95 722	Rangers	Scottish Cup 1st rd	18.11.30
Celtic	92 000	Rangers	Division 1	1.1.38
Hibernian	66 840	Heart of Midlothian	Division 1	2.1.50
Heart of Midlothian	53 496	Rangers	Scottish Cup 3rd rd	13.2.32
Partick Thistle	49 838	Rangers	Division 1	18.2.22
Clyde	52 000	Rangers	Division 1	21.11.28

St Mirren	47 428	Celtic	Scottish Cup 4th rd	7.3.25
Aberdeen	45 061	Heart of Midlothian	Scottish Cup 4th rd	13.3.54
Dundee	43 024	Rangers	Scottish Cup 2nd rd	7.2.53
Motherwell	35 632	Rangers	Scottish Cup 4th rd replay	12.3.52
Kilmarnock	34 246	Rangers	League Cup	20.8.63
Raith Rovers	31 306	Heart of Midlothian	Scottish Cup 2nd rd	7.2.53
St Johnstone	29 972	Dundee	Scottish Cup 2nd rd	10.2.52
Hamilton Academicals	28 690	Heart of Midlothian	Scottish Cup 3rd rd	3.3.37
Dundee United	28 000	Barcelona	Fairs Cup 2nd rd	16.11.66
Dunfermline Athletic	27 816	Celtic	Division 1	30.4.68
Albion Rovers	27 381	Rangers	Scottish Cup 2nd rd	8.2.36
Stirling Albion	26 400	Celtic	Scottish Cup 4th rd	14.3.59
Cowdenbeath	25 586	Rangers	League Cup quarter final	21.9.49
Ayr United	25 225	Rangers	Division 1	13.9.69
Queen of the South	24 500	Heart of Midlothian	Scottish Cup 3rd rd	23.2.52
Airdrieonians	24 000	Heart of Midlothian	Scottish Cup 4th rd	8.3.52
Morton	23 500	Rangers	Scottish Cup 3rd rd	21.2.53
Falkirk	23 100	Celtic	Scottish Cup 3rd rd	21.2.53
East Fife	22 515	Raith Rovers	Division 1	2.1.50
Dumbarton	18 000	Raith Rovers	Scottish Cup quarter final	2.3.57
Alloa	15 467	Celtic	Scottish Cup 5th rd	5.2.55
Clydebank	14 900	Hibernian	Scottish Cup 1st rd	10.2.65
Arbroath	13 510	Rangers	Scottish Cup 3rd rd	23.2.52
Berwick Rangers	13 365	Rangers	Scottish Cup 1st rd	28.1.67
Stenhousemuir	12 500	East Fife	Scottish Cup 4th rd	11.3.50
East Stirling	11 500	Hibernian	Scottish Cup 2nd rd	10.2.60
Forfar Athletic	10 780	Rangers	Scottish Cup 2nd rd	2.2.70
Montrose	8 983	Dundee	Scottish Cup 3rd rd	17.3.73
Brechin City	8 123	Aberdeen	Scottish Cup 3rd rd	3.2.73
Stranraer	6 500	Rangers	Scottish Cup 1st rd	24.1.48
Meadowbank Thistle	4 000	Albion Rovers	League Cup	9.8.74

Wembley Stadium for the 1926 FA Cup Final with nearly 92 000 present. Many of the clubs had witnessed record attendances during the period between the wars.

World's largest grounds

Brazil
Mario Filho (Maracana), Rio de Janeiro	169 000
	(present capacity)
Morumbi, São Paulo	150 000
Castelao, Fortaleza	130 000
Magalhaes Pinto, Belo Horizonte	110 000
Beira Rio, Porto Alegre	100 000
Olimpico, Porto Alegre	100 000

Egypt
Nasser Stadium, Cairo	100 000

England
Wembley Stadium	100 000

India
Eden Garden Stadium, Calcutta	100 000
Corporation Stadium, Calicur	100 000

Iran
Azadi, Karadj Auto Band	100 000

Indonesia
Senayan Main Stadium, Jakarta	110 000

Korea DPR
Pyongyang	150 000

Mexico
Aztec, Mexico City	115 000
Universitaria, Monterrey	100 000

Spain
Nou Camp, Barcelona	120 000
Santiago Bernabeu, Madrid	101 663

USSR
Central Stadium, Kiev	100 000
Lenin Stadium, Moscow	100 000

The giant Maracana Stadium in Rio de Janeiro, venue for the 1950 World Cup and the world's largest ground.

Index of General Subjects

Index to Teams